The Collected Letters of Canon Sheehan of Doneraile 1883–1913

A formal photographic portrait of Canon Sheehan taken at the time of his appointment to the Cathedral Chapter in 1904.

The Collected Letters of Canon Sheehan of Doneraile 1883–1913

EDITED WITH AN INTRODUCTION AND NOTES BY

James O'Brien

SMENOS

SMENOS PUBLICATIONS
smenosbooks@yahoo.co.uk
www.smenospublications.com
an imprint of
CARRIGBOY
Wells, Somerset, England
www.carrigboy.co.uk

ISBN 978–0–9575521–0–4 PB
ISBN 978–0–9575521–1–1 HB

A CIP catalogue record for this book is available from the British Library.

First print February 2013.
Revised second print April 2013.
Typeset in Caslon 11pt on 14pt.
Index compiled by Carrigboy.
Design and print origination by Carrigboy Typesetting Services.
Printed in Spain by GraphyCems.

Sister M. Ita

1929–2007

Contents

Acknowledgements

A debt of gratitude is owed to many persons who assisted with the compilation of this series of the letters of Canon Sheehan of Doneraile and readily made invaluable material and advice available to the editor. Particular thanks are due to: Sr Sheila Kelly, archivist of the Presentation Sisters, Southern Province, who very generously made their holding of Canon Sheehan's papers available for transcription and publication; Fr Fergus O'Donoghue, SJ, Archivist of the Irish Jesuit Province, who gladly facilitated consultation of the Sheehan/Russell correspondence in the Archives of the Province of the Irish Jesuits Fathers and to James Burke, the archivist at Lower Leeson Street, Dublin, who facilitated access to the correspondence; Shawn Weldon, assistant archivist, at the Philadelphia Archdiocesan Historical Research Centre, at Overbrook, Philadelphia, for access to the papers of Fr Herman Joseph Heuser; Allison Foley, archivist, St Mary's Seminary, Baltimore, for permission to consult the papers of Fr Joseph Bruneau, SS; Kevin Cawley, archivist at the University of Notre Dame, South Bend, Indiana, for providing copies of the Sheehan correspondence with Fr Daniel Hudson, CSC; James Bantin, manuscript archivist, Morris Library, University of South Illinois, Carbondale, for access to the papers of Katherine Tynan; Carolin Thissen of the publishing house J.P. Bachem Verlag GmbH, Cologne, for her assistance with regard to the archive of J.P. Bachem Verlag; Christoph Lienert of the Fram Museum for assistance with regard to the archive of Benziger Brothers held in Einsiedeln, Switzerland; Caroline Lyndsey Gould, deputy university archivist, Reading University, Berkshire, for information concerning the archive of Longmans, Green and Company; Mary Lombard, special collections, Boole Library, University College Cork, for much help with regard to the papers of Mrs. William O'Brien (Sophie Raffalovich); Professor David Burton of Bryn Mar, Pennsylvania, for kind permission to reproduce his transcripts of the Holmes/Sheehan correspondence conserved in the library of the Harvard Law School; Edwin Moloy, Historical & Special Collections, Harvard Law School Library for permission to publish Canon Sheehan's correspondence with Justice Oliver Wendell Holmes; James Harte, manuscripts department, National Library of Ireland who provided copies of the Canon Sheehan letters in the Castletown Papers and in the Doneraile Estate Papers.

In a special manner we also wish to mention the following: George Cardinal Pell; Raymond Leo Cardinal Burke; Mons. Joseph Murphy; Mons. Michael Crotty; Canon Gerry Casey; Fr Tobias Bluitt; Prof. D. Vincent Twomey, SVD; Sr Ursula Sheehan of the Convent of Mercy in Mallow; Dr Caitriona O Dochartaigh; Mr Jiří Sittek of the Czech Embassy to the Holy See; Prof. Dieter Böhler, SJ, St. Georgen, Frankfurt; Prof. Manfred Hauke, Lugano; Anthony Murphy; Prof. Joseph Hubbert, C.M., Niagara University, New York; Nora O'Keeffe, Doneraile; Michael O'Sullivan, Doneraile; William Cerbone, Fordham University Press; and Josette Prichard at Carrigboy.

Abbreviations

BSMS/JBP/*SB*	Baltimore, St. Mary's Seminary, Papers of Joseph Bruneau, Sheehan to Bruneau.
IJPA J27	Irish Jesuit Provincial Archive, J27 (Matthew Russell, SJ)
MS	Manuscript
MSS	Manuscripts
NLI/CP/MS	National Library of Ireland, Manuscripts, Castletown Papers
NLI/DP/MS	National Library of Ireland, Manuscripts, Doneraile Estate Papers
PA DON I	Presentation Sisters Provincial Archive, Doneraile Convent Archive, Section I
PAHRC/HJHP/SD	Philadelphia Archdiocesan Historical Research Centre, Papers of Herman Joseph Heuser, Sheehan to Canon Dallow
PAHRC/HJHP/SG	Philadelphia Archdiocesan Historical Research Centre, Papers of Herman Joseph Heuser, Sheehan to Lady Gilbert (Rosa Mulholland)
PAHRC/HJHP/SH	Philadelphia Archdiocesan Historical Research Centre, Papers of Herman Joseph Heuser, Sheehan to Herman Joseph Heuser
PAHRC/HJHP/SL	Philadelphia Archdiocesan Historical Research Centre, Papers of Herman Joseph Heuser, Sheehan to Sydney Royse Lysaght
PAHRC/HJHP/SP	Philadelphia Archdiocesan Historical Research Centre, Papers of Herman Joseph Heuser, Sheehan to Michael Phelan, SJ

PAHRC/HJHP/SR	Philadelphia Archdiocesan Historical Research Centre, Papers of Herman Joseph Heuser, Sheehan to Sr Raphael
PAHRC/HJHP/SRY	Philadelphia Archdiocesan Historical Research Centre, Papers of Herman Joseph Heuser, Sheehan to Miss Ryan
UCC U2/AP	William O'Brien Papers, Boole Library, University College Cork AP Canon Sheehan to O'Brien
UCC U2 AO	William O'Brien Papers, Boole Library, University College Cork AP (178) Canon Sheehan to O'Brien
UCC/WOB/PP/AS	William O'Brien Papers, Boole Library, University College Cork AS (44, 45a, & 49) Letters from Denis Sheehan to William O'Brien and Sophia O'Brien

Introduction

At the end of the nineteenth century, no writer in Ireland enjoyed a cosmopolitan literary reputation such as that of Canon Patrick Sheehan of Doneraile. Although he lived in Ireland, rarely left his parish, and while his works are permeated with Irish life, at the same time, it is difficult to regard him as a specifically Irish writer.

Sheehan saw himself as a Catholic writer and his literary activities as an apostolate. He averts to this in his correspondence with his editors maintaining that the only available vehicle of interpreting Catholic doctrine 'to the outer world' is the novel or the romance. Through the sugar coated pages of an entertaining tale, which would find ready public acceptance, he hoped to convey a deeper and more serious moral or religious lesson. As a Catholic writer, Sheehan's audience was without bounds and his readership supranational – though he did regard America as his happy hunting ground and Germany as his great Patroness and defender.

Unfortunately, Canon Sheehan never penned an essay outlining the literary theory, as he understood it, underlying the Catholic novel nor, indeed, did he deal with the theoretical question of the possibility of a Catholic novel or novelist. Nevertheless, some elements motivating his literary efforts in advancing religion in a secular world may be gleaned from his essay on Sir Joseph Noel Paton's pre-Raphaelite masterpiece *Satan Watching the Sleep of Christ* (1874) which was exhibited in Dublin (cf. *In a Dublin Art Gallery*, in the *Irish Ecclesiastical Record*, December 1881, republished in *Early Essays and Lectures*, Longmans and Green, London 1906). Here, he articulates a critique of Benjamin Disraeli's (Lord Beaconsfield's) materialist understanding of 'Nature' as the sole object of art – a theory which had been championed also by Ruskin prior to his conversion to the pre-Raphaelite movement. In this understanding of 'Nature', Disraeli confines the term to mean spatiotemporal phenomena and rejects the idea of art having any spiritual object – let alone a moral or religious purpose. On the other hand, Sheehan argues that art must have not only phenomena but also noumena – or spiritual things – as its object, otherwise it will not be able to reach or sustain the heights of its historical achievement. In his aesthetical critique of materialism, Sheehan expresses concerns and outlooks similar to many of the proponents of the *renouveau catholique* in French literature during the third republic – especially those of Charles-Marie-Georges Huysmans (1848–1907) after he abandoned the naturalism of Zola (cf. Richard Griffiths, *The Reactionary Revolution*, New York 1965).

In his choice of subject matter, the Catholic novelist, according to Sheehan, had ample imaginative scope, as well as wide opportunity to contrive plots, depict character and draw landscape. He does, however, admit that a Catholic writer, unlike his secular counterpart, is constrained in his choice and treatment of subject matter by propriety and service of the Truth (cf. *The Limitations and Possibilities of Catholic Literature. An Address to the Catholic Truth Society of Ireland,* in *Early Essays and Lectures,* Longmans and Green, London New York 1906). An example of that constraint could be found in his attitude to the modernist crisis – which impinged on all Catholic intellectuals at the end of the nineteenth century. While not a supporter of philosophical or theological modernism, he was aware of the issues at stake in the modernist crisis and had direct or indirect contact with some of its principle exponents, including George Tyrrell; the clerical circle associated with the *New York Review*, published from Dunwoodie seminary in New York between 1905–1907; the review *La Quinzaine,* published by Georges Pierre Fonsegrive-Lespinasse 1894–1907; and the Czech review *Nový život* published by Karel Dostál-Lutinov 1897–1907. Nevertheless, beginning in 1901, he insisted on having his writings examined by Prof. John Hogan of Philadelphia and by Fr Michael Maher, SJ, of Stonyhurst so as to ensure that they were theologically and philosophically error free.

The translation of Canon Sheehan's works into all major European languages ensured that he exerted a notable influence on Catholic literary, philosophical, theological, social and political circles in Germany, France, the Habsburg Dominions and in Italy. His extant papers, although probably only a fraction of their original extent, make clear that he was in contact with many contemporary Catholic literary movements: the literary circle of Fr Matthew Russell's *Irish Monthly*; the *Katolická Moderna* in Bohemia; the *renouveau catholique* in France and Germany; the Catholic literary and political circles associated with Professor Angelo Mauri in Milan; and the

Catholic publishing house of J.P. Bachem in Cologne which was closely linked to the political initiatives of the Catholic Deutsche Zentrumpartei. Moreover, the English language editions of his writings brought him into contact with Fr Herman Heuser's efforts in Philadelphia through the pages of the *American Ecclesiastical Review* and the *Dolphin;* with Fr John O'Brien's *Sacred Heart Review*, published from Boston; with Fr Peter Yorke's *Monitor*, published from San Francisco; and with Fr Daniel Hudson's *Ave Maria* journal, published from the University of Notre Dame, South Bend, Indiana.

At the time of his death in 1913, he was a literary phenomenon by any standards, enjoying enormous celebrity and maintaining a correspondence extending as far as British India and Java. Yet, by the end of the twentieth century, he was almost unknown outside of local circles in his native Co. Cork. Several reasons may be adduced partly to explain the eclipse of Sheehan's literary fortunes: the historical circumstances of post First World War Ireland; he had never operated within the Irish literary revival; a management policy of the heirs and beneficiaries of his intellectual property which conceded rights almost exclusively to Irish publishing houses; and the transformation or decline in the wake of the Second Vatican Council of many of the Catholic movements and publications with which he had been involved.

In Ireland, literary interest in his work tends to concentrate on the perspective of nationalism, the land and a narrow version of Catholicism – concerns of which Canon Sheehan was certainly conscious but which are too limited to encompass his literary work and his objectives. It is remarkable that little attention has been devoted to the translations of his novels; and to the motives of those who undertook rendering them into all of the major European languages. Notable exceptions in this respect are, perhaps, two brief articles published in the *Capuchin Annual* of 1952 to mark the centenary of his birth: one by Winefriede Nolan, the other by Liam Brophy; and a review of Michael P. Linehan's *Canon Sheehan of Doneraile* (Talbot Press, Dublin 1952) by 'Alcuin', published in the *Catholic Herald* (28 August 1952).

It is hoped that this collection of his letters, which can only be represented as a mere fraction of his actual correspondence and a *portiuncula* of his extant letters, may rekindle interest in exploring the circumstances which created the literary phenomenon that was Canon Sheehan of Doneraile.

PATRICK AUGUSTINE SHEEHAN

Patrick Augustine Sheehan was born in 1852 at 29 New Street, Mallow, Co. Cork, where his father kept a licensed premises and possibly also a bakery. He was the third of five children of whom only Sheehan and his younger brother, Denis, survived into adulthood – his parents, youngest brother, John, and both sisters died of consumption between 1863 and 1871. By February 1864, he was an orphan who had been placed under the guardianship of Fr John McCarthy (1815–1893), parish priest of Mallow and subsequently Bishop of Cloyne, who sent him to St Colman's College, Fermoy, to undertake a classical education.

In 1868, Sheehan decided to enter the priesthood and hoped to be sent to Rome for clerical studies. His health, however, and his poor academic results persuaded him to repeat his final year at St Colman's, at the end of which, he took first place in the examinations. He was accepted as a seminarian for the diocesan clergy and was sent to study at Maynooth College, which he entered in August 1869. From the outset, he disliked the place and he was plagued by ill health. The academic year of 1872–1873 was spent recuperating at home. He was eventually ordained at the Cathedral of St Mary and St Anne's in Cork on 18 April 1875.

Following ordination, he was appointed to the English mission and took up his position at the Cathedral of the diocese of Plymouth on 2 May 1875. After some months, and following on a controversy surrounding his part in the conversion to Catholicism of the well known Cornish antiquarian and Vicar of Morwenstow, Robert Stephen Hawker (1803–1875), he was transferred to St Nicholas' in Exeter. During his time there, he came into contact with the journalist and writer Wilfrid Meynell (1852–1948), who was appointed editor of the *Catholic Weekly Register* by Cardinal Manning in 1881.

Recalled to Cloyne in1877, he was appointed junior curate in his native Mallow where he became involved in promoting the Catholic Young Men's Society and various literary clubs. In 1881, he was transferred as curate to Queenstown (Cobh) where he remained until 1888 when he was diagnosed of cardiac hypertrophy and was obliged to take sick leave (September 1888 to July 1889), which was spent in Glengarriffe and Youghal. He resumed his ministry in July 1889 as senior curate in Mallow where he remained until his appointment as parish priest of Doneraile on 15 July 1895.

Canon Sheehan at the time of his ordination, April 1875.

As parish priest, he rarely left his parish except for the annual retreat and for his holidays, usually spent by the sea at Lisdoonvarna or Ballycotton. He conscientiously attended to the seven schools present in the parish and to numerous pastoral and charitable works. In this, he always had the support of the Convent of Presentation nuns in Doneraile. Several of the nuns were related to him and he confided much of the secretarial and administrative aspects of the parish to them, especially to Mother Ita O'Connell (1867–1950) and to Sister Columba Sheehan (1869–1918).

In September 1910, Canon Sheehan was diagnosed of a fatal tumour by the Dublin surgeon, Sir Charles Bent Ball (1851–1916). He told no one of his illness and carried on until late June 1912 when he suffered a collapse. Moved to the South Infirmary in Cork, he was placed under the medical charge of Dr T. Gelston Atkins (1855–1924) and Dr John Cremen (born 1844). The initial hospitalization period was expected to last about four weeks. He eventually left the South Infirmary in late November 1912.

By April 1913, he was no longer able to write and in August was confined to bed. In August 1913, he received a final visit from Oliver Wendell Holmes, of the American Supreme Court, with whom he had been in correspondence since 1903. Canon Sheehan died on 5 October 1913.

LITERARY CAREER

Canon Sheehan's literary career may be divided into four general periods: an early phase extending from his time in Maynooth to 1889; his first creative phase as a novelist covering the period 1892–1902; a second creative phase 1904–1908; and the final literary phase which ran from late 1910 to April 1913.

(a) The early period

Through the good offices of Wilfrid Meynell, Fr Matthew Russell, SJ, (1834–1912), editor of the *Irish Monthly*, came into contact with Fr Sheehan, who was then curate in Queenstown. In late January1883, Fr Russell wrote to Fr Sheehan asking him to become a contributor to his literary magazine, the *Irish Monthly*. While honoured by the invitation, he was diffident about his capacity to write for a publication of such high tone and he pleaded lack of time due to the large influx of emigrants then in the harbour town.

Parish Priest of Doneraile, 1898.

By 1888, however, he was regularly publishing poetical work in the *Irish Monthly* and continued to so for at least twenty years. Prior to January 1888, much of this was published anonymously and is, accordingly, difficult, if not impossible, to identify.

In addition to poetry, during this early period, Canon Sheehan wrote children's stories. These were printed in the *Children's Magazine*, published by a Mr O'Connell from Bray, Co. Wicklow. It appears that the magazine did not have the support of its projected market, the Catholic schools, and it soon folded. It was, however, in this magazine that Sheehan published his first piece of fictional prose. It was entitled *Topsy,* a story about a dog he owned while in England. An account of the plot is preserved in a letter of Mother Ita O'Connell to Fr Heuser (1851–1933) editor of *the American Ecclesiastical Review.*

A third literary genre characteristic of this early period of Canon Sheehan's career was the essay. From at least 1881 he published a long and consistent series of essays on literary, philosophical and theological subjects, principally in the *Irish Ecclesiastical Record*, the *Dublin Review* and latterly in the *Irish Monthly*. Many of these were subsequently re-published in 1912 by Longmans, Green and Company, in a volume entitled *Early Essays and Lectures.* The subjects ranged from religious instruction in intermediate schools, to Emerson and free thought in America, the German Universities to St Augustine and to Aubrey de Vere, whose work he greatly admired.

By January 1892, Canon Sheehan began to realize that there was not any great taste for poetry in the South of Ireland and that the philosophical and theological views propounded by him through his essays were not making great headway. While he still had a considerable number of poems and essays in his head, the demands on his time prevented him from making any further progress in committing them to paper. Despite the pastoral constraints on his time, and encouraged by Fr Matthew Russell, SJ, he began to look towards the novel as a more effective vehicle to convey his thoughts and theories.

(b) First creative phase as a novelist: 1892–1902

Encouraged by Fr Matthew Russell, SJ, Canon Sheehan began to experiment with novel writing in 1892/93. In reading circles, the novel had all but replaced the essay as the principle means of conveying and circulating ideas. Sheehan felt that his lack of success in drawing attention to his ideas, especially on education, might have been due to his use of the essay form rather than to the content of his writings. By May 1893, he had completed the first part of a story which he wished to see in print. This was his first novel, *Geoffrey Austin* (1895), 'a college story, but with a moral for men, and [formed] the prologue to a continuation in which [he was] working out some of [his] theories' on education, and particularly on the integration and role of religious instruction in education. In this respect, Canon Sheehan was much influenced by John Henry Newman's *Idea of an University* (1873). The novel was published anonymously by Gill and Company of Dublin and was hardly more successful than his essays – although his diocesan superiors acknowledged that he had identified a lacuna in the Catholic educational system – that religious instruction was not taught on a par with the classics whose influence, inevitably, dominated in the minds of young students. Canon Sheehan had first addressed this question in an essay entitled *Religious instruction in intermediate schools* published in the *Irish Ecclesiastical Record* in 1881. He indicated that this essay was an interpretative key to much of his writing.

Geoffrey Austin: Bohemian, the sequel to his first novel, was partly written by May 1895 and completed before June 1896. Burns and Oates agreed to publish the book but insisted on changing the title to *The Triumph of Failure* (1898) in order to distance it from the fate of its predecessor and to improve its market prospects. He outlined the plot of the book to Fr Russell saying that it would 'trace the steady downward career of G. Austin, as he plunges from classics into latter day philosophies, until, at last on the verge of despair, he is converted to his old faith: whilst Charlie Travers, taking up his vocation as lay apostle, runs a short but glorious career'.

Fr Matthew Russell, SJ, undertook something of a media campaign to ensure a positive literary reception for *The Triumph of Failure*. Through contact with Wilfrid Meynell, editor of the London *Weekly Register,* and Dr William Barry of Dorchester, he was able to promote the novel and soon afterwards favourable reviews began to appear in the English Catholic and secular press. In the United States, he approached Katherine Conway (1874–1926) of the Boston *Pilot* to secure a favourable review for *The Triumph of Failure,* as well as fifteen other literary magazines, including the *American Ecclesiastical Review*. In Dublin, he gave the book to Thomas Arnold, brother of Matthew Arnold, for review.

It was hardly surprising that a positive reception of *The Triumph of Failure* began to emerge by February 1899. In Britain it was well received while in colonial India glowing reviews had appeared in *The Indo-European Correspondence* of Bombay. Fr Russell's publicity campaign in the United States also produced the positive effects for which he had hoped. As far as the reception of the book in Ireland was concerned, Canon Sheehan was happy to relate to Fr Herman Heuser, editor of the *American Ecclesiastical Review*, that the new novel was 'attracting some notice at this side [of the Atlantic]. All the papers have been very kind; and extended articles will appear in the *New Ireland Review*, the *Irish Ecclesiastical Record,* etc.'. In March 1899, he reported to Fr Heuser: 'my last work has made me a thousand friends ... Now I am on the full swim of the tide ... it was weary work; only I felt I was working for Our Lord, and He would reward me. And He has a thousand fold'.

Canon Sheehan had planned a third novel in the *Geoffrey Austin* series. By late 1897, however, he had abandoned the idea partly because he felt that he might already have written sufficiently about the subject of education, but, more importantly, he had come into contact with Fr Herman Joseph Heuser. He had been in Dublin in July 1897 en route to the American College in Louvain when he chanced on *Geoffrey Austin: Student*. He immediately recognized the significance of the novel and especially its potential to influence a debate then going on in Germany concerning the place and role of theology in the civil Universities and in the *Gymnasia*. He arranged for a German translation of the book and, through Gill and Son, he wrote to the author inviting him to become a contributor to the *Review.*

As with his reply to Fr Russell's invitation to contribute to the *Irish Monthly* fifteen years earlier, Canon Sheehan, responding to Fr Heuser on 21 July 1897, expressed some hesitation. However, he looked forward to making contact with the American clergy and accepted the invitation. He regretted that he could not give him *The Triumph of Failure* for serialization as the rights had already been given to Burns and Oats. Instead, he proposed an article on literary criticism and a series on clerical education. Fr Heuser declined the latter as he had already commissioned a similar series from Prof. Hogan of Overbrook Seminary but he published the literary article as *Literary Criticism* in the June 1898 issue of the *Review*. At the same time, Fr Heuser pressed Sheehan to write a series of clerical sketches depicting ordinary priestly life. This was a curious coincidence as Canon Sheehan explained to Fr Heuser on 2 April 1898: 'I had already in my portfolio ten chapters on clerical life in Ireland, which I had intended to develop into a volume. They were, however, intended for popular reading: and my idea was to introduce my own ideas, suggestions, etc., under the sugared coating of a story. I venture to send you these chapters'. Thus was born *My New Curate* (1900) which was serialized in the *American Ecclesiastical Review* from May 1898 to September 1899. The novel was published in book form by Marlier and Callanan of Boston in 1900. It was a run-away success and quickly went through several editions and was translated into all of the major European languages. While well received in Britain, Germany and the United States, it garnered mixed reactions in Ireland where, in some quarters, it was perceived as an attack on the clergy and drew some pungent clerical criticism, including an article published anonymously in the *United Irishman* by a priest of the diocese of Cloyne which greatly offended Sheehan.

In January 1900, Canon Sheehan began the serialization of his fourth novel in the *American Ecclesiastical Review*. Originally entitled *Up Shepherds! Being the Harvest of a Quiet Eye*, he changed the title to *Luke Delmege*. It was a novel which explored contemporary clerical education, particularly in Ireland, analyzing the relevance or otherwise of a high proficiency in the theological controversies of the sixteenth century in a succession of particular pastoral contexts.

While well received in Germany, Britain and in the United States, in Ireland it unleashed a torrent of criticism, much of it of a personal nature. The anonymous critic among the Cloyne presbyterate once again penned a vitriolic attack on the book in the *Irish Independent*. More seriously, the February 1902 issue of the *Irish Ecclesiastical Record* published a long critique of the book. It was written by Fr John Hogan, Professor of Modern Languages at Maynooth College. Both the author and the place of publication lent a certain official allure to the article which set out to crush Sheenan's 'sly and pungent' criticisms of clerical training in Maynooth. Sheehan, sensitive at the best of times, was so upset by the article that in June 1902, writing to Fr Heuser in Philadelphia, he noted that although the verdict of the world was positive with regard to *Luke Delmege*, he was obliged to yield to the prejudices of his critics in Ireland by picking his steps more carefully and that he had 'determined not to touch this delicate clerical question any more, nay even, to rest altogether from literary work, and devote all my time to my parish and people'. With this he abandoned his plan to write a clerical trilogy and almost stopped writing altogether.

During this period, Canon Sheehan continued to write poetry, much of it being published by Fr Matthew Russell in the *Irish Monthly*. Among this material, he considered *Sentan the Culdee* (the *Irish Monthly*, January 1896) as his most important. It was the beginning of a planned series of poems on Irish idylls. This poem, together with several others which had been published since the 1880s, was republished in an anthology of his poetry entitled *Cithara Mea* (1900) produced by Marlier and Callanan in Boston.

He also published essays and articles in the *Irish Monthly* or in the *Irish Ecclesiastical Record* – among them *The Golden Jubilee of O'Connell's death* (the *Irish Monthly*, 1898), *Prêtres-Adorateurs*, (*Irish Ecclesiastical Record*, July 1894) on the movement founded by Pierre-Julien Aymard, and *Optimism v. Pessimism in Literature and in Life* (the *Irish Monthly*, 1897). In late 1902, he completed a large collection of essays which was serialized in the *American Ecclesiastical Review* and which were subsequently published as *Under the Cedars and the Stars,* initially by the Catholic Truth Society in Dublin but eventually by Benzinger Brothers, New York, when the Dublin edition was barred entry to the United States on copyright grounds. These essays, of a personal, philosophical and theological nature, were brought together in a collection modelled on Oliver Wendell Holmes' *Autocrat of the Breakfast Table* (1858) and Coleridge's *Table Talk and Omniana* (1835).

Between 1900 and 1901, Canon Sheehan granted translation rights to Fr Joseph Bruneau for French editions of *The Triumph of Failure*, *My New Curate* and *Luke Delmege*. Contemporaneously, he also granted rights for the serialization of the German translation of *My New Curate* to the *Kölnische Volkszeitung und Handelsblatt,* printed by the Catholic publishing house of J.P. Bachem in Cologne which was closely linked to the Catholic Deutsche Zentrumpartei; and for the serialization of an Italian translation by Angelo Mauri in *L'Osservatore Cattolico* in Milan.

Among the last things written by Canon Sheehan in 1902 was a dramatic play which he originally called the *Fate of Atropos* but changed to *A Lost Angel in a Ruined Paradise.* It was his only dramatic work and had been undertaken at the request of the Sisters of Charity to raise funds for Temple Street Children's Hospital in Dublin.

(c) Second creative phase 1904–1908

Having recovered from the crisis surrounding the publication of *Luke Delmege*, Canon Sheehan published his fifth novel, *Glenanaar*, in 1905. The book was serialized in the *Dolphin* and was published in book form by Longmans and Green, London and New York. It was a novel on the mercy of God woven around the historical events surrounding the Doneraile Conspiracy of 1829 and the ensuing trials brought against a number of

Bridge House, Doneraile: Canon Sheehan's Study *c.*1912.

innocent persons on the basis of perjured evidence supplied by an informer. The idea for the novel had been discussed at a Stations' breakfast held in the house of George Ellard of Lough Eagle who located a bundle of contemporary newspaper reports of the trials which had been preserved by his neighbours, the Linehans. Canon Sheehan regarded *Glenanaar* as his best literary piece.

Longmans, Green published Sheehan's sixth novel, *Lisheen*, in 1907. This was a social novel dealing with the agrarian questions of landlordism and rural depopulation based on Tolstoy's *Resurrection* (1898).

During the course of 1907/1908, Canon Sheehan completed his seventh novel, *The Blindness of Dr Gray*, in which he tries to preach … 'that above the iron laws of the Universe there is a higher command; or, as Tennyson puts it: That Love is Nature's Final Law'. The book was serialized in the *American Ecclesiastical Review* throughout 1909 and published in book form by Longmans, Green in time for the Christmas market. This was

Canon Sheehan's return to clerical subjects and he was 'sure to be carefully criticized here at home'.

Parerga, a sequel volume to *Under the Cedars and the Stars,* appeared in 1908, the title, apparently inspired by Arthur Schopenhauer's *Parerga and Paralipomena* (1851).

An unexpected development during this period, was the importance of the translations of Sheehan's work into other languages. The Canon authorised translations of *My New Curate* into Hungarian (1904), Dutch (1904), Czech (1906) and Spanish (1906). Permissions were granted to translate *Geoffrey Austin* into German (1904); *The Triumph of Failure* to German (1904); *Luke Delmege* to Hungarian (1905); *Glenanaar* to German (1907), to Czech (1908) and to Slovenian (1908).

(d) Final literary phase: late 1910 to April 1913

In September 1910, Canon Sheehan made a visit to Dublin for a medical consultation with Sir Charles Bent Ball. He was diagnosed of a cancerous tumour which, he was told, would prove fatal. He insisted on being told the likely development and progress of the disease. He was also given an approximate timescale for the disease to run its course.

In the months following his return to Doneraile, despite ill health, he embarked on a frenetic work schedule to complete as much as possible of the material he held in his literary portfolio, 'before the night fell'. In Februray 1911, Longmans, Green published his eight novel, *The Intellectuals.* Canon Sheehan had intended calling it *The Sunetoi* but the publishers insisted on an English title. Writing to Oliver Wendell Holmes, Canon Sheehan commented on the book: 'I intended it to be an Eirenicon between the rather furious parties into which Irish life is divided; but here again I am not over-sanguine, because the book will not be read except by a few, whose tastes and sympathies have already placed them beyond the zones of political antagonism. It is an unhappy and distracted country and the one thing that hitherto saved it – a certain kind of Celtic idealism – has now given way before the advances of materialism'.

The Queen's Fillet, a historical novel set at time of the French revolution, followed in the summer of 1911. This was his ninth novel and was particularly well received. His tenth novel, *Miriam Lucas*, was published in 1912. Writing to Lady Gilbert (Rosa Mulholland) in April 1913, Canon Sheehan confided: 'I am not now writing. I am too weak to attempt anything now. But I have a novel completed for the press'. This, his eleventh novel, was *The Graves at Kilmorna,* a study in idealism set in at the time of Fenian rebellion of 1867. It was published posthumously in 1915. A further novel, *Tristram Lloyd*, remained incomplete at the time of Canon Sheehan's death in October 1913. It was edited and completed by Henry M. Gaffney for publication in 1928.

In this final period, translation rights were given in 1910 for *My New Curate* (Spanish); in 1911 for *The Blindness of Dr Gray* (German); in 1912 for *Luke Delmege* (German and Czech); and *The Queen's Fillet* (German).

THE COLLECTED LETTERS

This collection of the letters of Canon Sheehan of Doneraile consists of 293 letters, drawn principally from three archival sources: the Sheehan papers in the archive of the Presentation Sisters, Southern Province; the Russell papers in the archive of the Irish Province of the Jesuit Fathers; and the Heuser papers in the Philadelphia Archdiocesan Historical Research Centre, Overbrook, Philadelphia. To them, some material has been added from smaller deposits: sixteen letters written by Canon Sheehan to Justice Oliver Wendell Holmes, Jr., of the American Supreme Court, which are conserved in the Library of the Law School of Harvard University; ten letters to Fr Joseph Bruneau, SS, of St Mary's Seminary, Baltimore which are currently in the Bruneau papers in the seminary archives; five letters written to Lord Castletown of Upper Ossory found in the Castletown papers in the National Library of Ireland; from the Hudson papers, conserved in the archives of the University of Notre Dame, South Bend, Indiana, four letters written to Fr Daniel Hudson, editor of the *Ave Maria* Magazine, and a letter to Fr Hudson from Fr Matthew Russell enclosing a letter from Sheehan; two letters of Canon Sheehan and three letters from his brother, Denis Sheehan, from the Mrs William O'Brien papers in the Boole Library of University College Cork; four letters in the Doneraile Estate papers in the National Library of Ireland; one letter in the Katherine Tynan Hinkson papers held in the Morris Library of the Southern Illinois University, Carbondale, in the United States of America; and one letter in the private possession of the Very Reverend Gerard Canon Casey, parish priest of Mallow, Co. Cork. A further two letters (nos. 115 and 125) are transcribed from Herman J. Heuser, *Canon Sheehan of Doneraile*

(Longmans, Green and Co., London and New York, 1917). These two letters were originally supplied to Fr Heuser in the winter of 1913/14 in preparation for the writing of his biography of Canon Sheehan. They are, however, no longer extant in the Heuser papers in Philadelphia.

Time constraints and practical considerations precluded adding further extant material which is scattered throughout several institutions both in Europe and in the United States. In particular, mention should be made of the business archive of the London publishing house of Longmans, Green and Company which is conserved in the library of the University of Reading, Berkshire, in the United Kingdom; the Sheehan papers in the Burns Library of Boston College in Massachusetts; and the Sheehan papers in the Cloyne Diocesan Archive, Cobh, Co. Cork – a relatively large collection of papers which currently appears to be in some disarray.

Research is required to locate the printing archive of Benzinger Brothers, Cincinnati, Chicago and New York, which had considerable contact with Canon Sheehan concerning the publication of American editions of several of his books. The company was acquired in 1968 by Crowell Collier Macmillan subsequently becoming Macmillan Inc. In 2007 the Benzinger name was acquired by the Texan company RCL (Resources for Christian Living) which then became RCL Benzinger. While the Benzinger archive, held by the Fram Museum, in Einsiedeln, Switzerland, does contain copies of the later German translations of Canon Sheehan's works published by the company, it holds no correspondence to or from him.

A further area requiring the researcher's attention is that of the often significant literary figures who translated Canon Sheehan's works. They were translated into at least ten European languages. Several of these writers were closely associated with the literary *renouveau catholique* movements. While some of their correspondence with the pastor of Doneraile survives in the archive of the Presentation Sisters, thus far, none of his with them has come to light – with the exception of his correspondence with Fr Joseph Bruneau of Baltimore who translated his work into French. In this respect, it may prove rewarding were it possible to locate and investigate the papers of Oskar Jakob and Anton Lohr, his German translators, Alois Koudelka who translated three of his novels into Czech, Izidor Cankar his Slovenian translator, Angelo Mauri his Italian translator, as well as the papers of his Hungarian translators – Victor Cholnoky, Viktor Kereszty and Lajos Cziklay.

(a) Canon Sheehan papers in the Archive of the Presentation Sisters

The archive of the Presentation Sisters includes that of the Presentation Convent, Doneraile and conserves, by far, the most extensive collection of material relating to Canon Sheehan. In addition to correspondence, it retains books, manuscripts, photographs, newspaper clippings of reviews of Canon Sheehan's writings, and memorabilia. Much of this material consists of the surviving papers of Canon Sheehan which were given to Mother Ita O'Connell by his executor, Denis Sheehan. In preparation for Fr Heuser's biography of Canon Sheehan, the material received from Denis Sheehan was sorted by Mother Ita who sent part of it to Fr Heuser and retained the rest in Doneraile.

With regard to correspondence, the Collection retains a large quantity of letters received by Canon Sheehan. This material is mainly in English with some items in German, French and Latin. While only a residue of Canon Sheehan's personal papers, it is indicative of the extensive international correspondence maintained by the parish priest of Doneraile throughout his literary career.

The archive of the Presentation Sisters contains two series of letters written by Canon Sheehan.

1. The correspondence with his cousin Hannah Sheehan of Mallow, subsequently Sr. Columba of the Five Wounds (1869–1918). This series consists of 22 letters, chronologically arranged from 1888 to 1899, including seven letters to which dates cannot be assigned. In this collection, these are designated: MS PA DON I/76 to MS PA DON I/97. Throughout, both the chronology and numbering system of the Presentation Archive have been retained.

2. The second series consists of letters written by Canon Sheehan to his cousin Hannah O'Connell, subsequently Mother Ita Ignatius (1867–1950). This material contains 100 letters written between 1900 and 1913. The letters were written to Mother Ita while she was ill or absent from the convent, or while Canon Sheehan was on holidays, during his absence at the time of his brother's illness in March 1909, during his confinement at the South Infirmary, Cork City (June-November 1912), and during his last illness in Doneraile (June-September 1913). The chronological series has integrated 4 letters (nos. 215, 216, 218, 219) from May Sheehan, his sister-

in-law, 4 letters (217, 220, 275, 276) from Denis Sheehan, his brother, and one letter (227) from an unknown person in the community of nuns attached to the South Infirmary, Cork City. These have been retained in the present collection. A number of items to which dates cannot be ascribed are appended at the end of the chronological series. While a small number of items, as is clear from internal evidence, are out of chronological sequence, these have been retained in the chronological order of the Presentation Archive. In this collection, the correspondence with Mother Ita O'Connell is designated: MS PA DON I/98 to MS PA DON I/197.

Mother Ita considered much of this material to be too personal to supply to Fr Heuser and retained it in the Presentation Convent Archive. It has not been previously published.

The transcriptions of this material were done from the original manuscripts in the winter of 2011 and during the spring and summer of 2012.

(b) Russell papers in the Archive of the Irish Province of the Jesuit Fathers

The archive of the Irish Province of the Jesuit Fathers contains some 52 letters addressed by Canon Sheehan to Fr Matthew Russell, SJ, editor of the the *Irish Monthly*. This collection is to be found among the Russell Papers and consists of a single bundle of letters which have not been arranged in any chronological series. The top two leaves are fragments of a letter and bear no date or signature. The top leaf is marked J27/27/1–53.

It appears that typed copies of these letters were made and supplied to Fr Herman Heuser, in Philadelphia for use in his biography of Canon Sheehan. Some eight of these letters were taken into the biography in whole or part. The counterpart of this correspondence, Fr Russell's letters to Canon Sheeehan, is conserved in the Library of Boston College.

Extracts from some of the letters in the collection appeared in two articles published by the Rev. Robert Forde, of the diocese of Cloyne, in a local historical journal entitled *Seanachas Duthalla* 1978/1979 and 1980/1981.

The collection has not previously been published in its entirety. Reference is made to it in Catherine Candy *Priestly Fictions* (Wolfhound Press, Dublin 1995). The collection was also consulted by Mary O'Keeffe in preparation for an MA thesis, presented at University College Cork in 1990 entitled *A view from the pulpit: the novels of Canon Sheehan.* The transcriptions in this collection are taken from 114 digital images of the originals made in July 2012.

For the purposes of this collection, a provisional chronology has been drawn up, according to which the first two leaves of the bundle have been tentatively identified as parts of letter no. 33 (2 July [1895]). In this arrangement, the collection amounts to 52 letters extending over the period from 31 January 1883 to 28 November 1911. They are designated: MS IJPA J27/127/1 to MS IJPA J27/127/52.

(c) Heuser papers in the Philadelphia Archdiocesan Historical Research Centre

The Sheehan material in the Herman Joseph Heuser Papers, conserved at the Philadelphia Archdiocesan Historical Research Centre, consists of two principal categories: letters sent by Canon Sheehan to Fr Herman Heuser; and letters sent by Canon Sheehan to other persons but transmitted to Fr Heuser by Mother Ita O'Connell, or others, in 1913/1914 in preparation for Fr Heuser's biography. Mother Ita explains in a number of letters to Fr Heuser that she sought Sheehan's letters from a number of people with whom she knew he had maintained a correspondence.

The Heuser papers also contain letters received by Canon Sheehan including sixteen holographs from Justice Oliver Wendell Holmes of the American Supreme Court – which have been edited and published by Prof. David Burton *Holmes-Sheehan Correspondence* (Fordham University Press 1993). The counterpart of this correspondence, Sheehan to Holmes, is conserved in the Wendell Holmes papers in the Law Library of Harvard University.

Unfortunately, not all of the material sent by Mother Ita reached Philadelphia – especially after the outbreak of the First World War. In fact, she relates to Fr Heuser that the war brought unforeseen obstacles to her already difficult task of organizing the writing of a biography in the United States from an all but enclosed convent in Ireland. The introduction of military censorship temporarily halted her sending packets to the United States inconveniently addressed to a German born national. However, by some means, she was able to come to an arrangement by which her packets of correspondence were sent directly to the office of the chief military censor in London from where they were cleared for passage to New York and eventually to Philadelphia. It is not to be excluded that Lord Castletown of Upper Ossory, a trusted advisor of the government, was of assistance in the matter.

1. Canon Sheehan's correspondence with Fr Heuser extends to fifty letters dating from 21 July 1897 to 13 October 1911. This collection has been catalogued and arranged in a chronological series. It is contained in the Heuser papers, Box 10, folder 6 – consisting of 51 items (one item being a typed copy of a letter in the collection).

For the purposes of this collection, the material has maintained the chronological series and is designated: MS PAHRC/HJHP/SH/1–50.

Some of this material appears in transcription, usually in edited form, in Fr Heuser's biography. It has not been completely published. The transcriptions in the present collection were made from electronic scans taken in May 2012.

2. The Heuser papers conserve a small number of letters addressed by Canon Sheehan to persons other than Fr Heuser. These are:

i. two letters addressed to Fr Michael Phelan, SJ, (1858–1934). These are designated: MS PAHRC/HJHP/SP/1 and 2;
ii. one letter to Lady Gilbert-Rosa Mulholland (1861–1941). This is designated: MS PAHRC/HJHP/SG/1;
iii. four letters to the poet and novelist Sydney Royse Lysaght (1860–1941). The letters are manuscript copies of the originals. These are designated: PAHRC/HJHP/SL/1–4;
iv. one letter to Miss Ryan of Kilkenny who wrote poetry for the *The Irish Monthly*. It is designated: MS PAHRC/HJHP/SRY/1;
v. two letter to Sr. Raphael of the Convent of Mercy, Mallow, Co. Cork. These are designated: MS PAHRC/HJHP/SR/1–2;
vi. Seven letters addressed to Canon Dallow of Birkinhead. These are designated: PAHRC/HJHP/SD/1–7.

The transcriptions in this collection were made from digital scans.

(d) National Library of Ireland

1. The collection also includes 5 letters from the Casteltown Papers which are conserved in the National library of Ireland MS 35,306. These are arranged in chronological series and designated: NLI/CP/MS 35,306.

2. Four items from Canon Sheehan are conserved in the Doneraile Estate Papers. They are arranged in chronological sequence and designated: NLI/DP/MS 34,034 and NLI/DP/MS 34,169.

The transcriptions were made from photocopies supplied by the National Library of Ireland.

(e) Boole Library, University College Cork

The collection includes transcriptions of two letters from Canon Sheehan to William O'Brien, MP, which are conserved in the Mrs. William O'Brien Papers in the Boole Library, University College Cork. They have been inserted in the chronological sequence of the collection and are designated: MS UCC U2 AO/581 and MS UCC U2/AP/178. The O'Brien papers also conserve three letters from Denis Sheehan to William O'Brien written in October and November 1913 which have been included in the collection. They are designated: UCC/WOB/PP/AS/45(A); UCC/WOB/PP/AS/4; and UCC/WOB/PP/AS/49.

The transcriptions were made from the manuscripts.

(f) The Archives of St Mary's Seminary, Baltimore

Ten letters of Canon Sheehan to Fr Joseph Bruneau, SS, are included in the chronological series. They extend over the period January 1900 to March 1902. In these letters Canon Sheehan is primarily concerned with arrangements for the French translations of *The Triumph of Failure*, *My New Curate* and *Luke Delmege*. From these letters, it also emerges that *My New Curate* was appearing simultaneously in serialization in French, German and Italian. More importantly, it is clear from his correspondence with Fr Bruneau that Canon Sheehan was in contact with Prof. Angelo Mauri, who wrote for *L'Osservatore Cattolico* in Milan, an organ of his politically and socially active Catholic circles, edited by Fr Davide Albertario (1846–1902). These letters have been designated MS BSMS/JBP/SB/1–10.

The transcriptions were made from scans taken in October 2012.

(g) Archive of Notre Dame University, South Bend, Indiana

The papers of Fr Daniel E. Hudson (1849–1934), conserved at the archives of the University of Notre Dame, South Bend, Indiana, contain four letters from Canon Sheehan and a further letter from him to Fr Mattthew Russell which is an enclosure of a letter of Russell to Hudson. From 1875–1929, Fr Hudson was editor of *Ave Maria* magazine. He was the first and longest established editor of a Catholic journal with a large circulation in the United States. These letters have been designated: Daniel E. Hudson Papers, University of Notre Dame Archives, Notre Dame, Indiana, USA (1–5).

(h) Morris Library, University of Southern Illinois, Carbondale

One letter (171) from the Katherine Tynan Hinkson Papers.

(i) Papers of Canon Casey, parish priest of Mallow

One letter (239) in the private possession of Canon Casey of Mallow.

(j) Letters transcribed from printed sources

A number of letters have been transcribed from printed sources because of their significance or because they are no longer extant in archival sources. They are:

1. Sixteen letters from Canon Sheehan to Judge Oliver Wendell Holmes of the American Supreme Court. The transcriptions are taken from David H. Burton, *The Holmes-Sheehan Correspondence*, Fordham University Press 1993. The source of these transcriptions is indicated in each instance. The originals are conserved in the Law Library of Harvard University.

2. Five letters have been transcribed from Herman Joseph Heuser, *Canon Sheehan of Doneraile*, Longmans and Green, London and New York 1917. The transcriptions have been made from the first edition of this work printed in November 1917.

* * *

Canon Sheehan's handwriting is ordinarily clear, distinct and easily legible. In those few instances where it is not possible to decipher a word, or where the text has been interrupted, or is missing, an omission is indicated by a long dash (—).

The system for dating letters has been standardized throughout. All abbreviated dates have been written *in extenso.*

A number of letters not by Canon Sheehan have been integrated into the series of letters held in the archive of the Presentation Sisters. These have been retained in the present series. The are indicated by placing the respective series' numbers in square brackets. The serial number of Fr Matthew Russell's letter to Fr Daniel Hudson is also placed within square brackets.

The letters are followed by short biographical notes on persons appearing in the letters or otherwise connected with Canon Sheehan.

A short autobiographical note written by Sheehan for Fr Matthew Russell, conserved in the archive of the Irish Province of the Jesuits, is included as an appendix. It was edited and published by Fr Russell in the January 1902 number of the *American Ecclesiastical Review.*

A list of publications occurring in the letters is also included as an appendix.

Biographical and Literary Chronology

1852 17 March: Born at 29 New Street, Mallow, Co. Cork.

1854 4 June: Birth of his brother, Denis.

1858 7 November: birth of his cousin Ellen O'Connell, daughter of John O'Connell and Johanna McAuliffe of Knockane, Ballyclough. She was subsequently Mrs Heffernan of Kidderminster.

1863 13 July: death of his father, Patrick Sheehan.

1864 6 February: death of his mother, Johanna Regan.
Becomes ward of John McCarthy, parish priest of Mallow, together with his two sisters, Margaret and Hannah, and his brother, Denis. Sisters sent to Loretto Convent, Fermoy, Co. Cork.

1866 Sent with his brother to St Colman's College, Fermoy.

1867 22 March: birth of his cousin Johanna O'Connell, daughter of John O'Connell and Johanna McAuliffe of Knockane, Ballyclough. She was subsequently Mother Ita Ignatius of the Presentation Convent, Doneraile.
17 December: birth of his cousin Lucy Sheehan (Loo), daughter of Patrick Sheehan and Frances O'Brien, Main Street, Mallow.

1868 7 November: death of his sister Margaret, Sr M. Augustine, Convent of Mercy, Mallow. She was born 5 May 1850.

1869 6 March: birth of his cousin, Hannah Mary Sheehan, daughter of Patrick Sheehan and Frances O'Brien, Main Street, Mallow. She was subsequently Sr Columba of the Five Wounds, Presentation Convent, Doneraile.
25 August: entered St Patrick's College, Maynooth, as a clerical student for the diocese of Cloyne.

1871 17 December: death of his sister Hannah, Sr Stanislaus, Convent of Mercy, Mallow. She was born 16 January 1848.

1872–1873 Ill health requires him spend the academic year at home in Mallow.

1875 18 April: ordained to the priesthood by William Delaney, Bishop of Cork, at the Cathedral of St Mary and St Anne, Cork City.
2 May: preached his first sermon, *On the Immaculate Conception*, at Plymouth Cathedral.
August: transferred to St Nicholas, Exeter.

1877 Recalled to the diocese of Cloyne and appointed junior curate in Mallow.
Makes a pilgrimage to Lourdes.
Published *Topsy* in the *Catholic Children's Magazine.*

1880 November: Foundation of the Catholic Young Men's Society, in Mallow.

1881 Transferred to Queenstown (Cobh).
September: *Religious Instruction in Intermediate Schools* in the *Irish Ecclesiastical Record.*

1882 October: *The Effect of Emigration on the Irish Church* in the *Irish Ecclesiastical Record.*

1883 March: *Gambetta* in *The Irish Ecclesiastical Record.*

1884 October: *Emerson: Free thought in America* in the *Irish Ecclesiastical Record.*

1886 June/August: *The German universities* in the *Irish Ecclesiastical Record.*

1887 January: *The German and Gallic muses* in the *Irish Ecclesiastical Record.*
December: *Recent Augustinian literature* in the *Irish Ecclesiastical Record.*

1888 June: *The poetry of Matthew Arnold* in the *Irish Ecclesiastical Record.*
July: *Recent Works on St Augustine* in the *Dublin Review.*
July: Became ill while on holiday in England; diagnosed as suffering from cardiac hypertrophy and ordered to rest.
Autumn of 1888 to May 1889: Recuperating in Glengarriffe.

1889 May-July 1889: Convalescing at St Mary's Presbytery, Youghal, Co. Cork.
During this period in correspondence with Dr James Field Spalding, Christ Church College, Cambridge, Massachusetts who had published *The Teaching and Influence of Saint Augustine* in 1886.
July: Senior curate at Mallow, Co. Cork.

1890 May/June: *The Life and Influence of St Augustine* in the *Irish Monthly.*
June/July: *The Two Civilisations* in the *Irish Monthly.*

1891 January: *Irish Youth and High Ideals* in the *Irish Monthly.*

1892 September: preparations for the publication of *Sermons.*
November: *Impressions of Tennyson* in the *Irish Monthly.*

1893 Holidays in Lisdoonvarna, Co. Clare.

1894 13 May: First part of *Geoffrey Austin:Student* completed.
July: *Prêtres-Adorateurs* in the *Irish Ecclesiastical Record.*
Holidays in Kilkee and Lisdoonvarna, Co. Clare.

1895 23 May: *Geoffrey Austin: Bohemian* partially completed.
2 July: *Geoffrey Austin: Student* offered to Gill and Son, Dublin.
2 July: Prospects writing a third novel *Geoffrey Austin: At Rest.*
15 July: Parish Priest of Doneraile, Co. Cork.
July: *Geoffrey Austin: Bohemian* in fieri.
July: Three chapters completed of *The Work and Wants of the Irish Church.*
29 August: Proofs of *Geoffrey Austin: Student* corrected.
29 August: *Sentan, the Culdee* completed.
7 October: *Geoffrey Austin: Student* goes on the market.
Took holidays in October.
His brother appointed auditor to the Board of Local Government and takes up appointment in Monaghan.

1896 January: *Sentan, the Culdee* in the *Irish Monthly.*
11 June: Proofs of 1st Book of *Geoffrey Austin: Bohemian* sent to Fr Russell for proofing; 2nd. Book completed and being revised; third book (of 5 chapters) and introduction to be written.
21 June: Title changed from *Geoffrey Austin: Bohemian* to *The Triumph of Failure.*

1897 July: Fr Herman Heuser, SJ, invites him to become a contributor to the *American Ecclesiastical review.* He also forwards *Geoffrey Austin: Student* to the Catholic publishing house of J.P. Bachem in Cologne to be translated into German and serialized in *Die Kölnische Volkszeitung und Handelsblatt.*

1898 2 April: Ten chapters on clerical life in Ireland supplied to Fr Heuser in Piladelphia.
28 May: Four chapters of *My New Curate* sent to Fr Heuser who serializing the book in the *American Ecclesiastical Review.*
28 May: *The Monks of Trabolgan* already written and refused by *The Catholic World.*
Geoffrey Austin translated into German and published by J.P. Bachem, Cologne.

1899 January 1899: *The Triumph of Failure* published by Burns and Oates.
17 February: a further five chapters of *My New Curate* completed; five more chapters to follow bringing the series to a conclusion with thirty chapters.
17 February: Herder of Freiburg and St Louis request rights for *My New Curate.*

13 March: Proposes a new series for *American Ecclesiastical Review* entitled *Up Shepherds! Being the Harvest of a Quiet Eye* (name changed to *Luke Delmege*).

5 April: Printer's proofs of eighteen chapters of *My New Curate* corrected.

8 April: Accepts offer from Marlier of Boston to publish *My New Curate* in book form.

30 June: Dr Joseph Bruneau of St Mary's, Baltimore, asks permission to translate *My New Curate* into French.

July: Holiday at Buxton in England.

18 November: Seven chapters of *Luke Delmege* sent to Fr Heuser for serialization beginning in January 1900.

20 December: Sent Marlier in Boston a preface to the second edition of *My New Curate.*

28 November: Burns and Oates to buy rights to a second edition of *The Triumph of Failure.*

1900 10 March: Receives manuscript of the French translation of *My New Curate* from Fr Bruneau in Baltimore. He forwards the manuscript for publication by Dumont in Limoges.

5 May: Burns and Oates have made an offer for *Luke Delmege.*

10 August: Fr Bruneau already working on the translation of *The Triumph of Failure.*

8 September: Next seven chapters of *Luke Delmege* arranged for serialization.

26 October: Five further chapters of *Luke Delmege* submitted for serialization.

6 November: Refers *Cithara Mea* to Fr Bruneau for translation into French.

26 December: Nine chapters of *Luke Delmege* sent to Fr Heuser.

27 December: Final chapters of *Luke Delmege* sent with two further to follow.

1901 13 February: Arranges with Fr Bruneau for the translation into French of *Luke Delmege*. The novel is to be serialized in German, by J.P. Bachem of Cologne and in Italian by Angelo Mauri of *L'Osservatore Cattolico* in Milan.

23 July: *My New Curate* running in the *Kölnische Volkszeitung und Handelsblatt*, translated by Oskar Jacob and published by J.P. Bachem.

23 July. *My New Curate* running in serial form in *L'Osservatore Cattolico* in Milan, translation rights having been granted to Prof. Angelo Mauri.

14 September: *On Retreat* sent to Fr Heuser to be published anonymously.

14 September: *Luke Delmege* has been given to Longmans and Green to be published simultaneously in London and New York.

1902 February: Dr Hogan of Maynooth attacks *Luke Delmege* in the *Irish Ecclesiastical Record.*

February: Degree of Doctor of Divinity conferred by Pope Leo XIII.

29 March: Fr Bruneau has finished French translation of *Luke Delmege.*

June: *Fr Mac On Retreat* published in *American Ecclesiastical Review.*

Holiday in Tramore, Co. Waterford.

26 July: Manuscript of *Under the Cedars and the Stars* sent to Fr Heuser.

29 August: *Writing Lost Angel of a Ruined Paradise* the rights of which are to be given to the Sisters of Charity for the benefit of sick children at Temple Street Hospital.

August: Degree of Doctor of Literature from the Albertus Magnus University, Wichita, Kansas.

23 October 1902: French copy of *My New Curate* arrived to him.

1903 25 August 1903: The Catholic Truth Society request rights for publication of *Under the Cedars and the Stars* through Brown and Nolan (Dublin).

28 November: American customs refuse entry to Brown and Nolan's printing of *Under the Cedars and the Stars.*

Autumn: Initial meeting with Oliver Wendell Holmes. There ensued a ten year correspondence.

26 December: Accepts appointment as a Canon of the Cathedral Chapter.

1904 January: *The Dawn of the Century* in the *Irish Ecclesiastical Record.*

28 May: Longmans publishing *Lost Angel of a Ruined Paradise.*

24 August: Instructs Longmans to forward a typed copy of *Glenanaar* to Fr Heuser for serialization.

28 August: Journey to Germany, visiting Cologne and Bad Nauheim.

24 September: returns to Doneraile

American printing of *Under the Cedars and the Stars* published by Brown and Nolan (Dublin) and Benzinger Brothers (New York) for the Catholic Truth Society (Dublin).
An unauthorized Hungarian translation of *My New Curate* published in Budapest by Fr Eziklay.
Appointed a canon of the Cathedral Chapter and assigned to the prebendary of Kilenemer.

1905 31 January: Benzinger Brothers request rights for a second edition of *Under the Cedars and the Stars.*
10 April: Herder in Freiburg request permission to publish a Spanish translation of *My New Curate.*
7 June: Assigns to the Bishop of Cloyne and to his trustees all of his literary property, including *Glenanaar*, for the support of the sick and aged priests of the diocese.
Holiday in Kilkee, Co. Clare.

1906 10 February: Fr Aloysius Koudelka informs that he has translated *My New Curate* into Czech and hopes to continue by translating *Luke Delmege* and *Glenanaar*.
Fr Koudelka's Czech translation of *My New Curate* published J. Otty of Prague with the poetical parts translated by Fr Karel Dostál-Lutinov.
Holiday in Ballycotton, Co. Cork.
Under the Cedars and the Stars, second printing by Benzinger Brothers (New York).
31 October: *Elements of Character* published in book form by Longmans.
23 November: Paul Maria Baumgartner, Munich, requests permission to publish a German translation of *Luke Delmege*.

1907 22 May: *Lisheen* to appear in book form.
22 May: Preparing a second series of *Under the Cedars and the Stars* (*Parerga*).
Holiday in Ballycotton, Co. Cork.

1908 Holiday in Ballycotton, Co. Cork.
23 September: Agrees to change title of new novel to *The Blindness of Dr Gray.*
23 September: *Parerga* pubished in England by Longmans.
13 November: Gifts the manuscript of *The Blindness of Dr Gray* to Fr Heuser.

1909 9 June: Poofs of *The Blindness of Dr Gray* corrected and returned to Longmans.
June: Holiday in Ballycotton, Co. Cork

1910 19 June: Mentions *A Review and A Forecast* published in *The Cork Free Press*.
June: Holiday in Ballycotton, Co. Cork.
8 September: Diagnosed as suffering from cancer by Dr Charles Ball of Dublin.

1911 3 January: Correcting final proofs of *The Intellectuals* originally called *Sunetoi*.
29 August: Comments on *The Queen's Fillet*.
8 September: Sends *Memoirs* to Fr Russell.

1912 31 March: Has a completed novel in reserve – *The Graves at Kilmorna*, published posthumously in 1915.
23 June: Enters the South Infirmary, Cork City.
October: *Miriam Lucas* published.
21 October: A visit from Archbishop Daniel Mannix, Coadjutor of Melbourne.
24 November: Returns to Doneraile.
Fr Alois Koudelka's Czech translation of *Luke Delmege* is published.

1913 13 June: testamentary dispositions for the disposal of effects.
5 August: Visit from Oliver Wendell Holmes.
5 October: Dies at Bridge House, Doneraile, Co. Cork.

Presentation Doneraile, *c.*1904

Front Row, L to R: M. Ignatius O'Brien, M. Teresa O'Callaghan, M. Alphonsus O'Keeffe, Canon Sheehan, M. Ita O'Connell, M. Agnes Hughes, M. Regis Harbison.
Middle Row, L to R: Sr Berchmans Fitzpatrick, Sr Alacoque Neligan, Sr Philomena Lane, Sr Columba Sheehan, M. de Pazzi O'Connell, Sr Dympna Whelan, Sr Evangelist Daly, Sr Augustine Cronin.
Back Row, L to R: Sr Veronica Conway, Sr Anthony Keneally, Sr Joseph Guiney, Sr Brigid Kearney, Sr Martha Conway, Sr Angela O'Connor.

THE LETTERS

1. FROM: QUEENSTOWN, 31 JANUARY 1883

Text: MS IJPA J27/127/1

Dear Fr Russell,

I received your very kind letter on yesterday morning and the magazine by a later post. For both accept my very grateful thanks. The poem by Helen Callanan is excellent. I have shown it to the Bishop,[1] who, I am sure, will be very gratified.

I do not know anything that could give me greater pleasure than to contribute to the *Irish Monthly*,[2] if considered, or could bring myself to believe, that I could write anything that would be worthy of its pages The little Magazine is an old friend of mine. I have had a great interest in its success since I knew Wilfrid Meynell seven or eight years ago in Exeter. He was at that time a contributor; and many a conversation we had about the *Monthly*, its success, and its prospects. I have again and again recommended it to the people both in public and in private, principally for its intrinsic merits, but partly also for the principle of supporting Irish Catholic literature. I am very much afraid that I could not write anything that would prove interesting to your readers, for the tone of the magazine is cast very high. Besides, I have really very little time to devote to literature. But if I improve very much, and can snatch a few hours from ordinary parochial work, it is just possible that I may be troubling you some day, and putting your charity to a very severe test. But I would not like to promise anything for I cannot say what I might be able to do; and the approaching four months will be a season of great labour, owing to the enormous influx of emigrants from February to May.

I am really thankful that you have such interest in the *Children's Magazine*.[3] I suspect that the editor has a very difficult task, and that the Magazine is not supported by Catholic schools, as it deserves. I think that

1 John McCarthy (1815–1893). As parish priest of Mallow, in 1864, he became guardian of the Sheehan family and saw to the education of Sheehan and his siblings. He became bishop of Cloyne on 1 September 1874. The character of Fr Tom Costelloe in *Geoffrey Austin* is partly based on him.

2 *The Irish Monthly* was published in Dublin 1873–1954 under the auspices of the Jesuits. It was founded by Fr Matthew Russell SJ and was intended as a magazine of general literature. Among its contributors were: Stephen Brown, Dora Sigerson, Rose Kavanagh, John O'Leary, Oscar Wilde, M. E. Francis, Katherine Tynan, Hilaire Belloc, and Alice Furlong.

3 Sheehan made his literary début in this publication with a children's story about his dog entitled *Topsy*. It was republished in *A Spoiled Priest and Other Stories*, Gill and Son, Dublin 1905

this is mainly the reason that it is not quite up to what might be expected. What you have said of the engravings and tales is only too true. The latter have been steadily deteriorating since April.

Again thanking you for your very great kindness,

I am, dear Fr Russell,

Yours faithfully,

P.A. Sheehan, C.C.

2. FROM: QUEENSTOWN, 20 FEBRUARY 1888

Text: MS IJPA J27/127/2

Dear Fr Russell,

I enclose Postal Order for 5/– a mite to help your young poet to the light. The title of the forthcoming volume would have made me shudder, if I did not remember that A. de Vere (who has been wasted by Providence on this generation) touched the ghostly Ossian and put flesh on him: and if he had not also a very vivid and pleasant recollections of some of Mr Yeats' work in the *Dublin University Review*,[4] particularly one very pretty dramatic idyll called Mosada.[5] It is not very Catholic in tone, but is very original and delicate. The refrains at the end of Mosada's dying speech are very touching.

The *Irish University*[6] has been, I believe, the most successful publication of this age. It has had a pretty large sale everywhere. It is really wonderful. I found in it a ballad, which I had been looking for for years – since, in fact I was a child and followed the singers — in wet and cold up and down the streets of Mallow. I cannot recommend it to you for publication for it is not — in my sense of the word: but I would like to see *Condemned to Death* by Bridget better known than it is. I think you inserted it in an obituary notice of the poetess in the *Irish Monthly*.

D. Bernard is 33 years old – a fine German scholar with excellent taste, with the consciousness that he is not perfect. I have been urging him to try other than national subjects. He has but little time to fire the Muses.

4 *The Dublin University Review* published by Trinity College, Dublin.

5 Published in the July1886 issue of the *Dublin University Review*, *Mosada* was separately circulated as an offprint and became Yeats' first separate publication.

6 *The Irish University* published in Dublin.

As for myself, my time is so occupied, that I can hardly read my office. I have just finished 50 pages of manuscript representing 15 pages of print for the April number of the *Dublin Review*;[7] 15 pages for July.[8]

I may possibly be seeking your good offices to revise some literary work (very light) in July or August.

I am,

My dear Fr Russell,

Yours most sincerely,

P.A. Sheehan

3. FROM: QUEENSTOWN, 15 APRIL [1888]

Text: MS PA DON I/76

My dear Hannie,[9]

I suppose you'll never speak to me again, and that you will tear up this letter into infinitesimal pieces. I have been saying *mea culpa* ever since I got Loo's[10] letter apprising me of your entry into Doneraile. The fault is all the greater, for when I was down in Youghal on 5th, whether I accompanied a young lady from this place, I found your fame had preceded me, and those courteous nuns were jealous because you were not seconded for themselves. And again Reverend Mother here wanted to know what I was doing in preventing your entry anywhere but here, with our 800 pupils, pension school, Intermediate Act, etc., etc., etc. I could only say it was not in my power to control the fancies of the young lady in question; but I would make representations, by ascertaining beforehand that Frank will go to Youghal and May[11] will come here. So please tell that volatile young lady who has swept so many prizes lately in Rathfarnham that she is booked, labelled and ticketed for the "City by the Sea".[12]

---

7 *The Dublin Review* was founded in 1836 by Michael Joseph Quin, Cardinal Wiseman and Daniel O'Connell. It ceased publication in 1969 when it was incorporated into *The Month*.

8 The article was entitled *Recent Works on St Augustine*. It was republished in *Early Essays and Lectures*, Longmans and Green, London and New York 1906, pp. 165–190.

9 His cousin, Hannah Sheehan of Main Street, Mallow, daughter of Patrick Sheehan and Frances O'Brien, born 6 March 1869, subsequently Sr Columba of the Five Wounds, St Joseph's Presentation Convent, Doneraile, Co. Cork.

10 His cousin, Lucy Sheehan, sister of Hannah Sheehan, born 17 December 1867.

11 His cousin May Sheehan, sister of Hannah Sheehan.

12 The "City by the Sea" is Queenstown (Cobh), Co. Cork.

It is good news that you are quite happy and at home, tho' I would expect that you might be a little lonely at first. That is inevitable. So you must not mind it. I suppose you are under the special patronage of St Augustine, and that you and de Pazzi have pleasant little rehearsals in the choir gallery. If Sister Cecelia[13] does not insist that you are to be called after her, perhaps you would place yourself under the patronage of St Stanislaus. So at least the Mallow nuns have decided.

I did not hear since from Rathfarnham:[14] nor do I suppose I shall. Sister Teresa has tired of corresponding. I shall go down to see you when?, when?, when?

When the days get long, and you are getting good. Meanwhile, pray for us all; and remember I positively will not preach at your profession unless I have a very good account of you.

If you should read so far, my kindest regards to Reverend Mother, Sisters de Pazzi, Augustine and de Chantal.

I am, my dear Hannie,

Yours affectionately,
P.A. Sheehan, C.C.

4. FROM: QUEENSTOWN, 20 APRIL 1888

Text: MS PA DON I/77

My dear Hannie,

Many thanks for your kind remembrance on my spiritual feast day – a day I, alas, would have forgotten but for the mementoes of friends.[15] You see what the distractions of the world can do, and what a blessed thing it is to be in the cloister, where you can remember so many things.

I am delighted to hear that you are surpassing yourself in cheerfulness and goodness; but in order to secure lasting peace of mind, keep out of politics especially with Sister de Chantal.[16] Poor William O'Brien: they are going for him again, the savages, and I am afraid he will succumb in the long run.

---

13 His cousin Cecelia Sheehan, sister of Hannah Sheehan, born 1 October 1876.

14 Convent of the Loretto sisters at Rathfarnham, Co. Dublin.

15 The anniversary of his ordination which he observed on the moveable feast of the patronage of St Joseph. See footnote 103.

16 Sr de Chantal Abbot (1823–1897) was English.

Pray for us all that we may be good. I'll keep to the letter your request about the beads and the Rosary.

Ever yours affectionally,
my dear Hannie,
P.A. Sheehan

5. FROM: QUEENSTOWN, 18 AUGUST 1888

Text: MS PA DON I/78

My dear Hannie,

I would have replied to your most welcome letter and appeared in person in Doneraile, as you desired, but I have been very unwell in England and am slowly convalescing at home. I am trying to creep though my duties as quietly as possible and regain my strength in that way. I have hopes of being all right in about a week.

I met Fr O'Connor yesterday and was delighted to hear how well you are, and how bravely you shook off that throat infection. Continue well and you'll please all.

I am reserving all I have to say until I go down to Doneraile which I hope will be soon. I trust Loo and May are keeping well, and that Frank is enjoying her vacation.

Give my regards to Reverend Mother, de Pazzi, Augustine, de Chantal etc. and say a wee prayer for

Your affectionate friend,
P.A. Sheehan

6. FROM: QUEENSTOWN, 4 SEPTEMBER 1888

Text: MS PA DON I/79

My dear Hannie,

Your letter reached me yesterday: and though I regretted exceedingly to hear that your admission to the holy habit has been deferred, still I was not quite taken by surprise. It is quite clear from your own and Reverend

Mother's letters that it was an accident of your health that influenced the sisters in putting off your reception for a time. Hence we may conclude that in every other way, you were not considered unfit for the order. It only remains for us to pray that your temporary indisposition may be speedily remedied and that you may have the happiness of being admitted to the white veil.

I am coming on slowly towards health, creeping, as it were. But, there again is the hand of kindness and I know it.

Keep a good heart and firm faith. We will all pray for you and none more than

Your affectionate friend,
P.A. Sheehan

7. FROM: QUEENSTOWN, 5 OCTOBER 1888

Text: MS PA DON I/80

My dear Hannie,

I heard the good news of your election today in Cork from Fr Carver. Need I say how very delighted I am to know that your first difficulties are happily got over?

Your faith and perseverance deserved it.

I have just returned from Youghal where I have been spending a few days.

I am not much improved as yet; and am going down to Banteer[17] tomorrow. Perhaps we may visit you!

Meanwhile say a prayer for me.

Kindest regards to Reverend Mother, and to Sisters de Pazzi, Augustine and de Chantal.

Yours affectionately,
P.A. Sheehan, C.C.

17 Canon Alexander Morrissey was the parish priest and a friend of Sheehan's.

8. FROM: QUEENSTOWN, 20 FEBRUARY 1889

Text: MS PA DON I/81

My dear Columba,

I sent you by way of a temporary the *Irish Monthly* for June, so long promised and so long deferred. It was truly a great pleasure to me to receive from Sister de Pazzi's letter. Nearly all my correspondents have dropped off since I got unwell; and I am delighted at it. I often wished I was a Carthusian with permission to receive one letter a year and that on Christmas day. But when a friendly letter comes now, it is a great relief.

You heard, I suppose, that I was in Dublin lately to see Dr Little; and that after all the treatment, or rather maltreatment of other doctors, he decided I was suffering from cardiac hypertrophy brought on by excessive action in preaching.[18] It will pass away in a few months, during which time I shall travel the globe, and return not as you expect to a village curacy, like Mallow or Doneraile, but to the City by the Sea[19] which I could not think of leaving on any terms. I was sorry not to have seen Loo in Dublin.

Take care of your junior postulant for we have all a special interest in her.[20] I am delighted that Augustine keeps so well.

Say a little prayer for me during our wanderings and I expect a lengthened and severe criticism of my poetry when I return.

I am, dear Columba,

affectionately,
P.A. Sheehan, C.C.

9. FROM: ST MARY'S PRESBYTERY, YOUGHAL, 18 MAY 1889

Text: MS IJPA J27/127/3

My dear Fr Russell,

I have to thank you very much indeed, for the letter and the volume (C.C. Maguire) forwarded to me at Glengarriffe. It was rather shortsighted of me

---

18 Between September 1888 and July 1889, Sheehan was on sick leave in Glengarriffe and in Youghal, Co. Cork.

19 A reference to Queenstown (Cobh), Co. Cork.

20 Another cousin of Sheehan's, Johanna O'Connell, daughter of John O'Connell (originally of Castlemagner) and Johanna McAuliffe of Knockane, Ballyclough, Co. Cork, born 22 March 1867. The future Mother Ita Ignatius.

not to have sent you my address: but I came away with Canon Keller, quite against all —— .

I have been taxing my memory these last days to recall the lines I had written in Queenstown. Of course, all my papers are locked up, and with them *The Rose*, and *The Leper Priest*. I am afraid I shall have to put off sending them until I return to Queenstown: and do not wish to send them in a mutilated form, and I should hardly come to see them in print so long as I am unable to resume parochial work. But, they are yours, sooner or later, for what they are worth. I have never used a *nom-de-plume*: and the Bishop would look aghast if he saw my name under a poem. He is a faithful subscriber to the *Irish Monthly*.

I am, dear Fr Russell,

Yours faithfully,
P.A. Sheehan

10. FROM: ST MARY'S PRESBYTERY, YOUGHAL, 23 MAY 1889

Text: MS PA DON I/82

My dear Columba,

Your letter and de Pazzi's were forwarded to me from Glengarriffe, which I left rather hastily, having been compelled and coerced by the kindness of Canon Keller to come on here to Youghal. I had spent two most delightful months in Glengarriffe, which I promise to be without exception the most beautiful place in the world. I cannot understand why people will be rushing across the turbid and boisterous sea to Harrogate and such like places, when there are such delightful little nooks and corners in our own little island.

But you are not patriotic enough to understand this so I will pass on.

To be very candid, and lest I be accused of not keeping my promises; I do not think I shall be able to go to Doneraile on 13th June. I don't know anything that would give me such pleasure as to see Hannah[21] clothed in the habit; but I don't think I can see you all until I am at work again. But one of the pleasures I anticipate from my recovery is that I shall be able to spend a half hour some day in the near future in Doneraile. 'Till then keep

21 Hannah O'Connell, subsequently Mother Ita Ignatius.

good. Is May coming down here this year? If so, I shall remain. If not, then for — parts.

I am, my dear Columba,

Most faithfully,
P.A. Sheehan

Note: Fr Keane, OP, wishes that Hannah's name should be Antoninus, not "Anthony". But the latter is a great saint.

11. FROM: ST MARY'S PRESBYTERY, YOUGHAL, 30 MAY 1889

Text: MS IJPA J27/127/4

My dear Fr Russell,

Take enclosed poems for what they are worth. I should like to divide *My Rose* into shorter lines as marked.[22]

Having no books near me that I could consult, I have been unable to give the Introduction – an extract from Heine; Essays to the effect that whilst Germany was ringing with his songs, and they were sung in camp, and university etc., the unknown author, a leper-priest, was tolling his leper-bell in a lager-house at Luneburg.

I cannot recall the last stanzas: neither can I fill them up. But as I do not intend either poem for publication, it makes little matter.

Yours, my dear Fr Russell,
very sincerely,
P.A. Sheehan

The *Irish Monthly* to hand strikes me as an especially good number. M. Griffin's essays are valuable, and I hope are intended to be published in book form. Who is J.D.? I envy him his beautiful piety and poetry. And lastly, your critique on the books submitted to you are excellent. Nothing wholesomer than to point out a blot where it exists.

I have been writing altogether from memory. Some expressions strike me as not quite befitting an Ecclesiastic. But you can expunge at will.

22 *My Rose* was published in *Cithara Mea*, Boston 1900, p. 183.

12. FROM: ST MARY'S PRESBYTERY, YOUGHAL, FRIDAY, NO DATE [ANTE 20 JUNE 1889]

Text: MS PA DON I/83

My dear Columba,

A line to wish you a happy feast and happy returns until you are as old as Melchizedeck.

I had good news about you from May, whom I see occasionally here on the strand; and still later from Fr O'Connor whom I met today. May says positively that you will not come down this Summer. Too bad!

Poor Loo was here about to stay a week; but she was called away unhappily after a day or two. Happy you away from all the disorder of the world.

All kinds of kind regards to the Sisters and the Reverend Mother.

Hoping very soon to have the great pleasure of seeing you all.

Yours,
my dear Columba,
P.A. Sheehan

13. FROM: MALLOW, 17 FEBRUARY 1890

Text: MS PA DON I/84

My dear Sister Columba,

Enclosed letter which I should have taken over the day of your profession. Hoping you continue well, and that Reverend Mother also is well and assuring you both of constant remembrance in my Mass and prayers,

I am, dear Sister Columba,

Yours sincerely in Christ,
P.A. Sheehan

Verso: Darling Loo, I got your letter this morning also M.M. Patrick's pencil safely. No news for the past few days, she is expecting operation any day this week, is in good spirits and well cared.

14. FROM: MALLOW, 6 JANUARY 1891

Text: MS IJPA J27/127/5

My dear Fr Russell,

You have the charity of an archangel. I never dreamt of seeing my literature in print again. I simply sent it for your amusement.

It is only my implicit trust in the same charity that has tempted me to disinter the enclosed papers written in Maynooth under the presidency of your distinguished uncle.[23] I have found them in an old notebook and send them just as they were written. I am afraid to look them over with a view to correct them, lest I should put them in the grave of many ambitious efforts of mine – the fire. I sacrificed 200 pages of the story on 8th December last, because on reading them over, I thought them of too secular a nature to put them in print. So I gave them up to our Blessed Lady: but it cost me some trouble.

I can only beg that you will "cut, burn and destroy" enclosed if you see in them anything faulty.

That was an excellent article on J. Boyle O'Reilly[24] by Count Plunkett.[25] It gave me quite new ideas about his character.

I hope to have a notice of *Whisper*! in our two Cork papers soon.

I dare not as yet write anything, though my mind is bubbling over with ideas and designs.

I am, my dear Fr Russell,

Yours always sincerely,
P.A. Sheehan

15. FROM: MALLOW, 2 JUNE 1891

Text: MS PA DON I/85

My dear Columba,

There was some delay about writing in the affair referred to you in your letter. But today I have written to Versailles, as Frances expressed a wish

23 Charles William Russell (1812–1880) was president of Maynooth College 1857–1880.

24 John Boyle O'Reilly (1844–1890). A poet, journalist and fiction writer, he was transported to Western Australia for his part in the Fenian rebellion of 1867. He escaped to the United States and subsequently became editor of the Boston *Pilot*.

25 Count Plunkett (1851–1948), father of the patriot Joseph Mary Plunkett.

that I should do so. She appears very anxious to get away.

I am not altogether sanguine that we shall succeed: but there is no harm in trying.

Ine (sic) is gone to Cork today to attend at the profession of Margaret Stanton. Everything is going well: better than ever before. I can truly sympathise with Reverend Mother in her trouble. But I sincerely hope that Mother Patrick's illness is not quite so bad as reported.[26]

Both shall have our prayers however humble.

'Till Tuesday, adieu!

I am etc.,
P.A. Sheehan

16. FROM: MALLOW, 16 JUNE 1891

Text: MS IJPA J27/127/6

Dear Fr Russell,

I am very distinctly of opinion that the last "fasciculus" I sent contains a great deal of rubbish. I think the lines "*In Memoriam*", "*When with a song of heavenly mirth*" are tolerable: and with your pruning pen you may be able to make passable *The First Sin: A Priest's Dream*. I think several lines in the latter are rather weak, if not puerile: but somehow, I am a little attached to it: and I think the last ten lines or so fairly good, as well as some ideas through the poem here and there.

P.A. Sheehan

I see in the newspapers this morning, that you will be one of the central figures in Belgravia next month, as you have already told me.
I have neither a hope nor a wish that you should publish enclosed except, in case of emergency, and then in an arcane place without my name.

26 Mother Patrick McNamara (1842–1913).

17. FROM: MALLOW, 12 JANUARY 1892

Text: MS IJPA J27/127/7

My dear Fr Russell,

I return by this mail the little volume of K. Tynan's poems which you have been good enough to lend me. Somehow I like her poems better in this shape than when I read them in the magazine: but I cannot get over a sense of too much artificial work in her poetry. In this way there is a decided contrast to Mr Yeats, who evidently "sings because he must". There are very few living poets, whose lines I can read with pleasure: but when I am wearied, I always can take up Yeats' little volume, or Joaquin Miller *Songs of the Sierras*[27] and glide through the lines without an effort.

I had a letter from Dr Spalding last Saturday. He is to be received into the Church on 15th at Washington by Fr Hogan. He says there is no truth in the report of the *Boston Herald* that his wife was coming over with him.

As for myself, I am come, alas! to that point in my career, when I have begun to ask the fatal question: "Cui bono?" I feel constantly, like Fr Faber, the "struggle between the poet and the priest, on account of the absorptive character of such a pursuit as poetry, and the exclusive character of such a calling as the priesthood". On me, poetry acts like opium and I have as much as I can do to keep my fancy in bounds. Then again: the game is not worth the candle. Here, in the South at least, literary tastes are not looked upon with much favour: and may be a decided drawback and disadvantage sometimes. I am afraid I settled my reputation by having acquired the name of a passion for poetry and metaphysics. I have decided, therefore, to enjoy quietly by myself, my own tastes; the world has enough wisdom already written for it, if it only cares to read.

This place now is a vast hospital, everyone stricken with influenza. With the exception of a slight cold, I have hitherto fortunately escaped. I am sorry to hear that the enemy didn't pass you by. All the victims declare that the disease is singularly depressing.

Keep up the *Pigeonhole Paragraphs*. They are by far the best items in the *Irish Monthly*.

With all good wishes

I am, dear Fr Russell,

Yours very sincerely,

P.A. Sheehan

---

27 Published in 1871.

18. FROM: DONERAILE, 19 MARCH 1892?

Text: MS IJPA J/27/127/8

I have just been made very happy by a volume of Malebranche[28] containing his *Meditations*[29] and his *Treatise on the Love of God.*[30] Have any expressions in these come under censure?

My dear Fr Russell,

I sent the only words on St Joseph I remember to have written. I am making it one of a series called *My Saints*. I have culled these discourses on the Saints from my written sermons: they would form a pretty little volume. I have also selected and arranged my sermons on our Blessed Lady, which I should also like to see in a little volume, to be called *Turris Eburnea*.

I have so many things on hands, however, that I cannot face the trouble of having them published. If, however, you think they are worthy of place in the *American Messenger*, and if you will kindly act as intermediary (for your *imprimatur* will carry weight, where an unknown quantity like myself, would be summarily rejected) I shall gladly send on both series to you, corrected and revised. They may serve some good purpose.

If you find any sentence in this discourse on St Joseph worth selecting, it will be a great favour. Perhaps, then, you could return the paper, to be incorporated in its proper place, in the series. Should you have a spare moment, when you are tired of editorial work, would you kindly read over *Thirza*;[31] and let me know is there anything objectionable in it. It is quite rough and unfinished from a literary standpoint: and I must polish and enamel it, when you send it back. But I want to be sure that no one will lift his eyebrows at it. Kindly let me have it as soon as you can.

I think the time is coming when I shall have to say in poetry all that I want to say.

Many thanks for the slip about Dr Spalding. I should like to see him lecturing on St Thomas or St Augustine, with both of whom he is well acquainted.

Always yours gratefully,
P.A. Sheehan.

---

28 The French Oratorian philosopher Nicolas Malebranche (1638–1715).

29 Published in 1683.

30 Published in 1699.

31 Published in *Cithara Mea*, Boston 1900, p. 235.

19. FROM: MALLOW, 14 MAY 1892

Text: MS PA DON I/86; a card.

My dear Sister Columba,

If we can get back in time from the station on Tuesday, I shall go to Doneraile. I am anxious to go, as I couldn't be present at the obsequies.

I would have gone over to see you before now; but I had written to Fr Murphy, Queenstown, for the volume *Monks of the West*[32] that contains the *Life of St Columba*. He promised to send it to Cork for me: but hasn't done so; and I dreaded all pains and penalties that were threatened if I went to Doneraile empty-handed.

I had a cheerful letter from Frances this week. She is very brave, notwithstanding her many friends.

I hope to find Reverend Mother
and all well on Tuesday,
Yours always sincerely,
P.A. Sheehan

20. FROM: MALLOW, 23 AUGUST 1892

Text: MS IJPA J27/127/9

My dear Fr Russell,

I have to thank you very much for your pretty little book which duly came to hand. I think you have found the secret of making our devotions really attractive, which cannot be said for a great many of the manuals of piety which are published at the present day. I was particularly pleased to find in an enduring form (not that I consider the *Irish Monthly* at all ephemeral) that very beautiful poem on the Blessed Sacrament by Mgr. de de [sic] Bouillerie of Carcassonne. I can read that poem over and over again with great pleasure.

Your notes on Dr Russell[33] are exciting a good deal of interest amongst priests, not alas! to the extent of making them subscribers but only borrowers

32 Charles Forbes René Count de Montalembert, *The Monks of the West*, Blackwood, Edinburgh 1861–1879.

33 Charles William Russell (1812–1880), president of Maynooth College 1857–1880.

of the *Irish Monthly*. I think, however, that when you have embodied them in a volume, it will have a large sale.

You heard of the sad defection of poor Dr Spalding. I had a letter a few days ago from Fr Hogan of Washington University in which he says that a weak and hysterical wife was the cause of his falling away. They are now separated: and there is a hope that he will speedily return to the Church. But he cannot repair his mistake in the eyes of men. What makes the matter more deplorable, yet consolatory to us all Catholics is, that Cardinal Gibbons had made the most ample and satisfactory provision for his temporal wants. The poor fellow needs all our prayers just now. If I knew his address I would write to him: because I am sure he will make an excellent Catholic yet.

As to myself, I am kept pretty busy with parochial work here. Yet my pen is not quite idle. I have any number of projected essays, poems, etc. in my head: but have no time to put them in shape. The demands on my time just now are very great: and promise to become more so.

I see you took no part in the projected Literary Association that held its inaugural meeting a few days ago. I am afraid angry politicians will bring that attempt to naught also.

I am, dear Fr Russell, with many thanks,

Yours sincerely,

P.A. Sheehan

21. FROM: MALLOW, 16 SEPTEMBER 1892

Text: MS IJPA J27/127/10

My dear Fr Russell,

I am quite distracted between my desire to do something for you, and my inability – the latter owing to pressure of time and the eternal "beware, beware" of doctors. I have had to say No! to a great many friends who have been asking me to do something for them.

We are now in the thick of a mission. But an inspiration, if it be an inspiration, struck me. I have 3 thick volumes of MS sermons most of which I preached in Exeter, England. I think they are fairly good, particularly one or two notices of the lives of the saints. There is one panegyric, if we may use the word of a saint, which I preached in Limerick on the occasion of the tercentenary of S. Alphonsus[34] a few years ago, and which has never been printed. I think it would suit the *Irish Monthly*, quite as well as that on S. Augustine which you printed some time ago.

If these volumes of sermons would be of any use to you, either for the *Monthly* or for *the Messenger* (in which I am much interested) I can send them to you by one of the Dominican Fathers, who leaves here on Monday for Dublin.[35] A post card on Sunday or Monday morning from you would help me.

I enclose *Carcassone* and the latest from Dr Spalding in the shape of a letter from your friend, Catherine Conway to Dr Hogan. He was always weak (as all converts are) on our devotion to the Blessed Virgin. I tried to knock the Catholic doctrine of the Incarnation into his head; but Protestants cannot understand or see our Divine Lord, except *in nubibus*. Hence then trouble about the Blessed Sacrament and our Lady.

You will send me back Miss Conway's letter and I shall return it.

And if you haven't lost that poem of infancy *A Priest's Dream* which I think I sent you, perhaps you would let me have it or as a souvenir.

I am, dear Fr Russell,

Yours always sincerely,
P.A. Sheehan, C.C.

22. FROM: EAGLE HOTEL, LISDOONVARNA, 28 JULY 1893

Text: MS IJPA J27/127/11

Dear Fr Russell,

I had to return to Mallow last Saturday, and found your letter and a volume of Miss Dora Sigerson's poems awaiting me.[36] Many thanks for both. I had barely time to look through the little volume which is very tastefully brought out. There are some very pretty poems there. A long and most

34 Saint Alphonsus Maria de Liguori (1696–1787), Bishop of Sant'Agata dei Goti, spiritual writer, philosopher and theologian, who founded the Redemptorists. He was canonized by Pope Gregory XVI in 1839. Pope Pius IX proclaimed him a Doctor of the Church in 1871.

35 Canon Sheehan eventually gave his collection of sermons to the *Homiletic and Pastoral Review* in New York believing that it was a clerical publication. He did not realize that it was a commercial publication, owned by the Wagner family, with an employed clerical editor. See footnote 174.

36 *Verses*, published in 1893.

favourable review appeared in the *Cork Examiner*[37] about a week ago from an unknown hand. I shall try to find it for you, if possible.

You shall have my scraps the moment I return, although they will be pigeon holed as valueless. Among all your contributors there is not one that feels more keenly than I the impossibility of carrying my good intentions into execution. I have projects and skeleton plans enough to fill twenty magazines but ...

I am, dear Fr Russell,

Yours always sincerely,
P.A. Sheehan, C.C.

23. FROM: MALLOW, 11 JANUARY [1894]

Text: MS PA DON I/96.

My dear Columba,

Many thanks for your good long letter. Don't hurry about the operetta: but send it as soon as it is presentable. Loo is better: but was quite unable to take part in Thursday's concert: at least, not unable, but thought it unwise to venture out in the cold. I have not heard a word about your epistle: and I had a long conversation on Wednesday with Loo. She never even remotely alluded to the matter.

I did write a long and — letter to Frank before Christmas and sent her a Christmas card: to which she has not as yet deigned to reply: nor has she written home lately.

I think Canon Keller although *dignissimus*[38] has done all in his power to escape the burden of episcopate. He has no expectation of becoming Bishop: and no wish.

The allusion to my soutane and surplice is a conundrum: which you will share when we meet.

I hope you are now quite well! And out of the infirmarian's hands.

Yours always,
P.A. Sheehan

---

37 The *Cork Examiner* was a Catholic newspaper founded in Cork by John Francis Maguire in 1841.
38 First on the list of names submitted to the Holy See for the provision of the diocese.

24. FROM: MALLOW, 15 MARCH 1894

Text: MS IJPA J27/127/12 (18)

Dear Fr Russell,

I have to thank you very much for your own letter and that of Mr de Vere, which I enclose. It is a great satisfaction for me to know that my paper pleased him so much: yet the statements he makes uncomplainingly about the reception of his works in Ireland is enough to fill me with sadness. I cannot help thinking that some day Irishmen will wake up: and condemn their very culpable neglect in such matters. I will take hold of your kind suggestions so far that I will get my sermons rewritten for press purposes. I shall group those on our Blessed Lady together: the three on the Blessed Eucharist: then those on the saints: and perhaps some day I may see these little meditations in book-form, and be able to assure myself that I have done something for God before I die. Nearly all these sermons were written in England, as you may have observed, and they were written straight off without transcribing. The greatest mistake I have made is that I never transcribe: for it has doubled my labour. I burned three years ago; and the — partly written, *The Work and Wants of the Irish Church* which if I ever complete it, will be an important work.

But I must go slowly. But I would dearly like to see my few reflections on our Lord and Blessed Lady in the hands of our nuns and pious young people.

This was Renan's ambition, you remember, but I hope my motives are somewhat different from his.[39]

It was the title *Hound of Heaven*[40] I objected to. I think it incongruous, because it implies the exact opposite of what the poet intends: and it is undoubtedly irreverent – the very antithesis of the "Good Shepherd". The poem is fine – the best he has written. I have no sympathy with his Platonic lovemaking: but the "Daisey" at Storrington[41] is very pretty. He was with the Praemonstratensians in that place:

I am, my dear Fr Russell,

Yours always sincerely,

P.A. Sheehan

---

39 Joseph Ernest Renan (1823–1892), French orientalist and philosopher, published his revisionist *Vie de Jésus* in 1863.

40 Published in 1893.

41 The priory of Our Lady of Storrington in West Sussex was founded for the Canons of Premontré by the 15th Duke of Norfolk in 1882. It became the refuge of the poet Francis Thompson.

25. FROM: MALLOW 10 MAY 1894

Text: MS IJPA J27/127/13

My dear Fr Russell,

Tempting as the subject is, and particularly so as the suggestion to write on it comes from yourself and Mr de Vere, I must nevertheless set it aside for the present, as my hands are full of engagements of various kinds. Somehow, too, I have come to think that the subject is a particularly delicate one: F. Thompson is an English man, with a strange religious bias. I think very highly of the man personally and expect good things from him. Would he heed much the opinion of a mere Irish priest?

I have not seen the works of Hon. G. Lancers to which you allude.

I hope you are not so dead to the world that we may not congratulate you on the well deserved and popular honours conferred on Lord Russell of Killowen. We all regard it as a step to the wool-sack; and then Sir Thomas More there once more!

Yours always, my dear Fr Russell,
P.A. Sheehan, C.C.

26. FROM: MALLOW, 13 MAY [1894]

Text: MS IJPA J27/127/14

My dear Fr Russell,

I have now completed, under some difficulties, the first part of a story, which I should like to see in print. It is a college story, but with a moral for men, and forms the prologue to a continuation in which I am working out some of my theories.

You have been always so kind, and I depend so much on your judgment, that I should take it as a favour, if you would permit me, [to] send you for an *imprimatur*. Perhaps you would give me some advice also as to publication, of which I know nothing. I have been in correspondence with some English friends[42] with a view to its being published in London. But these are all details.

I hope you are really well,

Always yours etc.
P.A. Sheehan

42 Wilfrid Meynell (1852–1948), editor of the *Weekly Register*.

27. FROM: MALLOW, 23 MAY [1894]; A CARD.

Text: MS PA DON I/91

My dear Columba,

I think, but I am not sure, that Loo has abandoned the idea of the Paris trip. I suspect she dreaded the journey. If Frank wishes to come home for the Summer, we would all be delighted to see her; but I think she should retain her hold on Nantes, as possibly she may desire to return in the Autumn, and I understand the sisters have been extremely kind to her.

I am quite sure we'll find her very much improved, if that were possible. How good and holy and happy creatures, like yourselves, do exaggerate your little troubles!! And see everything with a magnifying glass!! I am always saying that nuns never know how happy they are.

Nothing new here; but daily expectations of a telegram from Rome to announce our future master. There is some rumour in the wind that the Canon of Youghal[43] is very much before the minds of the Roman Congregation.

P.A.S.

28. FROM: MALLOW, 7 JULY 1894

Text: MS IJPA J27/127/15

My dear Fr Russell,

Returning from our annual retreat this evening, I found your letter before me. My time is so cut up by various demands that I am proceeding but slowly with my work: or rather works for I have three different literary venture on hands. It is curious how I dip into one today, and another, which requires quite a different train of thought, tomorrow, and so on. But the three things are moving steadily on to completion.

There is quite a feeling of national pride abroad about the Lord Chief Justice.[44] His is a most extraordinarily brilliant career. Where, and at what lofty summit will it end?

Tomorrow, I start for a three weeks' holiday, or three weeks' musing, at Kilkee and Lisdoonvarna. However, I shall be near the sea, and that is

43 Canon Daniel Keller, parish priest of Youghal 1885–1922.

44 Sir Charles Arthur Russell, brother of Fr Matthew Russell, SJ.

enough for me. I am very sorry I shall miss your Fr Hughes, who is coming to our nuns. I should so like to meet him and show him any attractions in my power.

I am getting the sermons transcribed in volumes: –

1. *Turris Eburnea* etc. (sermons on our Blessed Lady),
2. *My Saints* (from Elias down to Aloysius and Alphonsus),
3. *Vita Mystica* (on the Blessed Sacrament etc).

I am not idle at all.

Yours, my dear Fr Russell,
Always,
P.A. Sheehan, C.C.

29. FROM: QUEEN'S HOTEL, LISDOONVARNA, 22 JULY 1894

Text: MS IJPA J27/127/16

My dear Fr Russell,

Your letter was forwarded to me here. I am so pleased that you liked the papers on *Prêtres-Adorateurs.*[45] The French priest at Wilton,[46] Cork, who is the Director for Ireland, was in despair: and when by some accident I met him, and heard of this priestly devotion, I at once volunteered to send a few pages to the *Record*,[47] which the editor kindly admitted. The subject was so important, and I have always felt so strongly that we ought to bring devotion to the great central mystery of Christianity more to the front, that I considered it would be out of place to attempt anything like style. So I put the matter as tersely and as strongly as I could: and I think it will

45 This was an association of priests begun in 1879 (but first mooted in 1867) by Pierre-Julien Aymard, founder of the Blessed Sacrament Fathers, and approved by Leo XIII in 1881. By 1913 it had an enrolment of 120,000 members. According to the statutes of the association, members were obliged to devote and hour every week to Eucharistic adoration before the Blessed Sacrament; maintain a *libellus adorationis* to be sent periodically to the central offices of the association, and to offer Mass for the association once a year. Sheehan, who strongly supported the association, contributed an article to the *Irish Ecclesiastical Record* on the association's objectives, entitled *Prêtres-Adorateurs,* which was published in vol. XV (July 1894), pp. 577–585.

46 The house of the Society of African Missions.

47 *The Irish Ecclesiastical Record* was founded by Cardinal Cullen in 1864 but lapsed in the 1870s. It was revived in 1880 and published under Episcopal authority from Maynooth College. It had ceased publication by 1976.

touch many priests, and perhaps awaken them to the reality of the Divine Presence.

I shall be much interested in Fr Kolbe's papers. His writings are full of concentrated thought I can hardly imagine how he can say anything new on "*In Memoriam*". But he has said so many original and excellent things on all subjects, that I shall not be much surprised. His paper on the *Art of Thinking* deserved to be popularized in pamphlet form almost as much as yours on *Amethyst*, which latter should be found in every Catholic household. In my curious and various readings, I came across *Amethyst*, its — and its — in C[harles] Reade's *The Cloister and the Hearth.*[48] I am afraid I cannot argue with you about Dr Barry's novels. Only a few days ago I thought of *The New Antigone*[49] for a convent library. I couldn't recommend it. Yet where shall we draw the line? Our people will take no moral lessons except through the novel or romances. Yet who can write a useful and harmless romance without touching on dangerous subjects? And then — there is the "last account" — especially for a priest. It is a difficult problem.

This is a delightful place – too little known.

I am, dear Fr Russell,

Yours always sincerely,
P.A. Sheehan

30. FROM: MALLOW, 25 FEBRUARY 1895

Text: MS PA DON I/87

My dear Sister Columba,

Your letter this morning gave me a fit of introspection. I know I am getting old; but am I really becoming grumpy? It is a fine thing to be able to see ourselves as others see us; and I must watch the advance of years for the future, for I shall not like to become a sour old man.

The article on Priests — I have not in my possession; and it is not worth much. But I am deeply interested in the subject, particularly Lay-Brothers, and if I thought it were possible to institute this blessed practice in

48 Published by Everyman's Library, London, 1861.

49 Published by Macmillan, London and New York, 1887. Sheridan Gilley describes this as William Barry's masterpiece and "best-selling feminist novel". See his article *Canon Patrick Augustine Sheehan:Priest and Novelist* in Peter Clarke and Charlotte Methuen *The Church and Literature*, Ecclesiastical History Society, Warton (GB), vol. 48, 2012, p. 398.

Doneraile I would try and get you all the literature on the subject. Dalton, — I don't possess either; but I think Fr O'Callaghan has a copy; and if so, you shall have it.

I sent you today by Fr Lenihan two manuscripts written by Miss Sexton, who is now with the Little Sisters in Cork. They may interest you; and I know they are edifying reading.

Our little Sister Raphael[50] is still very feeble. She is still making a great struggle for recovery; but I hope she will come all right soon.

All well here; I wonder how is our little exile in Nantes?

Kindest remembrance to Reverend Mother,

Always sincerely,

P.A. Sheehan

31. FROM: MALLOW, 23 MAY [1895]

Text: MS IJPA J27/127/17

My dear Fr Russell,

I sent by parcel post, the MSS of a story (1st. part), called: *Geoffrey Austin: Student.*

The 2nd Part, which I have not yet completed, will be entitled: *Geoffrey Austin: Bohemian.*

The idea of the 1st. part is to show how dangerous is profane learning, divorced from religious training, as exemplified in the career of Geoffrey Austin: and how fatal is a young man's opposition to his vocation as exemplified by Charlie Travers.

The 2nd Part (if ever I finish it) will trace the steady downward career of G. Austin, as he plunges from classics into latter day philosophies, until, at last on the verge of despair, he is converted to his old faith: whilst Charlie Travers, taking up his vocation as lay apostle, runs a short but glorious career.

I should like a candid opinion from you: and if you notice any grammatical, or other mistakes, to correct them as you go: as I shall not see the MSS again until it is in the hands of the printers.

Always yours sincerely,

P.A. Sheehan

50 Sr Raphael Wiseman (d. 1936) of the Convent of Mercy, Mallow, Co. Cork.

I think I have changed the spelling of Charlie's name here and there. Make sure it is uniform – "Charlie": and let me know your opinion as soon as possible.

P.S. You will be glad to hear that my brother,[51] who called on you some time since, has obtained the coveted appointment as auditor of the Local Government Board, from 72 competitors. His head-quarters is at Monaghan.

32. FROM: MALLOW, 5 JUNE [1895]

Text: MS IJPA J27/127/18

My dear Fr Russell,

During the last three days, we have had the Bishop[52] on visitation and confirmation: and it has been a busy time for us. I had quite forgotten that I ever had the presumption to think of writing a book.

There is nothing that I could possibly object to in your kindly criticism. The more minutely you examine my MSS the better I shall like it.

I think if you knew our Southerners, and all the pranks that are played in our — and in the Queen's, Cork, you would not think the personification of the Frenchman extravagant.

You have guessed the opinion of Mayfield rightly. All the characters are, however, quite original and imaginary, except the O'Dells, of whom I have seen prototypes. So also, all the scenes etc. are an amalgam, except the *Aunt Sally* episode which really took place.

Should you see Charlie spelt differently, please make it uniform. You see I wrote it all (4 pages at the time) without copying or correcting: now I should not be surprised if there were several verbal mistakes. You are infinitely kind to take all this trouble.

The MS will never go to print until you assure me that there is not a word in it which I might regret at the last.

Always yours sincerely,
P.A. Sheehan, C.C.

---

51 Denis Sheehan (b.1854).
52 Robert Browne (1844–1935), bishop of Cloyne 1894–1935.

The original of Mr Dowling was a Mr Colclough or Coakley – a brilliant classicist who was in Gayfield[53] under J. O'Donoghue. But I have changed the presentiment considerably.

33. FROM: MALLOW, 2 JULY [1895]

Text: MS IJPA J27/127/19

My dear Fr Russell,

The MS has arrived safely.

You have put me again under a great obligation by your kindly criticism and the patient way in which you have examined the MS.

My object (for as you rightly say, I am a preacher rather than a story teller) is not to condemn the study of the ancient classics but to condemn the custom of familiarizing the young Catholic mind with Paganism, and pagan philosophy and all the natural attractions of pagan life, without equal, and parallel training in the truths and beauties of Catholicity. I have always thought the dangers of too-secular an education consisted in showing the attractiveness of Greek thought and philosophy, and putting Christianity in the background, thus teaching the young mind to argue: "Where was the necessity for a revelation when human thought and human life were so perfect".

I purposely laid the scene in a Civil Service institution lest any existing institution might fall under criticism.

In the 2nd part, to be called *Geoffrey Austin: Bohemian*: I run G. Austin's and C. Travers' subsequent careers side by side – the former drifting further away from God, yet never losing his faith – the latter, taught by his fall, commences a career of religious usefulness in the City, under the inspiration of Fr Aidan. On Charlie's deathbed the friends are brought together, and G. Austin's conversion commences. How that is worked out will be the subject of a few interesting chapters: and I may add a 3rd part: *Geoffrey Austin: At Rest*.

---

53 A private educational establishment dedicated to the preparation of students to sit the entrance examinations for the Civil Service. It was located at Donnybrook, Dublin, having been founded by Bishop Dunne of Brisbane as a training college for students for his diocese. When its original purpose ceased, it became a lay college directed by Fr. Edward O'Donohoe of Brisbane. By 1917 it was a novitiate for the Carmelites. John D. Colclough (Mr. Dowling in the novel) claims that Canon Sheehan entered Gayfield College in the winter of 1872 or spring of 1873. Cf. Colclough's article, *Canon Sheehan: A Reminiscence and an Appreciation* in *Studies*, vol. 6, no. 22 (June 1917), pp. 275–288.

About publication, some English friends, who have not seen the MS and who do not know its gist, recommended to have it printed in Dublin and published in London. This would mean journeying to London: and many other inconveniences. Besides, I may do a little more publishing, if God gives me strength: and I should like to have a publisher near at hand in whom I could confide. So I shall offer the MS to Gill, and Son, Dublin: and failing them, I shall give it to Eason, who is very anxious to commence the publishing business. Perhaps, however, you will add to your other favours by kindly advising me in such an important matter.

I would prefer to publish the little volumes separately.

G. Austin: Student has 450 MS pages with 164 words to a page. It would make a volume about the size of one of Marion Crawford's (265 pages of print) or a little less than one of Louis Stevenson's.

34. FROM: MALLOW, 15 JULY [1895]

Text: MS IJPA J27/127/20

My dear Fr Russell,

Mr Gill wrote me that under the depressed condition of the book-market, he could not purchase my copyright, nor undertake the entire risk of publishing: but he was prepared to print the book,[54] and take half-profits, half-losses with me. Considering the fact that I am an unknown author, I think this is only fair: and I am sure, it was only your intervention that secured such terms. I wrote in reply to say, that I would forward the MSS and reserve my decision until I should know what exactly would be the cost of printing: and for what amount I should make myself responsible. Mr Gill has the MSS now: and I am to hear from him in a few days.

Do you remember one page in the chapter: *Mr Ferris dismissed*: in which I give the interview between/with the brothers in the schoolroom. It is a good dramatic scene, I think: but I have a scruple about such expressions as "wifely fashion": "Your Aspasia": "Lais": "By H … I am beginning to respect you" etc. I should be glad to have your opinion.

I am informed that the Bishop intends to advance me to the pastoral charge of Doneraile – a pretty town – six miles north of Mallow, just now vacated by the resignation of Fr Ashlin. This will be a great compliment as

54 *Geoffrey Austin: Student.* The holograph manuscript of *Geoffrey Austin: Student* is conserved in Dublin: National Library of Ireland, MS 4674.

there are about 26 priests senior to me in the diocese. This will change all my plans for the future, but I think, after I shall have settled down there, I shall have more time for literature: and I think I could commence a serial story for the *Irish Monthly* in January.

I am getting on with *Geoffrey Austin: Bohemian*:[55] and I should like to submit to you four chapters which will give you an idea of the story. Also, 3 chapters of a more ambitious work, which probably I shall not finish for years: entitled *The Work and Wants of the Irish Church*.[56] But I am afraid to trespass too much upon your time and indulgence.

I am, my dear Fr Russell,

Always yours faithfully
P.A. Sheehan

35. FROM: MALLOW, 17 JULY 1895

Text: MS IJPA J27/127/21

My dear Fr Russell,

I arranged finally with M. H. Gill and Son today.

They have acted very generously. The entire cost of printing (of which I bear half) is 37–10–0: they undertake the binding. The profit, if 1000 copies can be sold, will be 11d. per copy.

I enclose specimen page and specimen paper, which, however, will be somewhat thicker. I would have preferred a larger page, with 28 lines to a page, I suppose it would be more expensive.

I hope I won't be tortured with scruples as to expressions here and there. That verdict in the *New Antigone* which I think your Archbishop Porter of Bombay was the first to pronounce, has been always before my eyes. But the little book is for the world: and the sequel will be a strong, vigorous sermon in favour of a more robust Christianity amongst us. And it is only by gilding the pill, our young men can ever be induced to swallow it. This is the reason I wrote no preface. But I shall put one in *L'Envoi* at the end.

I have asked that the first edition shall be without my name.

Always yours sincerely,
dear Fr Russell,
P.A. Sheehan

---

55 Published in 1898 under the title *The Triumph of Failure*.
56 This work was never published.

36. FROM: DONERAILE 29 AUGUST [1895]

Text: MS IJPA J27/127/22

My dear Fr Russell,

I was so glad to see your well known handwriting again. I had heard from Fr Hughes that you had gone to the University College. I was wondering how you would like the change. You will certainly have more time for literary work; and it is a wide, useful field but what about all those, brethren and people whom you have left desolate?

I am afraid my second vocation must remain undeveloped here for some time. This is a vast parish, somewhat neglected and rundown and there is a vast deal of uphill work before me. But, please God, all will come right in time.

In the midst of brick and mortar, and the uncongenial companionship of plumbers, masons, slaters etc., I have just finished correcting proofs of *Geoffrey Austin*. I sent back the last fasciculus last night. I think your conjecture that the printing is done in Scotland is correct. The printers' names are all Scottish. The work is done well. I thought several times of sending you proofs en route to printer knowing that you would detect errors where I couldn't see them. I am afraid I shall regret not having done so: but I dreaded trespassing on your time, and I did not know but that you might have been very busy. The whole thing reads well in print. My name doesn't appear on title-page: but I have given permission to H. Gill to let it be known that I am the author. I am pushing through *Geoffrey Austin: Bohemian* as fast as I can. I shall have a wide field here for preaching.

I have completed a long poem in blank verse, (18 pages, 33 lines each) the first of a series of "Idylls", of the early Irish Church. It is called *Sentan, the Culdee.*[57] There are some strong passages, which, I fear would make it somewhat unsuitable for the *Monthly* but I wish you could use it.

"We are puppets, man in his pride etc"? I am beginning to believe it. My highest ambition was a little cottage, down near the sea, 2 rooms, undisturbed peace with my books, and lo! Here I am, unexpectedly, in an immense parish, that would take the zeal of the Curé of Ars[58] to build up,

57 Published in the January 1896 issue of *The Irish Monthly*.

58 Jean-Baptiste-Marie Vianney (1786–1859), St John Vianney, patron saint of parish priests, notable for his priestly and pastoral ministry. He was devoted to the confessional, to the Blessed Virgin Mary and to Saint Philomena.

and in a mansion that would shelter a community. We have been obliged to furnish it in vice-regal style, of which I am most heartily ashamed. But it is all the will of the Supreme, and I must throw myself heart and soul into my work. At another time, I would have been tortured with doubts and misgivings: but I have got a great grace, and am making myself as happy as possible.

Always, I am affectionately,
My dear Fr Russell,
P.A. Sheehan

37. FROM: DONERAILE, 8 OCTOBER 1895

Text: MS IJPA J27/127/23

Dear Fr Russell,

I should have replied to your letter which awaited my return from a short holiday: but I have been hopelessly bewildered for these past weeks between duties and anxieties in this my sphere of life.

For the last few days I have had my pen in hand to thank you for the complimentary words in the *Monthly*: but again I have been prevented. I am afraid my present surroundings are anything but favourable to literary pursuits. I am full of worry and anxiety.

The publishers have sent the 1st number of *G. Austin* which has appeared, asking me to what special papers it should be sent for review: and stating that it would be placed on the market yesterday (Monday). But there was no publication in yesterday's *Freeman*.[59] The book is well brought out, printing and style excellent: but I have been appalled at the number of mistakes that are left uncorrected. I do not blame the printer, tho' I think he did not accept all my corrections: but I had to run through the proofs hastily. How I allowed, or ever wrote, such repetitions as "experienced experiences" etc. is a wonder to me. But perhaps, no eye but your own, will detect them. If ever the book reaches a second edition, I shall make many corrections. But the main thing that troubles me is, that the little volume cannot be rightly understood until its sister volume *G. Austin, Bohemian* appears. But I am always inclined to take a most despondent view of my work.

59 *The Freeman's Journal* a moderate nationalist newspaper founded by Charles Lucas in 1764. It ceased publication in 1924 when it was incorporated into the *Irish Independent*.

Is it customary for publishers to allow a dozen or 20 copies of volumes to the author for distribution among friends?

I am not the author of the article *Bridges*. I never saw it.

I am copying *Sentan the Culdee* for your perusal. I like to read it often, which may be a good or bad sign.[60]

How can I thank you for all your sympathy and advice, and for having quoted my poor philosophy amongst the immortals.

Always sincerely, my dear Fr Russell,
P.A. Sheehan, P.P.

38. FROM: DONERAILE, 24 OCTOBER 1895

Text: MS IJPA J27/127/24

My dear Fr Russell,

In sending you *Sentan the Culdee*, I know it was quite out of form: and was going to ask you to use the surgeon's knife freely. I was thinking mainly of the subject matter: and afraid you would think it too bold for the *Irish Monthly*.

To show you what a curious amalgam I am, I had marked several unascribed lines in Milton's *Comus* to defend myself against your criticism. But, notwithstanding my admiration for the great blind poet, I shall adopt all your suggestions. You can have the poem for December or January: and I shall be very much in your debt but I have two fancies about type: (1) that the heading (which will be *Sentan, the Culdee*) shall be in black letter or German text: and (2) that the type shall be large and the spaces wide – not so much, however, as to take up too many pages.

Sentan is the first of a series of Idylls on Christian Ireland which I have in contemplation, and partly written.

I am under great obligation to my critic in the *Freeman*: and to you for having told me his name. I think Gill might push the sale of the book in America. He has generously sent me 3 copies: and offered others @ 2/6 each.

But next after your own approval, which came first, and without which the volume would not have seen the light, I value very highly the letters I

60 *Sentan the Culdee* appeared in the *Irish Monthly* of January 1896.

have got from my diocesan Superiors. They tell me that I have touched a blot on the Irish system: and interpreted ideas that were in many minds.

Let me know whether you now care for *Sentan* and others.

Always yours most gratefully,
P.A. Sheehan

39. FROM: DONERAILE, PALM SUNDAY [29 MARCH 1896]

Text: MS IJPA J27/127/25

My dear Fr Russell,

I hope I did not forget to thank you for the valuable advice given in your second last letter about the choice of publisher. I have since received circulars from the Authors' Society which contain very alarming warnings to young authors; and promise great assistance but I think I cannot do better than follow the example of Mrs Hinkson. I think I ought to have *Geoffrey Austin* (2) finished before the 1st. of May. But I cannot be certain: as I have so many distractions here. Talk of a P.P.'s life and position as a sinecure! I have had thrice the work since I left the ranks of the C.C.'s. I enclose table of contents for 2nd. volume. I want you in your charity to tell me:

1. Would I give any offence to the Carmelites, if I made G. Austin, after many vicissitudes, conquered by our Lord's love, and invested with the Carmelite habit at Mayfield?
2. Besides the reproach of unreality, levelled against the 1st. volume, what are the principal heads of offence that poor book was guilty of?
3. I want the concluding passage in *The Hound of Heaven,*[61] where the sinner is overtaken by the mercy of God.

Allow me to shake hands metaphorically with Fr David O'Bearne, SJ for his paper in the *Monthly* which has just come to hand. Are we waking up at last? There are materials for the building up of a great Catholic literature in Ireland: only we are too much afraid of criticism particularly from the other side of the Channel.

61 Published by Francis Thompson in 1893.

I thought I might possibly be in Dublin this week, in which case I should call to see you: but my arrangements are now uncertain.

With renewed thanks,

I am, my dear Fr Russell,

Yours always sincerely,
P.A. Sheehan

40. FROM: DONERAILE 11 JUNE 1896

Text: MS IJPA J27/127/26

My dear Fr Russell,

With many misgivings as to the licence I am taking with your time and trouble, I sent on yesterday the 1st. book of my second volume, containing 9 chapters. I have also quite finished the 2nd. book of 18 chapters, and am finishing revising it. There remain to be written the preface and the 3rd. book of five chapters.

I wish you would exercise quite Inquisitorial powers on these chapters, for your kindness makes me blind to a good many of my faults in style and in idea. I would be glad if your would take the blue pencil of an editor, and expunge without remorse whatever seems to you unfit for appearing before the public eye. I have omitted one chapter — because it was a diversion from weighty matters, and yet not quite up to the level of that seriousness which the book requires. Might I say that the whole gist of the book is to ridicule the un-meaning and nebulous philosophy of our day – its object is to stimulate lay cooperation in the Church's work – its motto is – Christ!

I am deeply immersed just now in two strange books, Zola's *Rome*[62] and Huysmans' *En Route*.[63] The former is a deadly and dangerous book, not so much against morals, as against the Holy See – just such a book as would keep hundreds of converts from the Church – and imagine 600 pages published in London for 3/6. The latter, as far as I can see by cutting the leaves is a repulsive book, that Kegan Paul should never have translated into English.

One of our Canons (Dennehy)[64] has just published a 2 volume historical

62 Published by the Bibliothèque Charpentier, Paris 1896.

63 Published in 1895.

64 Parish Priest of Kanturk, Co. Cork. Canon Dennehy published a further novel *A Flower of Asia: An Indian Story*, Burns and Oates, London 1901. The book was also published in the United States by Benzinger Brothers.

novel: *Alethea*: by Cyril, 8/–. It has cost him £150 to produce it. I suppose it will be sent to you for review. I haven't seen it.

Mother Austin[65] has been very kind and speaks so warmly of you.

Believe me, my dear Fr Russell,

Yours most sincerely,
P.A. Sheehan

41. FROM: DONERAILE, 21 JUNE 1896

Text: MS IJPA J27/127/27

My dear Fr Russell,

I sent you yesterday the II Book. What an affliction I am imposing upon you.

I am recommended to change the title, so that it should not be like the former book. What do you think?

Edna L – has done so. I am undecided between:

A Young Reformer
The Triumph of Failure
Plato or Christ
etc., etc., etc.

We are in the midst of a mission here and very busy.

Always yours gratefully,
P.A. Sheehan

42. FROM: DONERAILE, 6 JULY 1896

Text: MS IJPA J27/127/28

My dear Fr Russell,

Irish Monthly and your letter to hand. In reading your opinion of second volume, I shall be more afraid of your leniency than of any hypercriticism. It will depend on your verdict whether I shall proceed with Book III.

65 Mother Austin Carroll (1835–1909) foundress of the Sisters Mercy in Alabama at Selema, and subsequently at Mobile in 1895.

I send on a MSS written by a friend, Fr Wilfrid Browne, O.M.I. I rather like it. Do you think you can find a corner for it in the *Monthly*?

You let Canon Dennehy down very gently.[66] I am just off for the deserts which means a week's penance, and very poor sleep. At home, I am a veritable Rip van Winkle.

Yours always,
P.A. Sheehan

The MSS in your hands should be read, side by side with Zola's *Rome* and Huysmans' *En Route*, two books I had not seen, until my manuscript was completed.

43. FROM: DONERAILE, 21 JULY 1897

Text: MS PAHRC/HJHP/SH/1

Rev. dear Father,

I am in receipt of your kind communication. I shall be very happy to correspond with your wishes. I have been anxious for a long time to get into touch with the American priesthood: and if I had had the opportunity, I should have published the sequel to Geoffrey Austin in America. I believe the volume, (which is practically a series of essays on the futility of human science compared with the great central science of the Church, knitted together by a narrative) would be more widely understood in America than at home. However, as no opportunity arose which would bring me into relation with an American publisher, I have now very nearly completed arrangements with Messers Burns and Oates, London, for the publication of the volume which will extend to nearly 500 pages. I enclose list of chapters.

I have been engaged for some time in putting together some ideas about clerical education. I have struck out the 6 chapters and design: and have written the first three chapters. The whole when completed will run thus:–

Book I. The Student

Chapter I: Clerical Equipment: *Piety*

Chapter II: Clerical Equipment: *Culture (Philosophy)*

66 Fr Russell reviewed Canon Dennehy's novel in *The Irish Monthly*.

Chapter III: Clerical Equipment: *Culture (Theology)*
Chapter IV: Clerical Equipment: *Culture (Ecclesiastical History)*
Book II. The Priest
Chapter I: the Priest as *Sacrificer*
Chapter II: The Priest as *Custos Domini*
Chapter III: The Priest as *Psalmist*
Chapter IV: The Priest as *Dispenser of Mysteries*
Book III. The Apostolate
Chapter I: The Apostolate of Preaching
Chapter II: The Apostolate of the Schools
Chapter III: The Apostolate of the Press
Chapter IV: The Apostolate of Literature
Chapter V: The Apostolate of the Laity
Chapter VI: The Apostolate of the Religious Orders.

The first chapters are written which I shall be happy to submit to you whenever you come to Ireland. I could not say, however, in what time I shall have the whole design completed for I have a great deal to do both in missionary work and in literature. The volume, too, was intended primarily for the Irish Church: but the Introduction alone is affected by that idea.

I shall be very happy to hear from you again and remain
Rev. dear Father,
Yours in Christ,
P.A. Sheehan, P.P.

44. FROM: DONERAILE, NO DATE

Text: MS PAHRC/HJHP/SH/2

Subsequent Chapters of *My New Curate*[67]
Chapter X: Over the Walnuts and the –
A conversation on fraternal correction, preaching, the temperance question, etc.

---

67 *My New Curate* was serialized in *The American Ecclesiastical Review* from July 1898 to October 1899. It was published in book form by Marlier and Callanan of Boston in 1900. Sheehan's American début began with a paper entitled *Literary Criticism* (see letter 45 of 3 March 1898) published in *The American Ecclesiastical Review*, vol XVIII (June 1898), p. 591.

Chapter XI: beside the Singing River
Secret Societies. Destructive of Religion.
Chapter XII: My Madonna
A little pathos about one of the school children; and the use of charms in Ireland.
Chapter XIII: Larry McGee
My curate attempts at church Improvements. His annoyances etc.
Chapter XIV: Winter Studies
The philosophy of the tramp-world.
Chapter XV: Captain Campion not at his Christmas Duty.
My curate's conference with him.
Chapter XVI: Christmas Morning.
The *Adeste* by the new village choir.
Chapter XVII: My curate on "Literature".
Chapter XVIII: The May Conference.
Gives the programme etc. of our Irish conferences; and how Dr Letheby startled the conference by his vehemence.
Chapter XIX: The *Star of the Sea* is launched.
Great success. Troubles.
Chapter XX: The factory opened. Great success. Troubles.
Chapter XXI: An Eviction.
Chapter XXII: Dr Letheby bankrupt.
His final success.
Chapter XXIII: The Bishop's Visitation
Chapter XXIV: I get the Mozetta and my curate is promoted to the Cathedral.
These are all of course subject to modification, as the history progresses.

45. FROM: DONERAILE, 3 MARCH [1898]

Text: MS PAHRC/HJHP/SH/3

Rev. dear Father,

Some months ago you were kind enough to request some contributions from me for your magazine. I have had neither heart nor time to do much since: but perhaps you would allow me make my debut in your journal with the enclosed paper on "The Higher Criticism".

I have personally only too much reason to be thankful for my treatment, as evidenced by yourself in your critique of *Geoffrey Austin* last year. But I think and feel that we are too prone to admire everything that comes from the opposite camps of infidelity and heresy instead of assuming the efficiency of the vast forces at our disposal.

It is quite possible, however, that this paper may not, in some respects, meet your views. In that case you would do me a great favour of returning the MSS as I rarely keep copies of what I write.

I am, Very Reverend dear Father,

Faithfully yours in Christ,
P.A. Sheehan, P.P.

The Editor
American Ecclesiastical Review
3 East 14th Street,
New York,
USA.

46. FROM: DONERAILE, 2 APRIL 1898

Text: MS PAHRC/HJHP/SH/4

Dear Rev. Father,

Many thanks for your letter and enclosure. (20 dollars). I quite approve your change of title in my paper. I had adverted to it: but I thought to give the paper a catching title.

In reference to your suggestion that I should write a series of papers on clerical life, it is rather a curious coincidence that I had already in my portfolio ten chapters on clerical life in Ireland, which I had intended to develop into a volume. They were, however, intended for popular reading: and my idea was to introduce my own ideas, suggestions, etc., under the sugared coating of a story. I venture to send you these chapters.[68] It is quite possible they will not meet your views, in which case I would thank you to return them.[69]

Should they be suitable for your paper, then I could easily direct them from the original purpose and make the remaining chapters more closely indicative of clerical studies, duties, etc.

68 See footnote 96.
69 These papers eventually became *My New Curate*.

In any case, it was my intention to offer the papers as a serial to some Catholic magazine.

With very many thanks,

I am, dear Rev. Father,

Yours in Christ,
P.A. Sheehan

I think Wilfrid Meynell, editor of the *London Weekly Register*,[70] will be much interested in my paper on criticism. He always notices your review.

I suppose that I have to thank you also for the fact that *Geoffrey Austin* is about to be translated into German.

47. FROM: DONERAILE, CO. CORK, 30 APRIL 1898

Text: Transcription from Herman Heuser, *Canon Sheehan of Doneraile*, p. 130.

Dear William,[71]

I deferred writing to thank you for the great favour done me by sending me an early copy of your new novel, until I should have had the gratification of reading it, and telling you what I thought of it. I have now gone carefully through the chapters; but last night I had to close the book at the 21 Chapter. *The Wreckers* quiet overpowered me by the dramatic intensity of the description. I am not acquainted with any chapter in fiction that equals the dramatic force. It challenges comparison with the famous storm scene in David Copperfield, which culminated in Steerforth's death; but the latter is easy reading. *The Wreckers* cannot be read without great nerve tension.

I think you have produced a memorable book. It is your greatest step towards realizing the vocation that many have foreshadowed for you – that of being the "Walter Scott" of Ireland. What will strike everyone most in the book is its peculiar Gallic flavour. You did a wise and artistic thing in giving the Irish expressions as they occurred and inserting the Irish idioms in the dialogue. But it must have cost you immense study – in history and language. It is a grand Irish novel; and will be taken to the hearts of the people. But it is all so pitiful. You have done justice to Sir John Perrot – a

70 A Catholic newspaper founded in London in 1881 which, in 1888, incorporated the *Catholic Standard* (founded 1849). It continued as *The Weekly Register and Catholic Standard.*

71 William O'Brien, MP (1852–1928).

figure almost too much neglected in Irish history. I hope you will deal yet with my deceased parishioners, Edmund Spencer and Raleigh.

There will be a peculiar attraction for the book just now, as it calls up so powerfully our past relations with Spain. And a very large percentage of our countrymen cling to these conditions, and give all their sympathies in the present war[72] to our old ally.

With most grateful thanks for your kind remembrance, and with all good wishes for your future, fraught with such vast consequences for Ireland, I am, dear William,

Yours affectionately,
P.A. Sheehan, P.P.

48. FROM: DONERAILE, CO. CORK, 6 MAY 1898

Text: Transcription from Herman Heuser, *Canon Sheehan of Doneraile*, p. 135

Reverend Dear Father,

I enclose corrected proofs. I received your letter and cheque (50 dollars) for which accept my thanks. The MS Registered came to hand also to-day, with proofs.

My original idea in writing those papers was to ventilate my own ideas on purely ecclesiastical subjects. Then I changed the plan and introduced a little romanticism. Now that you have kindly taken up the papers, I revert to the first design; and will make these papers of Irish life at the same time sermons in miniature.

I have rewritten, therefore, the remaining chapters, leaving out the romance – the story of the witch, etc. I have retained the chapter, or rather parts of it, *The Great House*, and renamed it *At the Station*. I have also retained the chapter *Our Concert* which is drawn from actual experience; and in which I desire to show what could be done in Ireland if we only wished. I have rewritten the chapter on secret societies, and have added two new sketches, *Severely Reprimand* and *A Lesson in Resignation*.

I have expunged all the rest, and confined the chapters to a priest's daily experiences in Ireland with all classes. I think you will find this satisfactory; but of course you can best judge what is suitable for the majority of your readers.

---

72 The Spanish American war of 1898.

If you have any suggestions to make as to the course which these papers ought to take, I shall be most happy to accept them, so far as I am able.

I shall send remaining chapters in a few days.

Thanking you very much for all your kindness,

I am, dear Father,

Yours faithfully in Christ,
P.A. Sheehan, P.P.

49. FROM: BRIDGE HOUSE, DONERAILE, 28 MAY 1898

Text: MS PAHRC/HJHP/SH/5

My dear Fr Heuser,

I sent by this mail, leaving Queenstown tomorrow Sunday 29th four chapters of *My New Curate*. I sincerely hope they will please you, and reach you in time for the July No. I am glad you have preserved my anonymity, altho' my friends here have guessed at once the author.

I would hardly care to write those pages, if I could not make them edifying as well as amusing: and it is, therefore, a source of great satisfaction to be assured by you that they must do good. I hope I shall succeed in not making any teaching too obtrusive.

You will see that I have altogether eliminated the romantic, and cut away all my scripture passages, which to an author, is equivalent to a surgical operation. I have introduced Campion for he belongs to a class that are likely to give trouble in Ireland. In most of our towns, professional men have great difficulty in approaching the Sacraments; and I want to show Dr Letheby's success there.

The *Station Picture* and *Our Concert* are drawn from life. Each has its own moral, that of the latter being – the ease with which village choirs may be organized, as I shall show in succeeding papers. The *Severely Reprimanded* speaks for itself. I enclose syllabus of succeeding chapters that you may know the drift of my work.

My great difficulty is to draw from life, and yet avoid identifying any character with living persons. And we are so narrow and insular here in Ireland, that it is almost impossible to prevent priests saying: That is so and so: That is Father – etc. But I shall steer clear without wounding charity.

I shall leave the correction of proofs in your own hands. A primitive mistake is of no consequence.

I hold a very good short tale on hands, called: *The Monks of Trabolgan.*[73] It was sent back from *The Catholic World*[74] on account of its length: 32 MSS pages. It would suit your series of papers as: *My New Curate's First Essay in Literature.*

With many thanks for all you kindness

I am, dear Father,

Yours in Christ,

P.A. Sheehan

A note in the left hand margin of the first page reads: The Bishop is taking around with him the May No. and reading it at the Visitation Dinners here in Cloyne.

50. FROM: DONERAILE, 27 AUGUST 1898

Text: MS PAHRC/HJHP/SH/6

My dear Fr Heuser,

Many thanks for your letter and enclosure (£8–0–0) just received. I am happy to know that these papers continue to give pleasure. I think they are attracting some attention at this side, as you may see by the slip attached at head of the letter.

I have also to thank you for cutting from the *Literary Digest.*[75] I showed it to Dr Matthew Russell, SJ, Editor of the *Irish Monthly*, who was staying with me at the time. It is a curious fact that Dr Russell and Fr Finlay, SJ, came simultaneously to the conclusion that *My New Curate* was my work, from purely internal evidence.

I had also had the pleasure of receiving the congratulations of Bishop Brady of Boston, who was in Clare with me, and to whom Dr Hogan,

---

73 *The Monks of Trabolgan* was originally intended as a sketch for an extensive work on monastic life. When Sheehan discovered Huysmans' *En Route* (see letter 121 of 28 May 1904) he abandoned the project. The story was rejected by the *Catholic World* because of its length. Fr Heuser declined to publish it as part of *My New Curate*. It was subsequently offered to Fr Thomas Finlay SJ, editor of the *New Ireland Review*, but withdrawn. It was eventually published by the Catholic Truth Society in Dublin and translated into Polish. See note 179.

74 *The Catholic World* was founded by Thomas Hecker in 1865. It continued publication in the United States under the auspices of the Paulist Fathers until 1996.

75 Founded in 1890 by Isaac Kaufmann Funk, the *Literary Digest* was published in New York by Funk & Wagnalls. It was a general interest magazine published weekly. It closed in 1938 following a controversial poll which it conducted on the probable outcome of the 1936 presidential elections in the United States.

SJ, revealed the authorship. His Lordship said that his assistants read the number eagerly. If you think there are any subjects on literature, poetry or philosophy that you think could be made suitable for your readers in the form of articles, I shall have some spare time during the winter months, and I might take them up. I have an article on Priestly Culture nearly completed. It was one of a series that I projected. It deals with the importance of the study of philosophy. But I suppose Dr Hogan (whose papers are learned and attractive) holds the field there.

I am, dear Fr Heuser,

Yours sincerely,
P.A. Sheehan, P.P.

51. FROM: BRIDGE HOUSE, DONERAILE, 10 SEPTEMBER 1898

Text: MS PAHRC/HJHP/SH/7

My dear Fr Heuser,

There is just one paragraph in the chapter *Beside the Singing River* of the wording of which I am not quite sure. I think it commences:

"It was a magnificent leap of imagination on Fr Letheby's part to connect Jews and Freemasons with etc., etc."

What I intended to convey was: 1. that, as in Europe, so in Ireland, anti Catholic Journals are run by Freemasons, and possibly Jews: 2. That Jewish and Freemason firms in these countries do a large business in making and selling devotional objects, beads, scapulars etc.: 3. That Jewish peddlers through the country, are often agents for the sale of pornographic literature.

It was not my meaning to connect this latter business with newspapers in Dublin or in Ireland. Would you kindly modify or omit. These papers are attracting a good deal of attention in Ireland: and I see the necessity of being very accurate and circumspect in what I publish, especially as I cannot see proofing.

Yours very sincerely,
P.A. Sheehan, P.P.

52. FROM: DONERAILE, 2 JANUARY 1899

Text: MS IJPA J27/127/29

My dear Fr Russell,

I do not quite know how to thank you all, yourself, Fr Brown, Mr Coyne etc., for all your great kindness to me. Mr Coyne's review was too flattering. May I depute you to convey to him my deep obligations and kindness. He truly described the book as *not* a great novel. I have the word. But I intended the book to be a psychological study of a troubled soul; and such my kind reviewer found it. Then comes your second paragraph in the January *Monthly*; and hot foot on all comes a letter from Dr Barry so kind and so appreciative that I feel very humbled and ashamed. I would send it to you, but I fear I should be violating all canons of modesty. He is writing a long review (signed) for a Catholic paper: and will push the book even with non Catholic journals. His own book is expected immediately. I suppose the "bitters" will come after all the "sweets" to me. My only regret is that no one has yet touched on Charlie's vocation, which I intended to be the real *motif* of the book after the first objects, as specified in the *L'Envoi*.

I nearly fainted when I read "Entice" for "Eager" on page 341. How did it escape your lynx-eyes?

Would you send me the *Monthly* for December and January?

Enclosed is a New Year's gift in the form of my subscription.

Always yours,

Most gratefully,
P.A. Sheehan, P.P.

53. FROM: DONERAILE, 7 JANUARY 1899

Text: MS PAHRC/HJHP/SH/8

My dear Fr Heuser,

Your letter just to hand with enclosure. Very many thanks for all your kind, encouraging words, which are a powerful stimulus to fresh exertions. And all kinds of good wishes, in reciprocity to your own, for the coming year.

I am quite disappointed to hear that my book has not reached you as yet. I am writing to B. and Oates about the matter. It is just possible that their agents Benzinger Brothers in New York have copies; but I directed that the press, especially yourself, should be supplied promptly. I am happy to say it is attracting some notice at this side. All the papers have been very kind; and extended articles will appear in the *New Ireland Review*,[76] the *Irish Ecclesiastical Record*, etc.

Dr William Barry of Dorchester, Oxford, is taking it up warmly, and is writing a long notice for a Catholic paper this week. But I look to America for the success of the book.

Again, with many thanks,
I am dear Fr Heuser,

Yours sincerely in Christ,
P.A. Sheehan

Just as I was closing it occurred to me to send you one spare copy, which I have by me. It will save time and be a Christmas souvenir.

54. FROM: DONERAILE, 17 FEBRUARY 1899

Text: MS PAHRC/HJHP/SH/9

Dear Fr Heuser,

I send by this mail five chapters, nearly 70 pages of MSS for April and May Nos. of the *American Ecclesiastical Review*.[77] I think you will find them quite equal to the preceding chapters. My next parcel will contain five more, making a total of 30 chapters, which will complete the history of Father Dan.

I hope you liked *The Triumph of Failure*.[78] It has been wonderfully well received by the entire Catholic press in these countries; and even the Indo-European correspondence of Bombay has been quite flattering. I have seen

76 *The New Ireland Review* was founded in 1894 by Fr Thomas A. Finlay, SJ as a literary magazine. Among its contributors were George Russell (Æ), James Cousins, Douglas Hyde, Thomas Kettle, Eoin MacNeill, George Moore, Horace Plunkett, T. W. Rolleston, Fred Ryan, George Sigerson, John Synge, John Todhunter, and W.B. Yeats. It was eventually subsumed into *Studies*.

77 Published in Philadelphia (1898–1927) and Washington (1927–1975). It was the first American theological journal.

78 *The Triumph of Failure* was not serialized in the *American Ecclesiastical Review* as rights had already been given to Burns and Oats, London and New York. The novel was published in book form in 1900. Edward McLysaght (edt.) in *A Literary Life: Essays and Poems*, Phoenix Press, Dublin, pp. 58–67 published a preface written in 1896 and intended for *The Triumph of Failure*.

nothing from your side as yet, except the excellent notice in *The Catholic World*. Some Berlin publishers are negotiating for a German translation.

Herder, of Freiburg and St Louis have written about the publication of *My New Curate*. I told him that you were in correspondence with some New York firms; and to communicate with you.

I hope you have escaped the New Yorkers' experience of the blizzard. It is as warm as June here; but rain! rain! rain!

I am, my dear Fr Heuser,

Yours always in Christ,
P.A. Sheehan, P.P.

Could you send me one June and one November number of the *American Ecclesiastical Review?*

55. FROM: DONERAILE, 13 MARCH 1899

Text: MS PAHRC/HJHP/SH/10

Dear Fr Heuser,

Most grateful thanks for your letter and enclosure (£10), for the extra numbers you have sent me; but, above all, for your kind encouraging words, which are worth more than gold. Your critique of my book was admirable. Altogether, I have reason to be most grateful. Your remarks about Dr Barry have been echoed here by very many gifted and holy priests: and I am quite sure they are correct. But, Dr Barry, our finest genius, has been literally fleeing into the hands of Protestants by the lack of sympathy in his earlier efforts. Fancy, he never received a line of encouragement during all the years he was writing for Catholic reviews. He is supporting his church and mission by his pen; and just now, is threatened with a bad breakdown in health, and must go abroad. I have written to him strongly urging him to take up the line of Christian apologetics: but he answers, who will read him in that department: yet, as in the case of the *Two Standards*,[79] he is able, by Protestant sympathy, to get an edition of 4,000 copies off his hands, before it is in print. I assure you, (comparing small things with great), my experience is almost similar. For the years I was writing for the *Irish Ecclesiastical Record*, I never received one word of encouragement. You and

79 Published by T.F. Unwin, London in 1898 and by the Century Company, New York, 1899 .

my dear friend, Fr Russell, are the only priests that have ever said a kindly word of my work hitherto. Now, I am on the full swim of the tide: and my last book has made me a thousand friends: but it was weary work ; only I felt I was working for Our Lord, and He would reward me. And He has a thousand fold. But venturing into the field of Catholic literature is a greater risk than many are aware of; and many a writer can say, as Dr Barry says, *aquae inundaverunt animam meam.*

Probably, I shall stretch out *My New Curate* a few chapters farther than intended: as I want to make the end interesting. And then, with your permission, I shall be able to open a new series entitled: *Up Shepherds! Being the Harvest of a Quiet Eye!*[80] This time to be told in the third person, and commencing with experience of English missionary life. Probably, I could give you the first chapters for September. You may, of course, have a more attractive series to offer. I hope you will. But let me know in time.

I am happy to know that our good nuns are reading my papers. I'll omit all the profanity, when the series appears in book form.

And now I thank you again for all for all your kindness, for your spirit of enterprise, and I hope, under Heaven, that you may be the means of inaugurating quite a new day in Catholic literature.

I am, dear Fr Heuser,

Yours always in Christ,
P.A. Sheehan, P.P.

56. FROM: BRIDGE HOUSE, DONERAILE, 5 APRIL 1899

Text: MS PAHRC/HJHP/SH/11

Dear Fr Heuser,

I forward by this mail (Sunday 7th) the six final chapters of *My New Curate*. I hope you will find them a worthy termination of the serial. I ran the XXX chapters so far – 18 or 19 pages – that I was obliged to pull up the last abruptly. Yet, I like closing a story with a certain amount of dramatic action.

I also forward printers' proofs of first eighteen chapters, corrected for press. Should you think advisable to give English translations (as footnotes) of the Italian and Latin quotations, it can be done. As to the illustrations, I

80 The original title of *Luke Delmege*.

have been looking for photos that might suit Father Dan and Fr Letheby; but none comes up to my ideals. And I feel that most readers here will be difficult to please in that matter, where faces are concerned. Scenery, of course, is easily managed; and there could be a few Sacred Pictures, suggested by the allusions, here and there, in the book.

I am just recovering from a short feverish cold; and am much debilitated.

Always gratefully,
P.A. Sheehan, P.P.

I have a lingering hope that some of your young priests may take up the syllabus of subjects, (given in the — chapters), metaphysical and historical, and build up articles for you, the same as I have suggested for Fr Letheby, and which eventually would form a comprehensive library on these important subjects.

Fr Charles J. Kelly, D.D., diocese of Scranton, Pa., called a few days ago to see the author "Daddy Dan".

57. FROM: DONERAILE, 8 APRIL 1899

Text: MS PAHRC/HJHP/SH/12

Dear Fr Heuser,

You have taken a great deal of trouble about my book; and I cannot see that I can do better than leave the matter unreservedly in your hands. It would be quite impossible for me to form an opinion, so far away from the centre of action. But it seems to me that Marlier's[81] offer should be accepted, unless some other, more advantageous, were offered before publication. The only person whom I consulted about the matter here, thought that it would be better to retain the copyright, and arrange only for edition by edition; but I dare say the publishers would not stereograph under such conditions. I cannot say anything, therefore, except I am quite sure my interests will be best safeguarded by leaving the matter absolutely in your hands.

In a few days, I shall forward the remaining chapters: this will leave me free for evolving the ideas of *Ye Shepherds*.

81 Marlier and Callanan of Boston.

Should good fortune waft you to this side during the coming Summer or Autumn, I shall take it for granted that you will pay me a welcome visit here.

I am, dear Fr Heuser,

Yours sincerely,
P.A. Sheehan, P.P.

I enclose letters.
[On the fourth page, the following German lines in *Kurrentschrift*]:

Nur etwas Liebe, etwas Muth,
nur festes Gottvertrauen;
das nützet mehr als Geld und Gut,
Du mußt's von dir erschauen.

Nur etwas Demut und Geduld,
nur vorwärts, nie zurück;
und irrest du nur, frei von Schuld,
so wohnt in dir das Glück.

58. FROM: BRIDGE HOUSE, DONERAILE, 30 MAY 1899

Text: MS PAHRC/HJHP/SH/13

My dear Fr Heuser,

I am in receipt of your letter and enclosure (£12–0–0) for which accept my hearty thanks. In a higher degree I feel intensely grateful for the last words of your kind letter, assuring me that our little serial has gone home to the hearts of the American priesthood, and that its lessons are likely to fructify there. The same mail brought me a letter from far Melbourne assuring me of the same thing. And I feel very humble, and most grateful to our Divine Lord that he has chosen such a weak instrument for so great a work. As to secular fame, I think I hardly value it; for one is always tempted to cry: *vanitas vanitatum*.

But to have spoken successfully to my dear brother priests and to have won their affectionate sympathy is a reward I never dreamt of expecting; and which is very sweet and consoling.

When Mr Marlier writes I shall tell him he can have the copyright; as I don't care to have too many burdens; and in this matter of copyright and the royalty, I shall accept his terms, already offered.

Let me add that your *Review* has earned unstinted praise (or shall I say its Editor) on this side of the Atlantic for its enterprise in rising above the usual leaden level of Catholic magazines. It is a tremendous lesson to many of our home journals.

I shall gladly accept any hints as to the future serials which you may be pleased to offer; or the line which I should follow. My Melbourne friend suggests the imperfections and drawbacks in clerical education: but I feel the subject is over done, tho' I have a few papers beside me on the subject.

With all gratitude and good wishes,

I remain, my dear Fr Heuser,

Yours in Christ,

P.A. Sheehan, P.P.

[59]. FROM: ST STEPHEN'S GREEN, DUBLIN, 18 JUNE 1899

Text: MS Daniel E. Hudson Papers, University of Notre Dame Archives, Notre Dame, Indiana, USA (1).

My dear Fr Hudson,

I think Fr Sheehan, the holy and gifted Parish Priest of Doneraile, Co. Cork, is not yet a contributor to the *Ave Maria*. Probably, you look at the *American Ecclesiastical Review* in which his serial *My New Curate* has attracted great attention. It is just coming out as a volume, and I expect its circulation will far exceed that of his previous work, *Geoffrey Austin* and *The Triumph of Failure*. Your American priests, readers of *My New Curate*, will, I think be prejudiced in favour of anything else by Father Sheehan. I enclose his note about the poem which goes to you by this mail. I think that in your establishment the bringing out of this as a tiny booklet quarto would be costly. *The Irish Monthly* will do its best to make it known if such a booklet issues from your press.

My publishers Burns and Oates said they had sent my last little eucharistic book *Close to the Altar Rails*[82] to eleven American journals. Bad

82 Published by Burns and Oates, London, 1899.

as they are, they cannot have overlooked the *Ave Maria*. But Mr James Bowden of 10 Henrietta Street, London, is not a publisher with any ecclesiastical connection, and therefore I will myself lay at your feet a book I am expecting now any day: *Idyls of Killowen: A Soggart's Secular Verses*.[83]

I hope your health is satisfactory at present. Mine still continues its imperturbable equanimity.

I am dear Fr Hudson,

Yours sincerely,
Matthew Russell, SJ

It just occurs to me to send you this Silver Jubilee Index of *The Irish Monthly*: not that it can be of any use to you.

Enclosure:
From: Bridge House, Doneraile, 10 June 1899

My dear Fr Russell,

I write to thank you for the *Austral Light* with the kindly review of Fr Watson; and to say I shall send you by this mail my poem, or paraphrase, of the *Magnificat*. I have only just given it the final touches; for I have been banished from all literary work for the past month or 6 weeks by the influenza, and the incessant demands of parochial work.

Should you give the *Magnificat* your *imprimatur* I would be thankful to you to forwards it to Fr Hudson. I am presuming it is too cumbrous for a magazine, like your own, or the *Ave Maria*; but my hope is that Fr Hudson might bring it out through the Ave Maria press in a tiny quarto booklet, for general circulation. Of course there would be no use in applying to any publisher at home.

I am out of reach of all literature at present; but I hardly like the tone of the new series of the *Weekly Register*. There is something about it that savours of dangerous novelty. Who is the editor? I am sure that W. Meynell must have resigned.

I hope you are well; and that you escaped "la grippe". It was my first experience and it attacked the weak spot – my chest. I am now all right, thank God!

Always yours,

My dear Fr Russell,
P.A. Sheehan

83 Published by Bowden in 1900.

60. FROM: DONERAILE, 15 JUNE 1899

Text: MS PA DON I/88

My dear Columba,

Sister Anthony must be praying for Margaret, for I had conditionally promised to consider another application this morning.

You will tell Margaret that I shall take her back on 2nd. or 3rd. week of July if she is prepared to come; but I don't intend to keep a grown second servant like Mary, because there is no work here for three servants and I cannot continue paying £36 a year any longer in wages. I shall get some young girl however, who can be trained and made fit for life, such as we had before. Let me have a decisive answer as soon as possible, as I shall be pestered with letters.

Yours etc.,
P.A. Sheehan

61. FROM: BRIDGE HOUSE, DONERAILE, 30 JUNE 1899

Text: MS PAHRC/HJHP/SH/14

Dear Fr Heuser,

Your letter with enclosures (for which accept my grateful thanks) has just reached me; and the American mail leaves in a few hours; so I am snatching a brief moment to thank you again for all your kindness. We go on retreat tomorrow; and then I go to England for a brief holiday.

As I said before I feel quite humbled and ashamed at all the praise my few papers have received. But my reward lies not there, for I know only too well what a passing thing is human praise or blame. But I feel great gratitude towards our Divine Lord for His having vouchsafed to use me for His own sacred cause; and it is a large and generous reward to be assured, as I have been assured so many times, that I have earned the goodwill and affection of the American priesthood, whom I have always revered since I had the happiness of meeting some of them, during my curacy in Queenstown. This week again Fr Yorke of San Francisco,[84] has been saying kind things of me in Maynooth; and yesterday I had a charming letter from one of your best contributors, Dr Bruneau, asking permission to have my books translated into French.

84 Fr Peter Yorke (1864–1925) editor of *The Monitor* and founder of *The Leader* newspaper.

But, assuredly all this would have been impossible, if I had not had the good fortune of having you as sponsor. No magazine at this side of the Atlantic would have published *My New Curate*. They are all old fashioned and conservative, forgetting that the Church must move with the age and that "The old order changeth, giving place to new." But I think your enterprise, and the success attending it, has caused some heart searching here in Ireland.

I shall certainly write a preface for the book; and introduce my obligations to the *American Ecclesiastical Review* and its Editor.[85] I have written to Mr Marlier accepting his terms, and also saying that he can have the copyright also. I do not see what use it could be to me, unless like Rudyard Kipling, I should have to buy it back at a big price in future years. The formal agreement, promised by Mr Marlier, I am expecting by every mail. The book will have a large sale here. I had forwarded to Mr Marlier a book of sketches and some loose photographs for his illustrations.

I had been thinking of asking you to commence the new series in January 1900, instead of next October, partly because it would synchronise better with dates, and partly because I am sometimes hard pressed with work. But I have refused to entertain any proposals, until the series, *Ye Shepherds!* has been ended in your magazine. Let me know what you think. Of course, I can supply you with copy for October in case you thought it advisable.

I shall be very much pleased if Mr Marlier and myself can become permanent friends, as we shall be. I am very anxious to bring out a volume of sacred poetry next year; and our publishers here are slow and unsatisfactory.[86]

I am so sorry I shall not have the pleasure of seeing you face to face this Autumn. Perhaps the fates will yet be kind, and let you come. I have a large house and garden in a very poor village: but the country around is beautiful and a few weeks here would send you back rejuvenated and refreshed to your desk. May it be so!

Again, with all thanks,

I am, dear Fr Heuser,

Yours in Christ,

P.A. Sheehan, P.P.

---

85 See footnote 95 below.

86 The volume, *Cithara Mea*, was published by Marlier and Callanan of Boston in June 1900. Holograph copies of poems from *Cithara Mea* are conserved in Dublin: National Library of Ireland, MS 4689.

62. FROM: BUXTON, 17 JULY 1899

From: The Eagle Hotel, Buxton, England, 17 July 1899

Text: MS Daniel E. Hudson Papers, University of Notre Dame Archives, Notre Dame, Indiana, USA (2).

Dear Fr Hudson,

I am here on a brief holiday: and shall remain to the 26th inst. Your most kind letter was forwarded to me. I am ever so pleased and gratified that I shall make my *début* in your fine journal with a poem, which, I hope, will increase in many hearts a great love for our Blessed Lady. I had an idea, when composing it, that it might suit, if illustrated, as a Christmas gift, like those which are issued in superabundance by the Protestant press. And the illustrations would not be too difficult to find, as you must have quite a number of beautiful pictures of our B. Lady, such as we have seen in the *Ave Maria* from time to time.

I see the *Ave Maria* regularly in Mallow Convent: but I should be very happy, indeed, if you would kindly send it to me.

For all your other kind words, accept my gratitude. Nothing has touched me as deeply as the generous appreciation of my work by my American brethren. I don't care much for secular fame, knowing how worthless it is: but I hope it is a legitimate pleasure to feel grateful for all the generous words that have reached me from beyond the Atlantic; and which are a powerful stimulus to renew efforts to keep on the course of Catholic literature.

I am, Rev. dear Father,

Yours gratefully in Christo,
P.A. Sheehan, P.P.
Doneraile.

63. FROM: BRIDGE HOUSE, DONERAILE, 2 SEPTEMBER 1899

Text: MS Daniel E. Hudson Papers, University of Notre Dame Archives, Notre Dame, Indiana, USA (3).

Dear Fr Hudson,

Very many thanks for your most kind letter, and for the magazines. The printing is a marvel of correctness. We could not do so well here, without proofs and second proofs. There are one or two alterations which I would suggest and which you will find on next page. I liked that article on Turner[87] very much. It had but one fault. It was too short. The writer could have given a most interesting paper on that very interesting subject. There is certainly one, and I think two, of Turner's landscapes in the National Gallery, Dublin.[88]

Whenever you want anything from me, especially in the poetic line, don't spare me. I have a large portfolio, that has never been printed as yet.

I am, dear Fr Hudson,

Faithfully yours,
P.A. Sheehan, P.P.

64. FROM: BRIDGE HOUSE, DONERAILE, 21 OCTOBER 1899

Text: MS Daniel E. Hudson Papers, University of Notre Dame Archives, Notre Dame, Indiana, USA (4).

Dear Fr Hudson,

I would be glad to have as many of the leaflets as you can send. Would fifty be too much? I am sure Fr Russell would give a notice of it in the December *Monthly;* and perhaps Gill, Dublin, could dispose of a few.

I send you herewith two poems, for better, for worse. Of course, Marlier will send you *My New Curate* for review.

Always in gratitude,
P.A. Sheehan, P.P.

---

87 Joseph Mallord William Turner (1775–1851).

88 The only pictures by Turner in the National Gallery of Ireland in 1899 were: St Alban's Abbey, Hertfordshire (NGI 2283) and Harlech Castle, Wales (NGI 2284). Both were presented to the National Gallery of Ireland by William Smith in 1872.

65. From: Bridge House, Doneraile, 18 November 1899

Text: MS Daniel E. Hudson Papers, University of Notre Dame Archives, Notre Dame, Indiana, USA (5).

Dear Fr Hudson,

Very many thanks for the two packages of leaflets just arrived. I think they are very well turned out. We could not do so well at this side.

I am opening a new serial in the *American Ecclesiastical Review* for January.[89] I wish I could do more for you; but you have a magnificent staff of contributors.

I think a good deal of our Catholic neglect of literature is traceable to want of literary training of taste in our colleges. And we have not yet grasped the idea that literature is our only vehicle of interpretation of Catholic theology to the outer world.

Give your readers more of your own notes and comments. These, as in the case of the *Irish Monthly*, are highly readable and attractive.

I am, my dear Fr Hudson,

Yours very gratefully and sincerely,
P.A. Sheehan, P.P.

66. from: Bridge House, Doneraile, 18 november 1899

Text: MS PAHRC/HJHP/SH/15

Dear Fr Heuser,

Yesterday, I posted 7 chapters, 100 pages of my new serial to you. I hope it will please you. If allowed by health etc., to perfect it I hope to make it quite as interesting, and more in structure than *My New Curate*.

I had a telegram on the 14th from Marlier about a preface to the book. I wired him to let you write it.[90]

Am I to blame? I have been so engrossed with the new serial that I had quite forgotten; and as I had not heard from Marlier (who, I supposed, was in touch with you) I thought the matter was praetermitted. Kindly accept

89 *Luke Delmege.*
90 See footnote 95 below.

all apologies, if I am responsible for the omission, which I hope will be now satisfactorily supplied.

Always yours,

My dear Fr Heuser,
P.A. Sheehan, P.P.

67. FROM: BRIDGE HOUSE, DONERAILE, 18 NOVEMBER 1899

Text: MS PAHRC/HJHP/SH/16

Dear Fr Heuser,

Yesterday I forwarded you seven chapters, 100 pages of copy for your January N[umber]. To-day I wrote to you explaining why the preface was forgotten until the last moment.

Your letter of this evening, which has just reached me, necessitates further explanations, and indeed, apologies.

There was so much correspondence with Mr Marlier about agreements etc., that my promise to write a preface completely escaped my memory until on last Tuesday Mr Marlier's telegram was placed in my hands. To this, I replied by wire, authorizing you to write the necessary preface. In truth, when I promised to write the preface some months ago, I thought that either you or Mr Marlier would remind me of it again; for across 3000 miles of water we have an idea that people are in constant touch with one another; and I was sure that Mr Marlier would keep you acquainted with the progress of the work, so that at the right time, you would remind me of my preface. Then as I say, I became so engrossed with other matters, the whole thing escaped me.[91]

I have always felt, and most cordially acknowledged your unwavering courtesy and kindness, to all classes of priests. I have told only one (and that one of your own Bishops) tho' several have inquired, the amount of pecuniary remuneration I have received at your hands; and I have said to all that I had rather work without remuneration of any kind for you, than for any editors in the home countries, for the simple reason that you have invariably encouraged and appreciated my efforts.

I am extremely sorry that these personal explanations (which are always so unpleasant) should be necessitated. If Providence had placed us nearer

91 See footnote 95 below.

to each other, they might have been obviated. But so far as my culpability is concerned, you have hereby a free and humble apology; and I regret very much that you should have been occasioned the least pain.

I am, dear Fr Heuser,

Faithfully yours,
P.A. Sheehan

You would have had the new MSS sooner, but I did not know that you had advertised it. I had been expecting to hear from you, and I have not seen any N[umber] since September.

68. FROM: DONERAILE, 28 NOVEMBER 1899

Text: MS IJPA J27/127/34

My dear Fr Russell,

Many thanks for your most kind letter.

I send you a handful of *Magnificats*: and shall write to Fr Hudson:[92] to send you more. Also, for your generous notice in the last *Irish Monthly*: and the big advertisement.

Burns and Oates wish to buy into the 2nd edition of *The Triumph* immediately: as the first is exhausted. I do not know their terms yet. They offer to buy copyright for a *modest* sum.

I am sure it will be all right with Fr Heuser. But I can never understand people getting cross over trifles.

One remark in our December *Irish Monthly* struck me – "Lady Gilbert is rather a poet than a novelist." It often occurred to myself: her strong aphoristic style gets too much diluted in prose.

I never had any quarrel with the *Record*. I ceased writing through ill health in 1888: and was never tempted afterwards. It was reported widely in England that I had offered *My New Curate* to the *Record*, and had been rejected. This is untrue: but of course, the *Record* will not publish anything lighter than hermeneutics etc: and I have no time now for deep study. I was downright indignant with the *Weekly Register* on Saturday for their onslaught on Fr Hogan's *Dante*.[93] You must be more kind: but this I needn't

92 Editor of *Ave Maria* magazine, published by the Congregation of the Holy Cross from Notre Dame, South Bend, Indiana.

93 *The Life and Works of Dante Alighieri*, Longmans, Green, London, 1899.

have said. I hope these onslaughts abroad will make the Irish cling more closely together.

I am deep in biographies – Stanley, Jowett, Romanes, A. de Vere.

When, oh, when, will you give us the "Life and Letters" of Charles W. Russell, D.D.: and the best of his essays?[94]

Always sincerely,
P.A. Sheehan

69. FROM: DONERAILE, CO. CORK, [3 DECEMBER 1899]

Text: MS PAHRC/HJHP/SH/19

Preface to the Second Edition [of *My New Curate*][95]

This issue of the second edition of *My New Curate* gives the author the much desired opportunity of publicly expressing acknowledgements that have hitherto been but privately and imperfectly conveyed. These papers were not originally intended for publication, except under very remote contingencies; but, having accidentally fallen into the hands of the able and enterprising editor of the *American Ecclesiastical Review*, he desired with singular sagacity and hopefulness to incorporate them with the weightier and more technical subjects of his important magazine. The enterprise of introducing lighter matter into the pages of clerical journalism, seemingly perilous, only because it was unprecedented, has been amply justified in the cordial, and always enthusiastic reception of these papers by the vast body of the American priesthood, and subsequently by their brethren in other countries. They owe the pleasure and profit, if such have been given, to the zeal and foresight of Father Heuser. The author is happy in the priceless reward of having secured an appreciative, as well as discriminating audience; and of having created for himself invisible, but invaluable friendships which are all the higher and dearer because generously extended to him by that great class, who are most cautious in their judgments, and guarded in their sympathies. And he regards this favourable reception of his writings in the wider light of a noble endorsement of what he has always regarded as a cardinal principle – that there must be a great future before Catholic literature, if we only try to make it larger in scope, though unique

94 Charles William Russell (1812–1880), president of Maynooth College 1857–1880.

95 Fr Herman Heuser explains in his biography of Sheehan (p. 164) that the preface was never published.

in its object; and far reaching and human in its sympathies and, without losing for a moment the sense of its vast responsibilities to souls, and its submission to the judgment of the divinely appointed representatives of truth and justice on earth.

Doneraile, Co. Cork
1st Sunday in Advent 1899][96]

70. FROM: BRIDGE HOUSE, DONERAILE, 20 DECEMBER 1899

Text: MS PAHRC/HJHP/SH/17

Dear Fr Heuser,

Very many thanks for your letter containing so many kind words and for the honorarium duly received. I am very much gratified to know that you like the new serial. I propose pointing out some of the dangers that lie in the paths of young priests abroad, especially when they begin to lead, or are thrown into dangerous circumstances. I shall complete the serial in five books of seven chapters each, altho' I may have to prolong it.[97]

Would you think it well to close the serial with the year 1900, and the 19th century, by giving 3 chapters in place of two in each No.? or would you prefer to extend it into the 20th century? This is a matter of no consequence to me; so decide as you think right. Also, suppress my name altogether except as *The author of My New Curate*. It always gives me the shivers to see my name in print: and the little notoriety I have attained has been productive of annoyance rather than pleasure to me. I am dragged hither and thither by all sorts of demands and as my health is always an uncertain quantity, I have to refuse all kinds of invitations to preach, lecture etc.

I sent Mr Marlier a brief, but pithy [text] for the 2nd. Edition, which is being printed.[98] I asked him to send it to you for revision, before printing.

There is some extraordinary delay in the issue of the book, and a good deal of grumbling at this side, when a good many orders are awaiting execution.

---

96 A note on the verso reads: "Fr Sheehan's Preface; Misleading, since I had suggested the topic and asked him to write it for the *Review*. He may have had it already, but that was not known to me". With regard to this matter, see letter 46.

97 The book mentioned here was *Luke Delmege*, published by Longmans, Green and Co., London and New York 1901.

98 Preface to the 2nd. Edition of *My New Curate*.

A great many thanks for your brilliant adverts in the *American Ecclesiastical Review.*

With all good wishes for the happy season.

I am dear Fr Heuser,

Faithfully yours in Christo,
P.A. Sheehan, P.P.

I had a few brief words lately with an old schoolmate, Rev. Morgan Sheedy of Altoona, Pa; he was very enthusiastic about the method, enterprise, and system, by which you have brought the *American Ecclesiastical Review* to success.

71. FROM: DONERAILE, 22 DECEMBER 1899

Text: MS IJPA J27/127/30

Dear Fr Russell,

I shall be glad to see the *Globe Review*,[99] when convenient. I enclose my subscription to the Magazine. I hope you will find us a new cover with the new type. The old cover is palefaced: and needs more pronounced lettering. I see *Donahoe's*[100] and *The Catholic World*[101] change cover every month. I think I saw your name in the former magazine for Christmas. What a wealth of beautiful illustrations!

Your paper in the *American Eccclesiastical Review* was devotional and inspiring. I looked up the great psalm again in my Bible: and found I had marked it, many years ago – Paschal's Psalm.[102] Give us many similar meditations on the office. There is such a temptation to slide over the

99 Published in Boston.

100 *Donahoe's Magazine* was founded in 1878 by Patrick Donahoe, one time editor of the *New York Pilot*. It was a general interest magazine with a Catholic orientation. It ceased publishing in 1902 when it was taken over by the New York *Catholic World* .

101 *The Catholic World*, a Paulist publication based in New York, began publication in April 1865 and ceased in 1996. See footnote 74.

102 The Great Psalm being Ps 118, the longest in the Psalter. The reference to Pashcal's psalm derives from 118:16 "*in iustificationibus tuis meditabor, non obliviscar sermones tuos*". On 23 November 1654, Pascal had an intense religious experience which he recorded in a note to himself beginning: "Fire, God of Abraham, God of Isaac, God of Jacob, not of the philosophers and the scholars…" and concluding with Psalm 118:16: "I will not forget thy word. Amen". This psalm is an acrostic poem, the stanzas of which begin with successive letters of the Hebrew alphabet and the verses of each stanza beginning with the same letter of the Hebrew alphabet.

wonderful melody and sublime meaning of the Psalms. All good writers should keep ringing the changes of the office and the Mass.

I have had some correspondence lately with Mr William H. Keatinge, 21 Belvedere Place, Dublin – the author of the letter in the *Nation*, signed "An Irish Catholic Layman". Is he related to your Fr Keatinge? He is a powerful and trenchant writer.

With all good wishes for Christmas: the New Year and the New Century.

I am, my dear Fr Russell,

Yours always,

P.A. Sheehan

72. FROM DONERAILE, CO. CORK, 26 JANUARY 1900

Text: BSMS/JBP/SB/1

Dear Fr Bruneau,

I had already written my publishers in Boston to treat with you about the translation, giving them full powers to deal with my interests, but asking them to deal liberally and generously with yourself personally.

That idea of a "trilogy" had already struck me; but the thought of introducing a seminarian is a novel and happy one. Perhaps, I may be inspired to treat that subject. *Nous verrons!*

I should say your work of translation must have been difficult, there are so many idiomatic phrases in the book. Would you kindly let me see it? And let me know your own views about the "royalty".

Always in Christo,

P.A. Sheehan

73. FROM: DONERAILE, CO. CORK, 10 MARCH 1900

Text: MS BSMS/JBP/SB/2 a postcard

Dear Fr Bruneau,

Your MSS arrived safely. I looked it through; but made no alterations, as none were needed: but forwarded it immediately according to address. It must have cost you much trouble in accommodating the idioms to the French.

Many thanks for your most kind remarks about the new serial. I think I shall make it quite as interesting, and even more practically useful than the former. Any hints or suggestions that may occur to you would be gratefully accepted.

Yours in S.C.J. et M,
P.A. Sheehan, P.P.

74. FROM: BRIDGE HOUSE, DONERAILE, CO. CORK, 5 MAY 1900

Text: MS IJPA J27/127/31

My dear Fr Russell,

Ever so many thanks for your kindness. You will read enclosed with pleasure. I had written to F. Lucas to be charitable enough to warn me off dangerous ground, if I approached too close in *Luke Delmege*. This is the reply. So kind, that I am wishing to hide myself away in a rathole, away from all this praise. I suppose I'll catch it for it some day.

Burns and Oates have already made an offer for "*Luke*". It would be a great comfort to me if all my books were in the hands of one firm and that at home.

Dr Barry returns with Fr Berry from Greece today. I have not had time to read his book as yet. But, a little note in the *Tablet* critique frightened me.

Tomorrow is the 25th Anniversary of my Ordination. Give me a remembrance in your prayers.[103]

Always sincerely,
P.A. Sheehan

103 This date corresponds with the moveable feast of the patronage of St Joseph which occurred on 6 May in 1900. In his article, *Concerning the Author of* My New Curate (*American Ecclesiastical Review*, vol. VI, January 1902), Fr Matthew Russell explains that Canon Sheehan was ordained on the feast of the patronage of St Joseph, which was observed on the third Sunday after Easter. In 1875, the feast occurred on 18 April. The feast is Carmelite in origin, having been permitted to the Order in 1689. Having spread throughout the Spanish territories, it was extended to all states and dioceses petitioning its use.

75. FROM: NO ADDRESS

Text: PAHRC/HJHP/SH/18, Printed receipt slip with autograph

Received from The *American Ecclesiastical Review* the sum of twenty pounds ten shillings and eight pence sterling for 10 chapters of *Luke Delmege.* Dated 11 July 1900. £20–10–8. P.A. Sheehan, P.P.

76. FROM: DONERAILE, CO. CORK, 6 AUGUST 1900

Text: BSMS/JBP/SB/3

Dear Fr Bruneau,

I have spent some days searching for that passage from S. Francis de Sales Letters; but I regret to say I have failed to find it. Nevertheless I am quite sure that S. Francis is the author of the quotation. You must only put it back into French again.

The *Kampener Thal* is the title of a work by Jean Paul F. Richter – a novel written to prove the immortality of the soul.[104] It is a very beautiful book, as the passages I have quoted indicate.

I am so glad you are making such progress in the translations. If I can help you in any other way, please command me.

I am just running off for a brief holiday.

Always yours in Christ,
P.A. Sheehan, P.P.

77. FROM: THE QUEEN'S HOTEL, LISDOONVARNA, 31 AUGUST 1900

Text: MS IJPA J27/127/32

My dear Fr Russell,

I have delayed offering you my most sincere sympathy in your great trial, coming so soon after your sister's death.[105] And yet I think the public loss to

104 Johann Paul Friedrich Richter (1763–1825) published *Das Kampaner Thal oder über die Unsterblichkeit der Seele; nebst einer Erklärung der Holzschnitte unter den 10 Geboten des Katechismus* at Erfurt in 1797. The book, along with other works, was translated into English in 1864 as *The Campaner Thal and Other Works* by Juliette Bauer, Thomas Carlyle and Thomas de Quincey.

105 Fr Russell's brother, Lord Chief Justice Arthur Russell died on 10 August 1900. Their sister,

Catholic interests is even greater than the personal bereavement of devoted friends. I intend the moment of return to say three Masses for the greatest Catholic layman of our age.

A few days ago one of our priests was travelling in North Wales and came across the footsteps of the Lord Chief Justice. In one case, the old priest at Carnarvon told him with enthusiasm how Lord Russell a few days before had clambered up to his eyrie, had asked for confession, and had left £2 for the missions. He was at Mass and Holy Communion the next morning. Again, at Beaumaris, the Lord Chief Justice of England was seen, coming up from the congregation and proffering his services as acolyte to a newly ordained priest. He was recognised at the little chapel and it occasioned a sensation.

These little traits affect us more deeply than all his great forensic and intellectual triumphs.

Requiescat!

I am writing amongst a crowd and in a Babel of voices.

Don't answer this. I am leaving here tomorrow.

Always sincerely,
P.A. Sheehan

78. FROM: BRIDGE HOUSE, DONERAILE, 8 SEPTEMBER 1900

Text: MS PAHRC/HJHP/SH/20

Dear Sir,[106]

In the absence of Fr Heuser, or with his permission on returning, would you kindly arrange that the next seven chapters of *Luke Delmege* should be given in the October, November, December Nos. of the *American Ecclesiastical Review*. It would be all the better if the three last chapters could be compressed in the December number which will be also a Christmas no.

The reason I make the request is that these chapters close the first part of the story: and that then I commence Part II with Luke's return to Ireland. The caption in the January No. should be: – *Luke Delmege, Part II, Conversion*, and so to the close of the story, which will terminate in the July or August Number.

Mother Baptist of San Francisco, had died on 6 August 1898. Cf. Matthew Russell, *The Life of Mother Mary Baptist Russell*, The Apostleship of Prayer, New York, 1901.

106 Edward Galbally (1872–1943), executive editor of the *American Ecclesiastical Review*.

Perhaps you could also kindly send me 2 or 3 copies of the July Number which passed out of my possession.

You will much oblige,

Yours faithfully,
P.A. Sheehan, P.P.

79. FROM: DONERAILE, 17 SEPTEMBER 1900

Text: MS IJPA J27/127/33

My dear Fr Russell,

I am much pleased to hear that my publishers have been so thoughtful. They sent me a similar copy: and it is really credible to their firm. Alas! the printer's errors! One even on the title page: but the most annoying on page 12 where in *Canto X*, 2nd. line, they printed *winds* for *minds* JF is so hard to reach across the Atlantic.[107]

The two first poems are to show that God is very close to us, even though we cannot see Him.[108] And the two last melancholy cantos in the 1st. part[109] are intended to show the despair of those who adopt the religion of "Humanity without God" – my pet dislike.

This poem is difficult. But it becomes easy with the key. I like best *Apotheosis* page 59: *The Soul's Farewell*, page 101: and *The Mart* 163. All the others are familiar to you. Should the poems ever pass into a 2nd edition and thus make themselves worthy of the dignity, I shall ask your permission to dedicate them to you.

We are not too sanguine about the new Catholic paper. I had great hopes of *The Leader*: but alas ! it has dropped rapidly into the gulf of personalities and abuse, like all our other papers.[110]

I have given Reverend Mother[111] your message: No one expected you to write in the first great shock of bereavement, which I hope has now passed away.

Always gratefully,
P.A. Sheehan

---

107 Marlier and Callanan of Boston had published his collection of poems, *Cithara Mea*, in June 1900.

108 The first two poems are entitled; *The Hidden*, and *The Revealed.*

109 *The Martin Song* and *The Dreaded Dawn.*

110 *The Leader* was founded by Fr Peter Yorke of San Francisco.

111 Mother Alphonsus O'Keeffe (1852–1938).

80. FROM: DONERAILE, CO. CORK, 23 OCTOBER 1900

Text: MS PAHRC/HJHP/SR/1

My dear Sr Raphael,

I mentioned so often the name of your mighty patron last Sunday, when preaching on October: that I could not overlook his rather diminutive client, especially as there is no one in the Doneraile community that has yet aspired to the patronage of an archangel.[112]

I would probably pay a visit to the convent tomorrow, but Fr Tim[113] has to be in Dublin on important political arrangements leaving here at 6 a.m. after saying the Convent Mass: and returning about 12 o'clock tomorrow night. He will return with great honours – Chief Director of Munster, etc., etc.

I hope you are all well, and not too worried about the new programmes. I believe that all the convents will have to send their most [underlined 4 times] intelligent and promising members to be trained here in object lessons, Kindergarten etc. So we have a chance of seeing you.

A good many convents are writing to us, but we are pretty reticent of our great secret, which is (I may tell you, and you won't mention it to mortal breathing) that they possess as chief instructor as well as Pastor,

Yours sincerely,
"Daddy Dan"

81. FROM: BRIDGE HOUSE, DONERAILE, 26 OCTOBER 1900

Text: MS PAHRC/HJHP/SH/21

Dear Fr Heuser,

I send you by this mail 5 chapters for the new year, the name of the story on title page etc. to be changed to *Luke Delmege. Part II. Illumination.*

Very many thanks for the critique in October No. Quite right in your conjecture. I hold that the music of poetry consists more in syllabic articulation than in merely metrical perfection. Milton, Keats, etc. have any quantity of redundant feet in their lines. But your notice was very generous.

112 In 1900, the feast of the Archangel Raphael was observed on 24 October.
113 Fr Timothy O'Callaghan, junior curate in Doneraile 1899–1902.

I am working in the dark with *Luke Delmege*. I have not heard a single opinion since I commenced it. If you notice anything you may think objectionable in the subsequent chapters (I have some doubts about introducing the Archbishop in the chapter: *A Great Treasure*) please correct, and you will oblige me.[114]

I am very busy and not a little worried.

Very sincerely yours,
P.A. Sheehan, P.P.

82. FROM: BRIDGE HOUSE, DONERAILE, CO. CORK, 6 NOVEMBER 1900

Text: MS BSMS/JBP/SB/4

Dear Fr Bruneau,

A copy of *La Quinzaine*[115] has been sent to me by, I suppose, P. Ardant. I must again write to congratulate you on your translation of *My New Curate*. It is remarkably well done. I have had no corrections to make: and the Irish colloquial idioms have been admirably supplied.

I hope you are translating *The Triumph of Failure*. I regard it as a far more important work than *My New Curate*; and I should say it would take well in France.

The final title of Luke Delmege will be: *Rev. Luke Delmege: First of First*. I suppose you would translate it with a French idiom. It means "Premier de la première classe". It will close in the August no. of the *American Ecclesiastical Review*: and probably appear in book form immediately. I do not know how it is taking in America: I have heard no opinions as yet.

Have you seen *Cithara Mea*? And would you face the translation of these poems? Some say they are difficult to follow.

114 Heuser retained the archbishop but made him a foreign one. Cf. Letter No. 85, p. 103.

115 *La Quinzaine* was a bimonthly literary, artistic and scientific journal published in Paris 1894–1907. It espoused a form of social Catholicism. The editor was originally Paul Harel (1854–1927). He was succeeded in 1896 by Georges Pierre Fonsegrive-Lespinasse (1852–1917). Fonsegrive, regarded as a *progressist* and supporter of the French republic, sided with Loisy in the early period of the modernist crisis and lauded his historico-critical method in biblical exegesis. Following the publication of *Lamentabili* on 3 July 1907, Fonsegrive closed the review. Under the *nom de plume* of Yves le Querdec he published a number of clerically inspired novels: *Lettres d'un Curé de Campagne* (1894) after serialization in *Le Monde*; *Lettres d'un Curé de Canton* (1895) after serialization in *La Quinzaine*; and *Journal d'un Évêque* (1896–1897) after serialization in the *Revue du Clergé de France*. Fr Joseph Bruneau dedicated his French translation of *My New Curate* to Yves le Querdec.

I hope you are very well. And, again, with thanks, I remain

Yours faithfully,
P.A. Sheehan, P.P.

83. FROM: BRIDGE HOUSE, DONERAILE, 5 DECEMBER 1900

Text: MS PAHRC/HJHP/SH/22

Dear Fr Heuser,

Many thanks for the postal order (20–5–4) just received.

Yes, I wish to drop "idiot" altogether. It was a mistake. I had its literal meaning before my mind: and did not sufficiently avert to its modern acceptation. If there be a reprint, I shall devise some other title, or modification. Print as I wrote: *Luke Delmege. Book or Part II. Illumination.*

In the XXVI chapter: *The King's Secret*, there is a passage representing old Fr Meade stooping down to kiss the forehead of the dead penitent. I should like to change that word "kiss" to "bless" if you thought well.

I shall send remaining chapter (12) to you before or immediately after Christmas: so that there would be time for alteration or correction. This will run the serial to September.

I think Fr Vassal in the November No. did not understand my metaphor: Thus: –

Where he spins syllogisms, (as a spider spins his web), and drew unsavoury flies (antagonists) into their (syllogisms) viscous and deadly clutches.

It makes no difference however.

I am, my dear Fr Heuser,

Yours faithfully,
P.A. Sheehan

84. FROM: BRIDGE HOUSE, DONERAILE, CO. CORK, 10 DECEMBER 1900

Text: MS PA DON I/98

My dear Ita,

It is very flattering to you, but I am sure you won't like to hear it, that we are all in the dumps about your slow recovery. I am sure there is nothing remarkable about it, because these troubles as a rule heal very slowly: and I believe the more slowly they heal, the better for the patient in the long run. But we are all agreed that whatever time it takes, you must be in no hurry to come home until you are absolutely and entirely well. Of course there will be a little cloud over the convent at your and Rev. Mother's[116] absence: but the good sisters must learn to be happy with the Crib, and other good things without you both, if necessary. All the same, if Norah Wallace brings you both back even at 11 p.m. on Christmas Eve, we won't stop the Band and the Bonfires.

Denis[117] writes to say he has seen you lately. I am so glad he calls occasionally. I hope you will be able to see 8 Waltham Terrace[118] before you return. Weather here very bad. Snow on the ground and frozen over. James Walsh, P.P. Ballyhea, to be buried tomorrow: and also Mrs Connors, Byblox, who has been happily released from all pain by death.

I suppose you saw the Christmas *Rosary*.[119] They pretend here to recognize me as the little boy in knickerbockers and stockings: and I let them have their little joke. Anything to amuse them now in their period of gloom. We are talking of breaking up tomorrow on account of the snow: Lent may hold on to Friday.

This is the "newsiest" letter I have written for an age to anyone. I hope I won't end up in the *Freeman*.

Kindest remembrance to Reverend Mother who has an anxious time just now.

Always sincerely,
P.A. Sheehan

85. FROM: BRIDGE HOUSE, DONERAILE, 27 DECEMBER 1900

Text: MS PAHRC/HJHP/SH/23

Dear Fr Heuser,

The nine chapters – XXX–XXXVIII were forwarded to you yesterday. You will thus have an opportunity of seeing the whole drift and scope of the serial. There remain but two chapters – XXXIX–XL and an *Envoi*.

116 Mother Alphonsus O'Keeffe (1852–1938), Superioress 1900–1906.
117 Canon Sheehan's brother, Denis Sheehan.
118 Blackrock, Co. Dublin.
119 *Rosary Magazine* founded by the Irish Dominicans in 1897.

In the chapter, entitled *A Great Treasure*, chap. XXVII: if you decide on retaining the Archbishop, please make him a foreign one, by the insertion of a few words.

With your large and liberal views you cannot form an idea of how easily offense is taken at this side.

With all good wishes,
I am, dear Fr Heuser,

Yours sincerely,
P.A. Sheehan, P.P.

86. FROM: DONERAILE, 8 JANUARY 1901

Text: MS IJPA J27/127/35

Dear Fr Russell,

The *American Ecclesiastical Review* just in: I have only time to say that it would be a very vain man who would not be thankful for your generous and kind notice. And as I am not very vain, I am correspondingly grateful. Accept this assurance and all good wishes for the New Year from

Your very sincere friend
P.A. Sheehan

87. FROM: BRIDGE HOUSE, DONERAILE, CO. CORK, 13 FEBRUARY 1901

Text: MS BSMS/JBP/SB/5

Dera Fr Bruneau,

A copy of *Cithara Mea* goes on to you by this mail.

The copyright of *Luke Delmege* will pass into my hands; and I shall arrange with you for translation. But, whilst the serial is running, it would be best to apply to the editor, Fr Heuser, for permission to publish single chapters in a magazine.

I have made no arrangements about publication until the Autumn, when the serial will be finished in the *American Ecclesiastical Review*. But it will be easy for us to come to terms about the translation.

The chief interest of the book lies in Ireland, not England: and I think I shall simply publish as *Luke Delmege* without any addition. The French title you must select.

How is the French edition progressing? It is now appearing in German and Italian.

I am, dear P. Bruneau,

Yours as ever,
P.A. Sheehan

88. FROM: DONERAILE, 16 MARCH 1901

Text: MS PAHRC/HJHP/SR/2

My dear Raphael,

I felt for some time that there was a fault somewhere: and as I could discover none in my conscience, I concluded it must be in my correspondence. But in the mighty stress of answering and docketing letters from Europe, Asia, Africa, Australia and Oceania, I must have forgotten your own diminutive self; and even forgotten to thank Sister Clare for that joyous but rather superfluous watch-pocket she so kindly sent me.

I have a shrewd suspicion, however, that in writing a second time, (which is an act of rare humility), you may perhaps, and only perhaps, be actuated by a well regulated curiosity to hear all about the wedding. So here goes!

I went to Limerick Junction the evening before; and met a large party there. I had a comfortable room: but no sleep from the external rumbling of trains all night. Next morning I started off and walked two mortal miles to a place called Solohead, hoping to be able to say Mass there. I found a fine church, which you can see from the train: but alas! all the glory of the king's daughter was not from within. I found the church empty. There was a missal on the Altar: and a joyous tub of holy water in the middle of the floor. That was all. And it requires not much knowledge of rubrics to know that you cannot say Mass with these. Mrs Darcey was nowhere to be found. So I had to walk back again 2 miles in a sour temper: but in hopes that S. Joseph wouldn't blame me. Then a long journey of 10 miles in a close carriage through the lovely villages of Oola, Dromkeen and Pallas: and Cloverfield. The guests were all assembled: and a particularly nice class the Limerick people are. Nice, refined, and simple with not a trace of that stuckuppishness you find in the Corkonians. Then the ceremony, during which the bridegroom pronounced his vows like a colonel commanding a regiment and the poor little bride broken down. Then congratulations and a dejeuner, just like a convent profession breakfast, speeches etc. and we darted back to the junction amid showers of rice, which I haven't got out of my hair as yet; and old slippers and the best feature was the presence of the poor in large crowds, and the enthusiastic: "God bless you Miss May, every day you live!" They all appeared very fond of her. We had "tay at the Junction": but that joke is lost, until you read the March No. of *Luke Delmege*: and I returned a sadder and wiser man.[120]

The young people are in London; and appear to be getting on gaily.

Now, for Mother Catherine's cold which I hope is improving by evaporating altogether. But it is dangerous weather.

I hope you will feel complimented by this letter. It is the longest and most undignified I have written for many a day. But, please burn it. It is one of those that must not appear in my biography.

Ever sincerely,
P.A. Sheehan

89. FROM: DONERAILE, CO. CORK, MAY 1901

Text: PAHRC/HJHP/SL/1, Manuscript Copy

Dear Mr Lysaght,

A line of grateful acknowledgement to you for your beautiful volume just arrived. In the midst of great hurry I could not resist the temptation of reading through *The Undiscovered Shore*.[121] Whether in their literal or allegorical meaning the poems are very beautiful. Just what I should like to have with me some warm afternoon in one of my sea-nooks down near Ardmore or Youghal. Of course the modern undertone of sadness runs through all; and the eternal yearning after the Infinite and the Ideal is the most touching and sad of all modern symptoms, yet one with which I, standing firmly on the shores of Faith, can readily sympathise. The great

120 A reference to chapter 26 of *Luke Delmege* in which two children travelling from Dublin are placed in the charge of the train guard. Tea is served to the children at Limerick Junction by most of the travellers on the carriage.

121 Part one of *Poems of the Unknown Way*, Macmillan, London 1901.

note of triumph, like those of Dante's *Paradiso*, will yet be heard and you, like so many stars, will come into harbor under the Great Pilot ... I shall be looking out for the reviews of you book ... P.A.S.

90. FROM: DONERAILE, 4 JUNE 1901

Text: MS PAHRC/HJHP/SH/24

Dear Fr Heuser,

What kind of story or moral would suit your new enterprise?[122] I hold in the stocks two skeleton forms of stories – one purely narrative, without any particular nature underlying the tale; the other, dealing with some complex question about labour etc. This latter would be the completion of the trilogy of which *My New Curate and Luke Delmege* are the first parts. It is an idea of forecasting a perfect civilization founded purely on religious lines. You will notice the refrain running through *Luke Delmege* – we must create our own civilization. I am anxious to formulate such a civilisation, founded on simplicity, self-surrender; and as alien as possible to all our modern cries of progress. You will perceive that Luke's failure sprang from his want of touch with the supernatural element.

Give me your ideas; and let me know is the enlarged *Dolphin*[123] to be consumed by laics only?; or as an occasional Friday dinner by ecclesiastics also?

Ever sincerely,
P.A. Sheehan

91. FROM: BRIDGE HOUSE, DONERAILE, CO. CORK, 29 JUNE 1901

Text: MS BSMS/JBP/SB/6

Dear Fr Bruneau,

Would you kindly let me know (1) how the French translation of *My New Curate* is progressing, and could I have a few copies for friends who are

122 The new enterprise mentioned here is the launch of the *Dolphin* magazine, a Catholic literary magazine published in Philadelphia 1901–1908.

123 In 1901, the literary section of the *American Ecclesiastical Review* was separated from the review and published independently as *The Dolphin*. It continued until 1908 under the direction of Edward Galbally.

importuning me for it? I got 3 copies from Limoges; but they were taken from me immediately.

Perhaps you would also do me the favour of letting me know whether you have had any correspondence with publishers about the French translation of *Luke Delmege*. I have not made any definite arrangements as yet; but your reply may be a guide in my determination as to whom I shall finally commit the publication of the book.

I am, dear Fr Bruneau,

Very sincerely,
P.A. Sheehan, P.P.

92. FROM: BRIDGE HOUSE, DONERAILE, CO. CORK, 23 JULY 1901

Text: MS BSMS/JBP/SB/7

Dear Fr Bruneau,

Very many thanks for your letter just received: and for all the trouble you have taken about the translations. You have done me great honour in making my works known so widely. The German translation of *My New Curate* is running through a Cologne newspaper; and Professor Mauri of Milan is bringing out an Italian version.

In arranging about *Luke Delmege* I shall stipulate with my publishers that I retain all rights of translation etc.; so that I shall have the pleasure of dealing solely with yourself.

I think the Introductory Chapter, as it stands, is a mistake. I shall commence the book with the 2nd. Chapter; and leave the death of Luke to the final chapter. I am pleased to know that this, too, is your judgment: and you can arrange your translation accordingly.[124] There are 9 chapters still to appear: so that the serial will not close until December. The August no. has not come to hand: but the July no. I send you by this post.

You will be pleased to know that your *Gospel Harmony* is well known to our ecclesiastical students at this side.

With renewed thanks,

I am, dear Fr Bruneau,

Yours faithfully,
P.A. Sheehan, P.P.

124 The French translation of *Luke Delmege* retains the first chapter of the original with its account of the death of Luke Delmege.

93. FROM: DONERAILE, 11 SEPTEMBER 1901

Text: MS IJPA J27/127/36

My dear Fr Russell,

Yes! suppress the heresy about Shakespeare and Burns, altho' some say it may become the orthodox faith. They are both mere national cults. I used to take *The Leader*, until one day I read:–

'What we need is a Burns in every village'.

Imagine that! And we with the *Irish Melodies*, and all the sweetest and purest songs in the world. It is the usual Irish self-contempt.

Also, suppress any circumstances and opinions, which may appear to your own judgment as farfetched or unwise. Just now, I must pick my steps. And above all, let the particulars be your own experience, so that nothing shall come from me.

Just now I am awaiting the decision of my London publishers.[125] I must push the book through the Press rapidly. Fr Heuser writes that great attempts are being made to pirate the book in America. Inquiries even have been made at the State Offices to see if it were legally copyrighted.

Always and sincerely,
P.A. Sheehan

You know that the Abbé Hogan is at present staying with Mrs Clarke near Lady Gilbert's, Blackrock. He is in feeble health.[126]

94. FROM: BRIDGE HOUSE, DONERAILE, 14 SEPTEMBER 1901

Text: MS PAHRC/HJHP/SH/25

Dear Fr Heuser,

I have been absent from home on a brief holiday; and found your letter before me. I sent *On Retreat*[127] in the hope you would keep it 'till next year, when *Luke Delmege* would have disappeared; as I should like to see my work occasionally in the *Review* which has been an excellent patron to me. And particularly I should wish to send you from time to time short little

125 The book referred to here is *Luke Delmege*.
126 John Baptist Hogan, SS (1829–1901). He died on 29 September 1901.
127 Published in the June 1902 issue of the *American Ecclesiastical Review*.

sketches, like this, which would not involve the wear and tear of examining Cyclopedias, but when I could call on my own material. Any suggestions of this kind I shall gladly accept from you.

I have given *Luke Delmege* to the firm of Longmans, Green and Co, London and New York, to be brought out simultaneously. Apart from Mr Marlier's shortcomings, and they were many, it is altogether pleasanter to be in immediate touch with one's publishers. Many thanks for typed chapters which came safely to hand. Messers Longmans will apply to you direct, or through me, for copyright.[128]

I have definitely declined (I never seriously entertained) the mission of collecting money in the States. It was morally repugnant to my feelings; and *physically* impossible to a wretched constitution, tho' I should have much wished to oblige our Bishop, who is naturally impatient under a load of debt.[129]

I am working through a mountain of correspondence. Sometimes I wish you had never drawn me out of my beloved obscurity. I am paying the penalty dearly.

Yours sincerely,
P.A. Sheehan

95. FROM: BRIDGE HOUSE, DONERAILE, CO. CORK, 25 SEPTEMBER 1901

Text: MS BSMS/JBP/SB/8

Dear Fr Bruneau,

I think it judicious to tell you that I have arranged with Longmans, Green and Co. to bring out *Luke Delmege* in New York and London in November; and that they claim half the profits of translations; I do know how this will affect you; but perhaps you would do well to correspond with them, or request Prof. Ardant to do so.

I am making a few alterations and a few omissions; so, perhaps, it would be well for you to delay publication of the translation until you have the book in permanent form before you.

---

128 In the author's hand, a note, in red ink, in the margin reads: "private for the moment".

129 A mission to collect funds in the United States for the completion of Cobh Cathedral on which works had resumed in April 1895.

I have received from Prof. Ardant 6 copies of the 2nd. Edition of *Mon Nouveau Vicaire* for which I must thank you.

I am, my dear Fr Brunneau,

Yours faithfully,
P.A. Sheehan, P.P.

96. FROM: DONERAILE, CO. CORK, 18 OCTOBER 1901

Text: BSMS/JBP/SB/9

Dear Fr Bruneau,

I wrote to you by last Saturday's mail.

In reply to your last, I have to say, that I make it a rule never to reply to criticism of my books. It does no good, but lends them additional importance. I have not seen the review in question. Should you deem it necessary to make a defence, use your own discretion. You understand the necessities of formalism in France better than I.

Longmans and Co. have written to say that the sheets of *Luke Delmege* as they are struck off, will be submitted to you from their house in New York.

Will you adhere to your own title of the book, or adopt mine?[130]

Always sincerely,
P.A. Sheehan, P.P.

97. FROM: DONERAILE, OCTOBER 1901

Text: PAHRC/HJHP/SL/2, Manuscript Copy

Dear Mr Lysaght,

After many interruptions I was able to finish the reading of *The Marplot*[131] last evening, and I hasten to thank you for the two volumes, and for the pleasure you have given me especially by your own work.

---

130 He did both. Bruneau's French translation was entitled *Ames Celtique et Ames Saxonnes: Luke Delmege*. The translation received a good review in *La Quinzaine*, tome XLIX, n.193 (1–16 November 1902), pp. 269–270.

131 Published in London and New York by Macmillan in 1893.

I am not enthusiastic about *Irish Ideals*. I suppose I am pretty tired of all the empiricism just now being practiced on this poor country and in which there seems but one hopeful future, viz. the return of alienated classes to their allegiance to the motherland … *The Marplot* is an exceedingly clever story. I agree cordially with one of your critics that "the descriptive passages rise to the level of genius".

I would have wished for more, but I suppose you have kept that great faculty under restraint. For the first time I have come across our real Munster idioms in print. I feel pretty sure you have been pelted with countless indignant letters from young ladies for having disposed of Elinora so suddenly and mournfully. I think the death of O'Connor and his insane idea about the dice-cast very dramatic and not at all beyond the reach of experience … I am going over *One of the Grenvilles*[132] again. It is an advance in many ways. You have a unique power of working out the plot of a novel. Some day you will give us a distinctively Irish romance but Calliope[133] is your goddess.

With renewed thanks etc.

P.A.S.

98. FROM: DONERAILE, CO. CORK, 5 JANUARY [1902]

Text: MS PA DON I/99

My dear Ita,

I was just about losing patience with your doctor about your slow progress, when your relic came to hand this morning in the shape of the extracted ligature. Now, all is well and we shall cease to be impatient.

Rev. Mother got a Royal Welcome.[134] I could hear the cheering from the back garden; and the illumination of the bonfires was equal to the conflagration at Todd, Burns and Co.[135] Rev. Mother is looking right well; but oh how glad to be at home again. It was a strange and novel experience.

---

132 Published in London by Macmillan & Co Ltd, 1899.

133 Καλλιόπη (the beautiful voiced), Homer's muse and inspiration for the *Odyssey* and the *Illiad* and, hence, muse of epic poetry.

134 Mother Alphonsus O'Keeffe (1852–1938), Superioress 1900–1906.

135 Todd, Burns and Co. drapery company of Mary Street, Dublin. Newspapers reported that "the flames illuminated the whole city and attracted an immense crowd, including the Lord Mayor. The reflection of the flames was actually seen by those on board a steamer forty miles out at sea" from the city. Three female employees were lost in the conflagration at the company's premises [*The Black and White Illustrated Budget*, January 1902, p. 487; cf. *The Sphere*, 11 January 1902, p. 31].

You have heard that there is a baby boy at 8 Waltham Terrace, Blackrock.[136] Poor May[137] had a rough time; but is better. I have been a little moody all the week about her. The last thing you could do is to drive out and be the fairy godmother. In any case be sure to visit them before you come back here.

John and Jeannette and baby were here to-day.

I hope Evangelist[138] is especially progressing.

Some evil person who had not the fear of God before his eyes introduced a new game, called ping-pong, into the Doneraile Convent; and there is general demoralization. Even the most grave and serious sisters have lost their heads. I hope the evil thing will be destroyed before you return.[139]

Kindest remembrances to Evangelist. I'll take up the sixths 'till she returns.

Always,
P.A. Sheehan

99. FROM: DONERAILE, 13 JANUARY 1902

Text: MS IJPA J27/127/37

My dear Fr Russell,

In the clash of arms and the front of fight we must not forget our duty to friends: so I enclose my annual tribute (7/–) to the magazine.

Can you spare time to run out to 8 Waltham Terrace, Blackrock to see my nephew, Bernard Augustine Sheehan. He nearly cost the poor young mother her life. She had a rough time.

Yes! The *Independent* has been very vicious and unscrupulous. Exactly the same hand in exactly the same manner attacked *My New Curate* last year, 1900 in the *United Irishman*. There were the usual letters and – silence. I'm afraid it is some priest of this diocese that is the author. I have received some disclaimers.

136 Canon Sheehan's nephew, Jeffery Sheehan, son of Denis Sheehan.

137 Canon Sheehan's sister-in-law, Josephine Mary Sheehan, neé Laffan, of Cloverfield, Co. Limerick, wife of Denis Sheehan.

138 Sr Evangelist Daly (1868–1942).

139 The ping-pong set was a Christmas gift from Canon Sheehan.

"Mulla"[140] wasn't wise. It is absolutely untrue to say there is, or ever has been, such a person as the "Canon" in this diocese. There is not one single character drawn from life but the Vicar General in England. The prototype there was old Dr Woollett of Plymouth, dead about 20 years. I ascertained by chance in Limerick on Tuesday last, that Barbara Wilson's self-sacrifice,[141] which I thought a mere tradition is founded on fact. A young Limerick lady did enter as a penitent and died as one to reclaim her brothers.

Miss Conway has a two column notice in the *Pilot*, need I say, only too laudatory. It is marked "I", as her generous pen will give the book another lift.

Other American letters to hand. They all seem to understand the *motif* of my book – an attack on positivism in dogma, and naturalism in practice: and an appeal to the heroic element in human nature.

As I don't wish worrying Dr Brown SJ with too many letters, would you kindly ask him to eliminate from our interview that passage when I expressed a fear lest my books might do harm. In face of a frontal attack, such an admission would be seized on immediately.

Always sincerely,

my dear Fr Russell,
P.A. Sheehan

100. FROM: DONERAILE, 5 FEBRUARY 1902

Text: MS IJPA J27/127/38

Dear Fr Russell,

Very many thanks for M.A.P. and *Monitor*. I think *Luke Delmege* has now run the gauntlet pretty successfully. American reviews not fully to hand,

140 A synonym for the river Awbeg taken from Edmund Spencer's autobiographical pastoral poem *Colin Clouts Come Home Againe*, published in 1595. The reference to Mulla occurs in verses 55, 90, 105, 115 and 140. Bridge House, Sheehan's residence in Doneraile, was situated on the south bank of the river Awbeg.

141 The pious Barbara Wilson, sister of Louis Wilson, in the novel *Luke Delmege,* enters the convent of the Good Shepherd in Limerick as a penitent maudlin in expiation for her brother's dissipated life. After ten years, her identity is discovered and she is eventually professed as one of the nuns. The theme of vicarious suffering was a constant of Catholic writers and most held their attention: Jules Barbey d'Aurevilly's *Un Prêtre Marié* (1865); Léon Bloy's *Le Déspéré* (1886); Huysman's *En Route* (1895), and *Sainte Lydwine de Schiedam* (1901); Emile Baumann's *L'Immolé* (1908), *La Fosse aux Lions* (1911) and *Le Baptême de Pauline Ardel* (1914).

except *Pilot* and *Ave Maria*[142] – all very good. I have some idea it will run *My New Curate* very close in circulation. I am expecting to hear of a new edition by every post.

The *Spectator*[143] is very good, indeed, but objects to introductory chapter. I see that some papers – *Tablet*[144] and *American Catholic Quarterly*[145] take that chapter as non-fictional; and derive from it evidence of haste, etc. What strange notions people take! Criticism is not a fine art as yet.

I should like much to have a few copies of that *Weekly Register* reprint which you gave in last *Monthly* – *Books I have Read*. They might serve me as references at some future time.

I have just refused an American offer of £300 for 30 lectures, all expenses paid. Nothing could induce me to go to America in a public capacity. Fr O'Donovan is young and vigorous; and should succeed. I find it hard to do serious work with all the correspondence that is pouring in. But perhaps that is good work too – at least, some poor souls are seeking light and guidance under strange and distressing circumstances.

Ever sincerely,

My dear Fr Russell,

P.A. Sheeehan

101. FROM: DONERAILE, 14 FEBRUARY 1902

Text: MS PAHRC/HJHP/SH/26

Dear Fr Heuser,

Some twelve months ago, a lady applied for permission to dramatise *My New Curate*. I refused it, unless her dramatic version were subject to ecclesiastical revision. I am now of the opinion that it would not bear dramatisation, and that it would not serve religion to put a dramatic representation of priestly life on the stage. I hope Mr Marlier will take a similar view.[146]

---

142 *Ave Maria* magazine was begun in 1865 by Father Edward Sorin, founder of the University of Notre Dame, South Bend, Indiana. It was published by the Ave Maria Press and focused on Catholic literature. It ceased publication in 1970.

143 Founded in London in 1828.

144 Founded in London in 1840 by Frederick Lucas, a Quaker convert to Catholicism.

145 Founded in Philadelphia in 1876 with James Andrew Corcoran (1820–1889), first professor of theology at Overbrook Seminary, as its editor.

146 A note in the author's hand, in red ink, at the top of the first page, reads: "Publish *On Retreat*

I am not losing sight of your brave attempts to bring something like intellectual matter under the notice of our Catholic laity. It is necessary (1) because otherwise they have to seek it elsewhere and probably in a vitiated state; (2) because it were very well for our coreligionists to know that intellectually the Church is not behind the world. And I say *brave,* because such an enterprise would mean, with us at least, a good deal of courage, and steady indifference to criticism, which would be lavishly and not too scrupulously levelled against such a work.

At present I have nothing I could offer you, although I have some work on hand. But soon I may be able to ask your consideration of a long series of paragraphs, under a fictitious title, and dealing with questions of literature and philosophy in such a way that there will be no strain in following them. Something, in fact, in homaeopathic doses, like Coleridge's *Table Talk.*[147] I have finished one part; but there are three others, and I can only labour at them in intervals.

Luke Delmege is doing well. Out of thirty English reviews, only 3 were unfavourable and these on political lines – *The Tablet*, *The W[eekly] Register* and the *Athenaeum.*[148] The English Catholics, represented by the two former, are ultra-imperialist in their politics.

Wishing you all success in you work,

I am, dear Fr Heuser,

Always sincerely,
P.A. Sheehan

102. FROM: DONERAILE, 23 FEBRUARY 1902

Text: MS IJPA J27/127/39

My dear Fr Russell,

Very many thanks for your kind words. There is not much danger of my being spoiled by these honours: but the delight of the poor people

anonymously. No remuneration; but continue to send me the *American Ecclesiastical Review* and *Dolphin*, until we resume literary relations".

147 This was the inception of his *Under the Cedars and the Stars*. Oliver Wendell Holmes' *The Autocrat of the Breakfast Table* (1858) was a similar type collection of essays.

148 A literary magazine published in London 1828–1921.

everywhere is a great source of gratification.[149] I am not quite so sure about the brethren.

Thanks also for cuttings. I think *The Dolphin* will be a success. At least, it is projected on the right lines. The only question is, will it find subscribers enough of mental calibre to appreciate its contents. I was hoping that your *St Stephen's* might develop into some such organ for our Catholic laity.

I have not seen the Irish *Ecclesiastical Record* for February.[150] In fact I have avoided seeing it. The momentary arrogance of such writing would suffice to build up 4 of 5 chapters of a good book. "And the night is coming etc."

When the first chapters of *Luke Delmege* appeared I had a long conversation with Dr Hogan in Maynooth about the motif and origin of the book. I explained that its was partly suggested by Fr Yorke's strictures on the College; and that I designed to show, that although a young student from Maynooth might be distinguished in College, he might easily be put to shame by flippant and foolish questions in the world; and that it would be well if the deep lessons of scholastic philosophy were made available for the man in the street" or "the man in the train". I told Dr Hogan that I also wished to show that the young man's fancy might be caught by the glitter of modern literature; and how, after many years and bitter experience, he might come to see the folly of criticising his college and his country by the light of a false civilization. Hence, as any one can read, all Luke's strictures on his College and country, are condemnatory of his own attitude, and such priests as Frs Martin and Cussan do not spare him. At last comes the great illumination told in pages 511, 512, 513, 514, 515 and Luke's final judgment on his country and race. The book, therefore, discredits not Maynooth teaching, and certainly not scholastic teaching, but <u>those who try to discredit such teaching from afar</u>.

Of course, it would be too much to expect that Dr Hogan would have remembered this conversation in July 1900; and it would also be too much to expect that one so busy with his classes could read the entire book of 580 pages. Several have told me that they understood my meaning only after a second or third reading. Yet strange to say, the girls in the Boston Reading

149 In 1902, Sheehan received an honorary doctorate in divinity from Pope Leo XIII. The Dominican University of St Albertus Magnus, in Wichita, Kansas, conferred a degree of doctorate in literature in August 1902.

150 This is a reference to John Hogan's devastating critique of *Luke Delmege* published in February 1902. Cf. *Irish Ecclesiastical Record*, vol. XI [1902], pp. 145–157.

Circle have grasped the whole teaching of the book at a glance. I suppose it is the absence of the "literary sense" which still characterizes us; and which makes a University such an absolute necessity.

I forwarded a paper to Fr Brown on Friday last. It will be (sic) need to be rewritten, that is if it ever is to appear in type. We must measure our words now.

Young B.A. Sheehan is developing a temper. How do you account for it by the laws of heredity? Father and mother are the meekest of mortals: and surely it did not come from me?[151]

Ever sincerely,

my dear Fr Russell,
P.A. Sheehan

103. FROM: DONERAILE, 29 MARCH 1902

Text: MS BSMS/JBP/SB/10

Dear Fr Bruneau,

I am pleased to know your translation is finished. I hope to see it soon; and that it will be as great a success as its predecessor. But, it must have cost you considerable trouble.

For the present, I am letting the clerical novel in abeyance. I have had to suffer a good deal of abuse and misunderstanding on this side by reason of some misinterpretations which were set afloat by a Dublin paper concerning *Luke Delmege*. So I prefer dealing with other subjects just at present.

Later on, I may return to your trilogy. I am not unmindful of it.

Luke Delmege has been a great success. Over 10,000 copies have been sold up to March 1st. So, on the whole, my work has been successful.

Very many thanks for all your kind felicitations. The distinctions conferred by the Holy Father have given great pleasure to many friends.

I am, dear Fr Brunneau,

Yours always,
P.A. Sheehan, P.P.

---

151 An ironic allusion to Emile Zola's theory of heredity as a means of explaining social behaviour.

104. FROM: DONERAILE, 2 JUNE 1902

Text: MS IJPA J27/127/40

Dear Fr Russell,

You are very good to sacrifice the *Sacred Heart Review*.[152] It is, I think, the best notice that has appeared as yet, altho' *Mosher's*[153] and *The Guidon* are very close, not to speak of the *Austral Light*.[154] It seems to have interpreted my mind rightly. Altogether, the book has got a wonderful reception. I cannot make out why Longmans is not bringing out a new edition. He had struck off 13,000 for the 1st.; of which 10,000 have been sold at the end of March, 4,500 in America alone.

I hope you are keeping well. I had only a chance word with you in April, when I had so much to say. I hope you visit Waltham Terrace sometimes.[155] You cannot imagine what pleasure you give them.

To make up for the great world, I have had plenty of local troubles, principally with teachers, who are very unsatisfactory sometimes. But this is the eternal balance.

Always sincerely,
P.A. Sheehan

105. FROM: DONERAILE, 13 JUNE 1902

Text: MS PAHRC/HJHP/SH/27

Dear Fr Heuser,

The paper: *Fr Mac on Retreat* took me by surprise this morning.[156] I was not expecting it; and, indeed, I had almost forgotten its existence. I expect

152 Published in Boston 1888–1918 by Fr John O'Brien, parish priest of the Sacred Heart Church, in East Cambridge. The publishing archive of the *Sacred Heart Review* is conserved in the library of Boston College. See letter no. 183 of 27 April 1909.

153 *Mosher's Magazine*, which began publication in 1884, became the official organ of the Catholic Summer School of America and of the Reading Circle Union. It was edited and published by Warren Mosher from Youngstown, Ohio. The Catholic Summer School of America was a University outreach programme which settled firstly at New London, Connecticut and subsequently at Cliff Haven, New York. Among the prominent supporters of the Summer School were Cardinal Satolli and the Reverend Morgan Sheedy of Pittsburg.

154 *The Austral Light* was published in Melbourne 1892–1920.

155 The residence of his brother in Blackrock, Co. Dublin.

156 *Fr Mac On Retreat* was published in the June 1902 issue of the *American Ecclesiastical Review*.

there will be diversity of opinion about it, as about my other work; but in view of the hostility that has been raised against me in clerical circles at this side, on account of *Luke Delmege* I would urge upon you the advisability of keeping the authorship of *Fr Mac on Retreat*, a profound secret.[157] Attempts may be made to discredit the authorship; but I am aware that many at this side would be glad to be able to quote it as another example of my desire to lampoon and discredit the Irish priesthood. Although the verdict of the world is the other way, we must yield a little to those insane prejudices; and I had determined not to touch on this delicate clerical question any more, nay even, to rest altogether from literary work, and devote all my time to my parish and people. But, you will see the necessity of maintaining the anonymity of the article intact.

Hoping that you are quite well,
I am, dear Fr Heuser,

Always sincerely,
P.A. Sheehan

106. FROM: DONERAILE, 26 JULY 1902

Text: MS PAHRC/HJHP/SH/28

Dear Fr Heuser,

You will receive by this mail a fasciculus of 116 pages, sent for your consideration as to their adaptability to the pages of *The Dolphin* or the *Review*. They are simply my own reflections made, day by day; but I thought they might be useful to your readers as homoeopathic doses of literature and philosophy.[158]

Please examine them carefully, <u>especially the purely philosophical portions</u>. If acceptable, you might commence in the October no. and finish this fasciculus in December. I shall have the other portions ready, and all could be completed in a year.

---

157 It remained so until Fr Herman Heuser published his biography of Canon Sheehan in 1917.

158 These were serialized in the *American Ecclesiastical Review* in 1903 and eventually published in book form in 1904 in the United States by Benzinger Brothers, New York as *Under the Cedars and the Stars* . See also notes 161 and 172. A manuscript draft of *Under the Cedars and the Stars* is conserved in the library of Boston College.

I received Dr Henry's very beautiful book of Leo's poems;[159] but thought it advisable to forward the volume to the *Athenaeum* office, as they wish to issue their own notices, and are jealous of the interference of outsiders.

Have you seen the *Edinburgh Review*[160] for July?

I am, dear Fr Heuser,

Always sincerely,
P.A. Sheehan

107. FROM: DONERAILE, 29 AUGUST 1902

Text: MS PAHRC/HJHP/SH/29

Dear Fr Heuser,

I beg to acknowledge with many thanks your letter and enclosure (75 8).

Altho' I wrote from Tramore to you about preserving the anonymity of the papers, I now accept your opinion in the matter; and leave it to your own discretion to publish with my name if you please. I hope to have a little volume constituted out of these papers at the end of the series.[161]

The only fictional work I have been engaged in, I am handing over to the Sisters of Charity, Temple Street, Dublin, for the benefit of the sick children in their care. It is a trifle of 12 chapters in a dramatic form; and deals with school-girl life.[162] So it would not suit either *American Ecclesiastical*

159 H.T. Henry, *Poems, Charades, Inscriptions of Pope Leo XIII*, The Dolphin Press, New York and Philadelphia, 1902.

160 Published in Edinburgh 1802–1929.

161 The papers were published in book form as *Under the Cedars and the Stars* initially by Brown and Nolan for the Catholic Truth Society, Dublin (1903); and subsequently by Benzinger Brothers, New York (1904) acting agent for the Catholic Truth Society; a second printing was published by Benzinger Brothers, New York in 1906.

162 The drama was *Lost Angel in a Ruined Paradise* which was translated into French and published in 1907 as *Ange Egaré d'un Paradis Ruiné* by Éditions P. Lethielleux, Paris. Sheehan explained to Fr George O'Neill, SJ, professor of English at University College, Dublin, that his original title for the work was *The Fate of Atropos*; "but the Nuns asked me, under the inspiration of a priest, to change it to the present title" (cf. letter 125 of 24 August 1904). Fr O'Neill taught James Joyce who subsequently lampooned his view that Francis Bacon was the real author of Shakespeare's plays. When Joyce died in 1941 a general silence was observed in Jesuit circles with the sole exception of Fr O'Neill, then in Australia, who recalled his first encounter with Joyce, forty years earlier at Clongowes Wood College. Writing in a forward to Paul Grano's *Witness to the Stars: An Anthology of Australasian Verse by Catholic Poets*, published in 1946, he wrote: 'I have introduced to college life a very small boy destined to regrettable celebrity as the author of *Ulysses*, and put a Catholic choir-book into his little hand'.

Review or *the Dolphin*. I have nothing else in contemplation at present; and it will put me to the pin of my collar to have the papers (*Under Cedars and Stars*) ready for you. I am glad to know that your *Dolphin* is much read and appreciated. Could we give it a push here? The *Monthly Register* notices it always favourably.

I have just been made the recipient of the Degree of Doctor of Literature from Albertus Magnus University, Wichita, Kansas, U.S. Do you know anything of this University? It cannot be Catholic.

Always sincerely,

My dear Fr Heuser,
P.A. Sheehan

108. FROM: DONERAILE, 6 SEPTEMBER 1902

Text: MS PAHRC/HJHP/SH/30

My dear Fr Heuser,

Your letter and the *Dolphin* have come together. I see that in this, as indeed in other matters, your judgment is always right. It was not dread of criticism (I am pretty hardened now) but an idea that there was so much of my own personality in these papers, that made me sensitive about appearing above my name. I had an idea that the papers would read better from an unknown or obscure writer – I mean, unknown by reason of his anonymity. However, all's right now: and you have given me a grand send-off. I only hope the papers will realise all your expectations.

If the *Dolphin* once gets hold, it must prove a valuable organ of instruction to the laity. I always think that our own people are starved for want of wholesome intellectual food. We must try and push it here. Dr Russell is doing his best in the *Irish Monthly*.

I have received a copy of Dr Henry's fine book. Please thank him for me. I should like to know what Leo[163] himself thinks of it. He must be gratified exceedingly.

Always sincerely,

My dear Fr Heuser,
P.A. Sheehan

163 Pope Leo XIII (1810–1903), elected on 20 February 1878.

109. FROM: DONERAILE, 14 OCTOBER 1902

Text: PAHRC/HJHP/SD/1, Manuscript Copy

My dear Fr Dallow,

Very many thanks for your cordial letter. I am so pleased that you liked the book.[164] It can never be as popular as its predecessor, although it has had a wider sale. But I am sure it will last longer. It is just now in French, also published by Lethielleux, Paris.

What you say about your note–translations is quite correct. A great many lay-people have written me on the subject. It blocks their interest in the book, to find anything concealed or unintelligible. I must see about it in a new edition.

I hope your own pen is not idle. We all work, while it is day: for the night cometh.

Yours sincerely etc.,
P.A. Sheehan

110. FROM: DONERAILE, 23 OCTOBER 1902

Text: MS IJPA J27/127/41

Dear Fr Russell,

Very many thanks for the *Quinzaine*. It is the first I have seen and it leads off well.

Yours is the only opinion I have received about the new papers. *The Dolphin* has not quite six readers in Ireland. I suspect Fr Heuser will incorporate these papers in *American Ecclesiastical Review* later on or perhaps immediately.

The French copy made its return journey safely.[165]

The scene at Gracie's bedside in *The Fate of Atropos*[166] had this signification. Dr Latouche, in his extreme anxiety about his wife, and

164 *Luke Delmege.*

165 This is the French translation of *My New Curate*, published as *Mon Nouveau Vicaire* by Pierre Dumont of Limoges. The translation was done by Fr Joesph Bruneau, SS, of St Mary's Seminary, Baltimore. Fr Bruneau dedicated *Mon Nouveau Vicaire* to Yves le Querdec, the *nom de plume* used by Georges Pierre Fonsegrive-Lespinasse. See note 115, p. 101.

166 *The Fate of Atropos* was the original title of Sheehan's *Lost Angel in a Ruined Paradise.* See footnote 162. Two holograph versions are conserved in Dublin: National Library of Ireland, MSS 4684–4685.

probably too self reliant, snatches the chloroform from the hands of Fitzmaurice, and administers it. Whether it arose from his want of skill or Grace's weakness, the experiment had nearly proved fatal. And Fitzmaurice utilized it afterwards to play on the suspicions of poor Grace, by hinting that her husband wanted to get her out of the way. His object was to create jealousy in Grace's mind, so that she would strain every nerve to remove Lilian White from London. This could only be done by her marriage with Fitzmaurice. Here money was the only obstacle, as it was the only thing Fitzmaurice coveted, as his suit with Lilian was hopeless. He finally succeeds in getting Grace to apply to her father for her dowry, so that she could make restitution to Lilian for the wrong done her and her father by Grace's father. He gets the cheque payable to Lilian, forges the latter's name, and is blocked at the bank by Lehmann. Then flies the country.

You have not touched on my great difficulty – whether in view of all the criticism now leveled at convent teaching – the brusquerie of the young girls might not be used as an argument against our Convents; and whether there may not be something approaching to levity in the brightness and gaity of Eva Farrell – Sister Felicity.

I always find that the points on which I am most apprehensive in my books, seem to affect no one else; and that I cannot see the points they make with others.

Do go back to your den! I feel quite queer writing to that un-metropolitan locality.

Always etc.,
P.A. Sheehan

III. FROM: DONERAILE, 3 MARCH 1903

Text: MS PAHRC/HJHP/SH/31

Dear Fr Heuser,

Very many thanks for letter and cheque just received.

From some communications I have received, I fancy these papers in the *Dolphin* are finding their way into unusual and unexpected places, and I think are likely to effect some good, at least, perhaps, they may liberate us Catholics from the ordinary charge of obscurantism.[167]

167 An idea promoted by Saint-Simon in France and by the National Liberal Party, under Rudolf von Bennigsen, in Prussia during the *Kulturkampf*.

I should prefer to allow the remark about Chapter LXI to go unnoticed. These criticisms are generally suggested by vanity, and it merely flatters such vanity to notice them. The expression, of course, "exiled from the blisses of Heaven", is not theologically exact; but my meaning was quite apparent. Perhaps I should have said "exiled, according to our selfish conceits, from the blisses of Heaven, though enjoying the Beatific Vision etc".

What a wonderful literature we would have, if even one tenth of our cities would write something themselves!

Ever sincerely,
P.A. Sheehan

A few days with you here will be a rare break in the monotone of my life. But let me know the when of your coming.

112. FROM: DONERAILE, EASTER MONDAY [13 APRIL], 1903

Text: MS IJPA J27/127/42

My dear Fr Russell,

Very many thanks for the *Catholic World*, William Sillard's letter and your corrections. The article in the *Catholic World* would be a curious, and not uninteresting comment on Fr Gallery's notice, if they were placed side by side. I cannot help feeling very grateful to Mr Sillard; and I am writing to him to say so.

My authority for attributing the article on Keats in *Blackwood*[168] to Terry is Mr Lowell in his *Essays on English Poets*,[169] although, of course, it is but a conjecture, as I believe the authorship has never been definitely ascertained. I have noted the other corrections in my proof copy.

With regard to your suggestion it seems to me that the random and irregular paragraphs would be more consistent with my original idea of giving the public my thoughts as they occurred, than if I were to bracket them together under headings. I can see however (indeed I experience the difficulty myself now) how puzzled a reader would be in searching out a particular passage. But I think I shall complete a short index with some notes of explanation at the end.

---

168 *Blackwood's Edinburg Magazine* was published in Edinburg and London by William Blackwood and Son 1818–1980.

169 James Russell Lowell (1818–1891), *Essays on English Poets,* London 1888.

Besides I have this idiosyncrasy, that I cannot bear going over anything that I have written. I never rewrite anything. The pages go to press under the first copy. Hence, correcting proofs etc. is the greatest task I can face. I would rather commence at once a second book. But it has occurred to me that I ought submit the initial paragraphs, dealing with metaphysical questions to some expert, like Fr Maher of Stonyhurst,[170] lest there should be any phrases or ideas that might be misconstrued. I asked Fr Heuser as a particular favour to submit these paragraphs to the Professor of Philosophy at Overbrook; and I understand he made some changes.

What do you think of the idea? Did you like the April number quite as much as the preceding one?

Always gratefully and affectionately,
P.A. Sheehan

113. FROM: DONERAILE, 18 APRIL 1903

Text: NLI/CP/MS 35, 306

Dear Lord Castletown,

I return with very many thanks *The Geographical Journal*[171] so kindly lent. It is very interesting especially to those who have visited these places.

I am, dear Lord Castletown,

Very faithfully yours,
P.A. Sheehan, P.P.

114. FROM: DONERAILE, 25 AUGUST 1903

Text: MS PAHRC/HJHP/SH/32

Dear Fr Heuser,

The Catholic Truth Society of Ireland has asked me to allow them to publish in book form *Under the Cedars and the Stars*. They have done and

170 Fr Michael Maher SJ (1860–1918), psychologist and noted neo-scholastic philosopher from Leighlin Bridge, Co. Carlow.

171 The journal of the Royal Geographical Society, *The Geographical Journal* began publication in 1831. The journal specializes in original research papers and review articles relating to geography.

are doing such good work, that I have yielded to their request, and the volume is now in the hands of their printers, Brown and Nolan, Dublin. These latter are so particular about terms etc., that I must ask you to send me the transfer of copyright as soon as you can. I feel I would have done better for the success of the book, if it had been published through Messers Longmans; but it may do more good in this way.

Must we abandon all hope of seeing you this Autumn?

Always sincerely,
P.A. Sheehan, P.P.

115. FROM: DONERAILE, 12 NOVEMBER 1903

Text: Transcription from Herman Heuser's Biography of Canon Sheehan of Doneraile, pp. 184–185. The printed version does not have an incipit but is addressed to Fr Heuser.

I received in good condition and time your edition of *Under the Cedars and the Stars*. The type and all were so familiar and beautiful, I had the impertinence to write to the office for a few more. And they sent me six, which, considering the limited nature of the edition, was very generous. I suppose by this time the Irish edition has come to your hands. I have improved it by marginal notes and a table of contents which seems attractive.[172]

I am now kept very busy lecturing, mostly in Dublin. It is a form of literature I don't like. I prefer my desk, and pen and lamp, and I find the physical effort of talking for over an hour very distressing, as lungs and heart are both weak. I am ploughing through a paper for the Maynooth students to be read on December 1st. The late president, Dr Gargan, wrote so urgently I could not refuse him; and the present President[173] urged the matter again. So there is no getting out of it. Besides, of all audiences, I like students best. I hope your *Homiletic Review* will do well. The New York

172 Fr Heuser explains that when the serialization of *Under the Cedars and the Stars* was completed, in agreement with Sheehan, the Dolphin Press published the series in a limited edition book form. The book was not for commercial purposes but sent as a gift to the subscribers to *The Dolphin*. The plates from the edition were subsequently used by Benzinger Brothers, New York, for the printing of the American edition of the book (cf. Biography 184).

173 Daniel Mannix (1864–1963), a fellow priest of the diocese of Cloyne and subsequently Coadjutor and Archbishop of Melbourne. The paper delivered was *The Dawn of the Century*. It was reprinted in Edward McLysaght (edt.), *The Literary Life: Essays and Poems*, Phoenix Press, Dublin, pp. 121–150. See footnote 303.

man, Wagner,[174] has two bound volumes, MSS, of my sermons which he is doling out. I understood that this was a priestly undertaking, under the exclusive management of priests. Otherwise I would not have sent them.

Need I say how glad I shall be to see you here? Thanks for the President's letter.

I had a few interviews here in the Autumn with Chief Justice Holmes, the son of the author of *The Autocrat*.[175] He was a most interesting man; and when we got on philosophical topics he talked well … I know I am exacting: but could you send him a copy of the *Cedars and Stars*? He lives in Boston.

Always sincerely,

my dear Fr Heuser,
P.A. Sheehan

116. FROM: DONERAILE, 28 NOVEMBER 1903

Text: MS PAHRC/HJHP/SH/33

Dear Fr Heuser,

Advises from Benzinger state that the New York customs refuse to allow my book to pass, because copyrighted in the United States, and set up in British Isles. Dublin publishers think you could interfere with some effect by stating book already printed in the States etc.[176]

The fates, otherwise propitious, intend that I shall practice my own philosophy, and never enter the Temple of Mammon. I have just heard that Mr Marlier, of Boston, has sold out all his property and mine to a Mr Whithaker; and decamped with about £600 of my money. He had promised the week before Fr McQuaide, of Scranton, to remit my money. He had previously mortgaged the plates, in which I had a claim, for 12,000 dols. He had not even the grace to restore me copyright. I wonder how will he face eternity.

---

174 Joseph F. Wagner was the founder, in 1900, of *The Homiletic Monthly and Catechist* which changed its name to *The Homiletic and Pastoral Review* in 1919. The review, initially edited by William Brady of Dunwoodie Seminary, featured a sample sermon for each Sunday and Feast Day of the year together children's catechetical material. See footnote 35.

175 Oliver Wendell Holmes, Sr (1809–1894), *The Autocrat of the Breakfast-Table*, originally published as a series of essays in *The Atlantic Monthly* in 1857 and 1858 and in book form in 1858.

176 This is the Dublin Catholic Truth Society's printing of *Under the Cedars and the Stars*.

I heard there were some good reviews of my book appearing in America. If so, some cargoes must have passed through.

I am, dear Fr Heuser,

Yours faithfully,
P.A. Sheehan

[Along left margin] If my publishers fail to get in the Irish Edition to the States, they must, I suppose, set up an American edition.

117. FROM: DONERAILE, 19 DECEMBER 1903

Text: Transcribed from David H. Burton, *Holmes-Sheehan Correspondence*, Fordham University Press, 1993.

Dear Mr Holmes,[177]

I have received and read your speeches, since I wrote. Accept my thanks for the pleasure they have given me. My sympathies were altogether with the "war" and "academic" speeches. They are full of that fire and vitality that go to make real eloquence. But I think your "law" speeches were a greater triumph, though I could not read them with the same sympathy. But to command the dry bones to rise up and be clothed, as you have done, was a Prophet's work.

Why have you not gone into Congress, where you would have a much wider field?

With all good wishes for the New Year,

I am, dear Mr Holmes,

Yours very sincerely,
P.A. Sheehan, P.P.

I had no idea that you had gone through the Civil War. When will its real history be written?

177 Oliver Wendell Holmes, Jr. (1841–1935), Associate Justice of the American Supreme Court.

118. FROM: DONERAILE, 26 DECEMBER 1903

Text: PAHRC/HJHP/SD/2, Manuscript Copy

My dear Canon,

A great many thanks for your most kind letter, and for the dainty little piece of music you were good enough to send.

I read with the greatest interest your list of lectures and addresses. It is very full, and sufficiently liberal and wide for all tastes. You are doing valuable work, somewhat uphill, too, I expect, but that is the best part of valour.

Believe me, dear Canon Dallow,

Yours most sincerely,
P.A. Sheehan

119. FROM: DONERAILE, 3 FEBRUARY 1904

Text: Transcribed from David H. Burton, *Holmes-Sheehan Correspondence*, Fordham University Press, 1993.

Dear Mr Holmes,

I am very grateful for your generous appreciation of my book. You have been much before my mind these latter days. On reading over the book for corrections and index, I stumbled across one or two expressions and thought with a little qualm or regret: "Judge Holmes, I fear, will be grieved at this". Then a paper came to me from Taunton, Mass., with your portrait and some account of your entering your new house. Then finally came your letter, containing such a nice expression about my book.

Would you let me assure you that there is no antagonism between us? We differ in our interpretation of human life and the universe around us; but that fact, so far as I am concerned, in no wise diminishes my esteem for you. I respect your conscientious convictions; nor have I any right to intrude within the sacred sanctuary, where each should be alone with God. Conscience is the supreme monitor. I would that all men believe as I do, for I believe that this faith is not only the solution of what is otherwise inexplicable, but also the great proof and support of the human soul under the serious difficulties of life. But I have no right to force this conviction on you; and the fact, that you see with other eyes than mine, should in no way imperil or diminish the friendship, which I take the privilege of assuming, should subsist between us. I assure you I esteemed it a great kindness on the part of Lord Castletown to afford me an introduction to you, first, for your good father's sake, whom I have learned to love from his kindly, humane writings, and then for your own sake.

I am a great believer in the words of St Paul: "There remain faith, hope and charity; but the greatest of these is charity". I have toleration and friendship for all, but one class – the aggressive and intolerant. You might read this in my book. I think that anyone that deliberately hurts another, in feeling or person or property, is very much to be reprobated. Life is such a tragedy to so many, that anyone who seeks to accentuate its trials, is unworthy of human fellowship. We have one supreme obligation – to be kind to each other. And I must say, that is the spirit of my Church today. In the past, things were different all around. There is a new spirit in the world today.

But I cannot regard with equanimity the efforts of non-believers to destroy the faith of the masses by scoffing and proselytizing their disbeliefs. Hence although German rationalists have done a great deal to destroy Christianity, they have approached the subject at least with reverence unlike the wretched French, so closely imitated by modern writers who ridicule what they are incapable of understanding; and dishonestly destroy the great prop and support of a tottering race. That class of propagandists raises my anger; and yet perhaps even there, there is pity too.

See how much one word in your letter (ever again to be eliminated) has drawn from me. I assure you that your acquaintance was a pleasure; your friendship a source of permanent and unalloyed gratification. I have just space to wish you many happy years in your new home.

Yours sincerely,
P.A. Sheehan

120. FROM: DONERAILE, CO. CORK, 20 FEBRUARY 1904

Text: MS PAHRC/HJHP/SRY/1

Dear Miss Ryan,

Very many thanks for your kind and generous words, and for your still more generous appreciation of my latest book. The only part of your letter with which I disagree was where you spoke of yourself as "stranger". I do not think "Ulices Esmond" is a stranger" to most in Ireland; least of all to me, who have read your fine poems again and again, and keep your volume enshrined in my bookcase between Keats and C. Patmore. I hope you have not broken your pen: for altho' trial and suffering have been yours, the best things the world hold (sic) in fee, have been solicited by trial; and I think I have quoted the lines somewhere about poets, who learn in sorrow what they teach in song.

I flatter myself that my literary trials are over. They were sharp enough while they lasted. It was hard for one like me to feel that I was creating enmities, whilst I was trying to preach charity to the world.

But I think it was the severity of the criticisms which were passed upon my books, that has always deterred me from writing *A Life of Christ*. I should dearly like to do so, if only to bring back the world to His feet. But I felt it would be rather cruelly attacked and but poorly circulated, at least amongst the class for whom I should mainly write – the poor and the afflicted.

I see you are in the Marble City – the City of the Churches.[178] I liked it much a few years ago when I was there; but perhaps it was all the kindness I had from priests and nuns.

Once more, thanking you cordially,

I am, dear Miss Ryan,

Yours most sincerely,
P.A. Sheehan

121. FROM: DONERAILE, 28 MAY 1904

Text: MS PAHRC/HJHP/SH/34

Dear Fr Heuser,

I was pleased to see your handwriting again, although I expected to have the larger pleasure of seeing yourself.

The Jesuit Fathers can, of course, make whatever use they please, for the benefit of their patients, of any of my books. I am only too glad to be able to keep their afflicted ones.

178 Kilkenny City.

I am just bringing out through Longmans a little dramatic tale, called *Lost Angel of a Ruined Paradise*. I have written it for the benefit of the Children's Hospital, Dublin, and have given over copyright and all other rights to that institution. For the sake of the children, if not for any merit of its own, I am sure you will keep it on. When I wrote *the Monks of Trabolgan* some years ago, I had in view a large work on the monastic life, such as you have suggested. But I found I was anticipated by Huysmans;[179] so I left it a mere sketch.

I am laboring at a labour and capital novel; but am making no headway. The agony of the thing does not strike us; and all my sympathies are with the poor and the laboring classes.

Marlier, although still publishing *My New Curate* has ceased to send any returns. He owes me £300 for 1902 according to his own estimate; and I presume an equal sum for 1903. I am trying to get a publisher at this side; as he has sacrificed copyright, according to our agreement.

Always sincerely,
P.A. Sheehan

122. FROM: DONERAILE, 13 JUNE 1904

Text: MS PAHRC/HJHP/SH/35

Dear Fr Heuser,

Very many thanks for letter and cheque just received.

I think Brown and Nolan, Dublin, will publish *Under the Cedars and the Stars* under the auspices of the Catholic Truth Society of Ireland. There were a good many reasons why I had to retain the publication in Ireland.

I have been thinking a good deal about your Socialist novel; but it is a good deal outside my sphere of thought. What should be the underlying principle? Do atheism and socialism go together? How to keep the golden mean between labour and capital? What of Christian socialism? These are a few of the questions that keep cropping up when I allow myself to think on the matter. And, are not the conditions of labour in America (for I should plan the scene there) very deplorable? I never think, without a shudder, of

179 Joris-Karl Huysmans (1848–1907) wrote two novels with monastic themes: *En Route*, Paris, Tresse Stock (1895) and *L'Oblat*, Paris, Stock (1903). From the chronological context, and given its expansive description of monastic life, Canon Sheehan is probably referring to *En Route*. See note 73.

your mills and tenement-houses and the environments of the poor. Books are no guide. One or two facts about socialists would guide me better.

Benzinger has most favourable terms from our Catholic Truth Society as their American agent. He gets 50 p.c. off. This may be a guide to you but regard it as a private matter.

I am ever so sorry you didn't take up *Luke Delmege* and this book. It would have been great gratification to me to know that my books were keeping on the course of great Catholic literature, for which you are doing so much.

I hope you keep the plates of last work safe. They may be useful.

Always most sincerely,

My dear Fr Heuser,

P.A. Sheehan

123. FROM: DONERAILE, 24 AUGUST 1904

Text: Transcribed from H.J. Heuser's *Canon Sheehan of Doneraile*, p. 369.

Dear Sister,

We have been reading all your letters with avidity. To-day we are very anxious about Sr E. I fear it will be a very critical operation, and we shall be watching for your telegram. I am so glad now that you went with them. It was clearly indispensable. Poor Sister A. We all have the deepest feeling, and there is much sadness in the Community. *Fiat Voluntas Dei!* I think all the papers are now signed. Sister P. is very clear-headed on the matter and I think my part of the work is done. I would advise postponing the question of the gas until later on. When you come back (next week, I hope) we must attack the school question seriously. All well, D.G., but hurry back. The nuns are all so good, so sympathetic, so affectionate, so anxious. They are beyond all praise.

P.A.S.

124. FROM: DONERAILE, 24 AUGUST 1904

Text: MS PAHRC/HJHP/SH/36

Dear Fr Heuser,

I have instructed Messers Longmans, London, to forward to you direct, as soon as it is typed, copy of a new Irish novel, *Glenanaar*. They were about to issue it in bookform; but the pleasant but too angelic visits, of Messers Galbally and D. Walsh, induced me to hope that probably you might find the serial rights of the novel useful for the *Dolphin* and *Ecclesiastical Review*. The right of ultimate publication in book form belongs to Messers Longmans. Should you not care to use it as a serial, would you kindly return to Messers Longmans' house in New York.[180]

I like to let my books speak for themselves, so I shall not say what I think of it. But I should wish you to push it through the magazines as rapidly as possible, so that Messers Longmans might publish early in the Summer. I just snatched the serial rights our of the hands of a big American magazine, who were eager to get it.

Could you at all manage to get me back *My New Curate* from Marlier? It is no further use to him, I believe, and has gone out of print. He owes me, on his own showing, £300 for 1902. I am presuming he owes me a similar sum for 1903. I fear the book will become of common property.

I shall be from home (in the Vaterland) from 29 August to 24 September.[181]

Believe me, dear Fr Heuser,

Always sincerely,

P.A. Sheehan

125. FROM: DONERAILE, 24 AUGUST 1904

Text: Transcription from Herman Heuser's biography of Canon Sheehan, pp. 366–367

Dear Fr O'Neill,

I assure you it was an unqualified disappointment to us that we had no opportunity of seeing you here during your sojourn in our neighbourhood. I say "us" because the Nuns would have liked very much to see you: and the profession ceremony and Dejeuner, which seemed so formidable to you, was a very informal and undress affair, which you would have enjoyed immensely.[182]

To myself personally, a visit would have been one of the Temporal Works of Mercy. If I could have pinned you down to a seat in my garden, and in the most secluded part thereof, and let you talk at me for a couple

180 *Glenanaar* was serialized in *The Dolphin* 1904–1905. The autograph manuscript of *Glenanaar* is conserved in Dublin: National Library of Ireland, MS 25,007.

181 Sheehan's 1904 holiday at Cologne and Bad Nauheim.

182 The profession of Sr Dympna Whelan took place on 28 July 1904.

of hours, it would have brightened my existence very much for me. For you cannot conceive how much I feel the loss of some communication of ideas with those who, like yourself, could bring into a secluded and solitary life some of the ideas that are stirring the world outside. You do not feel the need of those stimulants, because you are everyday meeting men who talk your own language; but to me an hour's conversation on those subjects that interest me would be a pleasure akin to that of hearing one's mother-tongue in a foreign country. See what you deprived me of. And worst of all, you went away hungry and footsore from our door. And a Dives' banquet at the convent.

I am pleased to have the correct edition of St Teresa's bookmark in your lines. I had always a suspicion that there was something lacking; but I took my own as the orthodox version.

The reason I like Shelley so much is that he seems to me the most spiritual English poet; and he also seems to me to be the one poet who has shaped his language to his thought, and not his thought to his language. Rhythm seemed to come at the back of thought; whereas in Tennyson and others rhyme seemed to be framed first, and the thought called upon to fill in the spaces.

It cost me an effort to write as I did about Keats whom I like so much. I feel that I was disloyal to a friend.

I would send you my last book, if I thought it worthy of your acceptance. The reviews seem to make the mistake of regarding it as an attempt to create a masterpiece, instead of regarding it as a *jeu d'échecs* written off to help a charity. I was unfortunate in the title. My own title was *The Fate of Atropos*; but the Nuns asked me, under the inspiration of a priest, to change it to the present title. The 2nd. scene *After the Carnival*, which Fr Russell thinks unreal, is a *verbatim* report of a conversation between three young ladies overheard in a carriage between Cork and Queenstown.

I am, dear Fr O'Neill,

Yours sincerely,
P.A. Sheehan

126. FROM: NO ADDRESS.

Text: MS PA DON I/191; September [1904]

Dear Reverend Mother,[183]

Arrived here safely last evening.[184] It is a long and fatiguing journey; and such jolting in crowded trains, each about the length of Buttevant Lane. But it was interesting to see such vast crowds of all nationalities under the Sun.

We are agreeably surprised with this place. We formed the idea of a remote and — — place, whereas it exceeds Buxton or Harrogate. But of course it is all hotels. Ours is very quiet and comfortable. Only a few people here as season is over.

The Catholic church is a poor specimen; but they are building a handsome new one. Imagine two tiers of galleries, one over another, and one of these running right around and over the Altar.

I met at Mallow two American nuns who were just starting over to see us. They knew me from photos and challenged me at once. We came on together to Cork. I urged them strongly to go over to Doneraile as they had engaged a car. But they said no! There was nothing further to be seen!!! Alas!

The sea was like glass all from Cork to Milford and from Ostend to Dover, or rather vice versa.

I think I shall like this place, and yet be glad to get home.

We searched every inch of Cologne Cathedral yesterday. The shrine of the Magi is gorgeous. A huge mass of ornamentation all in gold.[185]

Will write again soon,

Always,
P.A. Sheehan

I hope de Pazzi[186] won't forget to have the schools' opening announced on Sunday.

183 Mother Alphonsus O'Keeffe (1852–1938), Superioress 1900–1906.

184 Bad Nauheim in the Grand Duchy of Hessen und bei Rhein.

185 The shrine commissioned by Archbishop Philipp I von Heinsberg (1130–1191) in 1180 from Nicholas of Verdun to house the relics of the three Wise Men which had come to Cologne in 1164. The shrine was completed in 1225.

186 Sr de Pazzi O'Connell (1852–1941).

127. FROM: DONERAILE, 24 SEPTEMBER 1904

Text: MS PAHRC/HJHP/SH/37[187]

Dear Fr Heuser,

Just arrived from Germany to find your letter before me. I have only time to say that you may omit anything you deem in individual expressions prejudicial to the interest of the story. The expression which I think you object to was used not long ago to a friend of mine, who regarded it as a joke.

I intended, as in the case of my priestly characters, to make the "Yank" a lovable character; but I find that in cases of racial or clan prejudices, people won't reason, and prefer to fasten on a cause or complaint.

Always sincerely,
P.A. Sheehan

128. FROM: DONERAILE, 24 SEPTEMBER 1904, EVENING

Text: MS PAHRC/HJHP/SH/38

Dear Fr Heuser,

Last night I wrote you a hasty letter lest I should miss the Queenstown mail. Since then I have gone over the first chapter;[188] and except that one word: Hell! I can see nothing objectionable. If I were publishing in book form, I would not change that; but as I have given you the serial for the benefit of your magazine, I leave you at liberty to alter it. I must say I think the opinion of your Irish American friend as unreasonable as the opinions of some of the Irish clergy about *My New Curate*. The fact is, that if an author once begins to accommodate himself to the whim of every class of the public he must lay down his pen. I am quite sure that landlords, Fenians, the Education office, will all find fault with the book; and a good many in Ireland will be severe on my too generous treatment of an "Informer's son". I think when you read the MSS through, you will see this.

Did I ever ask you to send honorarium by Postal orders, not by cheques, which take a month to get cashed.

---

187 Note in pencil, top right corner, first page, reads: *Glenanaar*, Nov. 1904.

188 Of *Glenanaar*.

I am quite enthusiastic about all I saw in Germany. Equally depressed by the contrast with my own poor country, which the Irish in America are steadily depopulating.

I think *Glenanaar*, though short, is the most perfect piece of work I have yet executed.

Always sincerely,
P.A. Sheehan

129. FROM: DONERAILE, 29 SEPTEMBER 1904

Text: Transcribed from David H. Burton, *Holmes-Sheehan Correspondence*, Fordham University Press, 1993.

Dear Mr Holmes,

There must be a sympathy in facts, as well as an association in ideas, for just as I got your letter of the 6th inst., you were brought to mind vividly by a picture of the house at Cambridge where O.W. Holmes was born; and by the quotation in the same magazine from Paul Bourget, which runs thus:

"One of the most eloquent of the Magistrates of Massachusetts, Judge Oliver Wendell Holmes, Jr., has said in one of those short speeches so full of soul, in which he excels: 'Even if our mode of expressing our wounds, our awful fears, our abiding trust in face of life, our death, and of the unfathomable world, has changed, yet at this day, even now, we, New Englanders are still leavened with the Puritan ferment'"

The Lord and Lady Castletown are here just now; and I have heard that you have written. So all around you occupy a pretty space in my thoughts these days. If I cannot write all I think, set it down to the fact that I have just returned from a brief holiday in Germany, and that there are six inches high of letters before me.

I am very much pleased to learn that you feel as thoroughly well after your years of labours; and refreshed by your holiday for new work. I consider your office an extremely arduous one. At least it would be so for me. In all my mental processes, the one that affects me most by its strain upon the mind, is the balancing of facts and arguments towards the formation of a judgment. Strange to say I can give free rein to the imagination for hours together without the slightest fatigue. And I can concentrate my thoughts on a process of reasoning, although I find this distressing. But weigh and balance, and judge – that is an ordeal I always avoid when I may. I am sure you don't feel it so; partly because you are trained to that habit of thinking, although your extraordinary powers of eloquence are mostly associated with the imaginative faculty. But I can conjecture what mental anxiety you must have suffered in the case you mentioned, where you had to face the dilemma of maintaining your judicial integrity and the possibility of displeasing friends. These are the things that make grey hairs, even while they elicit and develop all that is wholesome and virile in a man.

About Plato. I lean much towards him. I do not care for Aristotle. He had too little fancies and too many facts for me. And after all, I am every day becoming more and more convinced that the best of our thinking is done with the heart and not with the brain. Yet, Aristotle is one of the Saints of our Church. St Thomas has built his stately pile on his shoulders; and Aristotelian philosophy is the foundation of all Catholic theology. But, all my own predilections lean towards idealism rather than realism, towards St Augustine rather than St Thomas; towards Plato rather than Aristotle. Hence, I am utterly unqualified to be a judge, or a bishop. If I were the former, I should leave all discussion to a jury; if I were the latter, I would put my crozier in Chancery.

Arnold and Clough, whom you dislike, are two of my favourite poets. I think the latter very much over praised and the former very underrated. But I feel a curious pleasure here in my safe retreat, where problems of life do not touch me personally, in going out and experiencing that strange melancholy that seems to be charisteristic of our times, and of which these two poets are perhaps the best interpreters. I suppose it is the same feeling that makes one listen to the storm and the rain on a wintry night, when one is safely housed, and the curtains are drawn and the fire is bright, with a peculiar, and almost selfish pleasure. But I can read Arnold a hundred times over when I cannot touch Tennyson. He seems to me to have felt more deeply. I cannot dissociate Tennyson from my idea of an artist, who is always aiming to be out "on the line".

I had a pleasant three weeks in Nauheim, Germany. All that a good government, solicitous for the progress of its people, could do, has been done for this charming place. And the people! – a calm, grave, courteous people, enjoying life without noise or excitement, and infinitely polite to each other and to strangers. I could not help thinking of my own poor country, where everything is so tragical and sad.

Keep well; and do not deem me impertinent if I say, hold fast, as you have always done, to the great principles of justice and truth, so often controverted and repudiated in these days.

Always and most sincerely,

My dear Mr Holmes,

P.A. Sheehan

130. FROM: DONERAILE, 18 OCTOBER 1904

Text: MS PAHRC/HJHP/SH/39

Dear Fr Heuser,

Very many thanks for your Postal Order received today.

I spelled the name of the romance phonetically, – Glenanaar, as it is usually pronounced here. But perhaps, I would spare myself some criticisms from the Gaelic League if the word were printed correctly:

Glananair.

I see you have the correct spelling in the *Dolphin*.

The greater part of this valley is in my parish, Doneraile.

Always sincerely,

P.A. Sheehan

131. FROM: DONERAILE, 29 OCTOBER 1904

Text: MS PAHRC/HJHP/SH/40[189]

Dear Fr Heuser,

Some weeks ago Mr Galbally wrote me kindly offering plates of *Dolphin* for a 2nd. edition of my book *Under the Cedars and the Stars*. Up to the present moment, I have not been able to make any arrangements; and I would ask you to withhold use of plates from <u>any and every publisher</u>, until you hear from me, and understand the terms of my agreement with the publishers I shall select.

Very sincerely,

P.A. Sheehan, P.P.

189 Marked "Private and Confidential", top left corner, first page.

132. FROM: DONERAILE, 4 NOVEMBER 1904

Text: MS PAHRC/HJHP/SH/41

Dear Fr Heuser,

The reason I wrote you last Saturday to keep back *Dolphin* plates was that up to then I had received nothing from publishers on the American edition.

After six months waiting they have forwarded me this week £46–0–0, retaining for themselves £120, out of an edition struck from your plates, and without risk or trouble on their part.

I do not wish this to be repeated; and I think you should withhold your plates until such time as I am able to enter into a more equitable agreement with these gentlemen.

I shall be glad to know how *Glenanaar* takes with the public.

Ever sincerely,
P.A. Sheehan, P.P.

133. FROM: DONERAILE, 31 JANUARY 1905

Text: MS PAHRC/HJHP/SH/42

Dear Fr Heuser,

Benzinger Bros. have written me re a new publication of *Under the Cedars and the Stars*. I have written them to say that as you have kindly placed the *Dolphin* plates at my disposal, they can have them by complying with my terms, which are: £50 payable in advance on each edition of 1000 copies.

I got nothing for the use of these plates for the 1st. edition, believing that the publishers in Dublin would deal generously with me; but I was disappointed. They shall not have all the profits this time.

I am pleased to know *Glenanaar* is doing well. You are certainly giving it a splendid advertisement.

Always sincerely,
P.A. Sheehan, P.P.

134. FROM: DONERAILE, 21 MARCH 1905

Text: NLI/DP/MS 34,034

Dear Mr Mitchell,[190]

I have informed Mr O'Keeffe that I have no objection to a tournament in Doneraile for which you have kindly given the use of a field, provided that every precaution is taken that there shall be no intemperance; and that the Sunday peace shall not be disturbed.

Very sincerely,
P.A. Sheehan, P.P.

135. FROM: DONERAILE, 7 JUNE 1905

Text: MS PAHRC/HJHP/SH/43

Dear Fr Heuser,

I have assigned to my Bishop and trustees all my literary property, including *Glenanaar*, for the support of the sick and aged priests of this diocese.[191]

I write to ask you to continue to them the favour you have so generously bestowed upon me, of holding for them the *Dolphin* plates of my book. I don't know whether my publishers have brought out a second American edition from these plates; but I am quite sure the Bishop will manage them better than I have been able to.

Probably you will hear from his Lordship on the subject; and I am sure, that, considering the object for which I am transferring all my property, you will grant him all the facilities in your power.

Always sincerely,
P.A. Sheehan, P.P.

---

190 Land agent for the Doneraile estate. Tournament was the contemporary term for a hurling match.

191 Robert Browne (1844–1935), bishop of Cloyne 1894–1935. The business management of Sheehan's benefaction devolved on his secretary and nephew, Fr William Browne.

136. FROM: DONERAILE, 26 JUNE 1905

Text: MS PAHRC/HJHP/SH/44

My dear Fr Heuser,

At the risk of wearying you, I am sending you MSS of an article on the Gealic League, written by a young friend of mine, Mr J.J. Horgan, Cork, a young gentleman, who has already made his mark in literature this side. He is one of these splendid young Catholic laymen, on whom so much of our future depends. A valuable book of his on *Great Catholic Laymen*[192] is in the press, and will be shortly in your hands. He is a subscriber to the *Dolphin*, and is anxious to get into touch with you with a view to becoming a contributor, as we have nothing this side to compare with the *Dolphin*. I wish that you would write him a note; or ask Mr Galbally to correspond with him. You will find him everything that could be desired as a well-educated, zealous, Catholic layman.

There are a few slips in the MSS – which your printer will easily correct.

Glenanaar just out. I think it will take at this side.

Always sincerely,
P.A. Sheehan, P.P.

137. FROM DONERAILE, 8 JULY 1905

Text: MS UCC U2 AO/581

My dear William,

Your kind invitation was before me when I returned this morning from retreat.

It is the keenest disappointment to me that I have an engagement in Limerick on Monday, on my way to Kilkee. I shall be in Kilkee a little more than a fortnight; and my first duty on my return, shall be to visit you at Rockforest, and you must come over and see our nuns and children here.

If the good people of Mallow leave you any time at your disposal, you might cast your eyes over this little book *Glenanaar*, which I sent you, not

192 John J. Horgan, *Great Catholic Laymen*. [Andreas Hofer, Gabriel Garcia Moreno, Ozanam, Montalembert, Frederick Lucas, Windthorst, Pasteur, Daniel O'Connell.], Dublin, Catholic Truth Society 1905. The book carried a forward by Sheehan.

for its worth, but as a pledge of unbroken friendship that has subsisted between us so long that it makes one grave to contemplate it. How many times I have yearned to have a quiet talk with you on the many subjects that interest us both! As the universal hope is that you have now come to remain amongst us, I hope at least to have the opportunity I have so many times desired.

Please say to Mrs O'Brien that I joined in spirit in the warm welcome accorded you both by our fellow townsmen; and that I look forward to the pleasure of meeting her soon again.

Ever affectionately,
my dear William,
P.A. Sheehan

138. FROM: THE ROYAL MARINE HOTEL, KILKEE, CO. CLARE, 13 JULY [1905]

Text: MS PA DON I/100

My dear Ita,

The Bishop[193] has written to say that he has forwarded to you that bit of paper. I am so much impressed with the necessity of silence concerning it that I write to ask you to keep it secret, for a while at least, from everyone. Let it appear it came from an obscure benefactor.[194]

We are all well here. Good weather, very few visitors and the hotel is comfortable. I say Mass every morning at the convent which is quite near, and lounge about the rest of the day, keeping mostly to myself.

I hope you are all well: and that the schools are keeping up the average.

Imagine there is nearly a week gone.

Always sincerely,
P.A. Sheehan

193 Robert Browne (1844–1935), bishop of Cloyne 1894–1935.

194 This appears to be a reference to a gift of £200 which Canon Sheehan gave to the Presentation Convent.

139. FROM: THE ROYAL MARINE HOTEL, KILKEE, CO. CLARE, 18 JULY 1905

Text: MS PA DON I/101

My dear Reverend Mother,[195]

This is glorious news. God bless the anonymous donor; and if he is dead, God rest his soul! The first demand will be a doubly glorious feast for the children on 2nd August. You must give them at least 2/8 tea, as this is the standard to which our poor women go! I return the bishop's letter. I suppose he will tell you sometime who your benefactor is. What a pity it was not left to a less wealthy community, like Queenstown or Charleville.

I am not getting on well. Mass every morning in the Convent. I thought I was incognito but the second morning I found my name in the largest and roundest hand in the book, which I would not sign.

On Sunday morning there was a rush: but the other mornings I have no delay because the brethren prefer saying the *Lavabo*[196] out among the waves. There is an awful crowd of blackcoats here – C[hristian] Brothers, seculars, Redemptorists, camping out under tents.

I made off after breakfast and hid myself from all human observation in the awful rocks, reading or thinking for four hours 'till luncheon. Then I read in my room 'till my bath at 4.30: then tea. Dinner at 7. And away to the rocks until 10.

There are a good many Americans here. There was one young imp called Gladys, the ugliest little creature I ever saw, and the torment of her mother. She talked never endingly, talked with her mouth full, talked with spoon in her mouth, etc.. the mother was almost insane and several times threatened the "priest". I am afraid the "priest" had not much effect. "He looks severe, my child, very severe; but perhaps he is not quite so severe as he looks. We must not judge by appearances". This in my hearing. It is a lesson, I hope.

---

195 Mother Alphonsus O'Keeffe (1852–1938), Superioress 1900–1906.

196 A reference to the prayer of the Mass said at the washing of the priest's hands which is taken from Psalm 26:6–12 "*Lavabo inter innocentes manus meas, et circumdabo altare tuum, Domine: ut audiam vocem laudis, et enarrem universa mirabilia tua. Domine, dilexi decorem domus tuæ, et locum habitationis gloriæ tuæ. Ne perdas cum impiis, Deus, animam meam, et cum viris sanguinum vitam meam: in quorum manibus iniquitates sunt; dextera eorum repleta est muneribus. Ego autem in innocentia mea ingressus sum; redime me, et miserere mei. Pes meus stetit in directo; in ecclesiis benedicam te, Domine*".

My vis-à-vis last evening at dinner was Canon McInerney,[197] who had the action against the *Irish Times*[198] for libel – a gentle, typical, good Irish priest.

Several Americans have called here – some Canadians etc. All nice.

I expect Denis this week, probably on Thursday.

I enjoy the place very much. So far it is the quietest holiday I have had. I am as much alone as Robinson Crusoe: and the savage rocks are delightful.

The church is visited all day long by crowds, in and out the whole day long. It is nice to see ladies bringing their children to morning Mass and the Afternoon Visit; It carries out all that I said of the place: although there is a fair share of other things also.

I am glad that James Burke[199] has got some appointment. But I fear he will find Youghal more trying than Doneraile.

I suppose there are whole scale changes.[200]

Keep well and don't spend all that might fortune 'till I return.

Always and Sincerely,
P.A. Sheehan

140. FROM: THE ROYAL MARINE HOTEL, KILKEE, CO. CLARE, 22 JULY 1905

Text: MS PA DON I/102; *Addressed:* Rev. Mother, Presentation Convent, Doneraile, Co. Cork; *Franked:* Edward VII, penny red; *Postmark:* Kilkee, PM, Jy. 22 05 and verso Buttevant AM, 2.30, Jy 23 05.

My dear Ita,

Your letter and pleasant enclosures to hand. I return the letter. The book is doing fairly well.[201]

By no means change the dates for the feast and play: but set theme remains as arranged. I was mixing them up.

197 John McInerney, from 1906 parish priest of Kilrush, Co. Clare, and subsequently Dean and Vicar General of Killaloe.

198 *Irish Times* was founded by Lawrence Knox in 1859 as a Protestant nationalist newspaper. It was purchased in 1873 by Sir John Arnott of Cork who introduced a Protestant unionist editorial policy for the newspaper. See also note 264.

199 James Burke was curate of Youghal 1905–1912, after when he was transferred to Castletownroche. He is listed in the *Irish Catholic Directory* as John Burke.

200 Clerical changes.

201 *Glenanaar.*

The place continues delightful. Denis came up on Thursday and will remain 'till I return. May and Jeff were going to come. May dreaded the Journey and it is trying.[202]

The place is quite cosmopolitan – English, American, Australians etc. I try to keep to myself as much as possible. The weather is favourable: but we had much rain last night.

I fear Youghal will try Fr Burke very much. The confessional is severe. I am afraid I praised him too much to the Dean.[203]

It will save me from much questioning when I return if that plea is put forward that is suggested in your letter; viz: that it will be extremely embarrassing to Canon Sheehan to have it suggested that he [*were* erased] is the donor, if he [*were* erased] is not. It will be a distinct hint: Go thou and do likewise!

We will talk about postulants etc., when I return.

Always
P.A. Sheehan

141. FROM: THE ROYAL MARINE HOTEL, KILKEE, CO. CLARE, 26 JULY 1905

Text: MS PA DON I/103

My dear Reverend Mother,

As Denis is going home tomorrow (Thursday), and this hotel is becoming uncomfortably crowded, I have decided to return home tomorrow.

I sent you a telegram this morning. Annie[204] could tell Kate so that a car could be sent to Buttevant to meet me at the evening train.

Hoping to find you all well.

I am always and sincerely,
P.A. Sheehan

---

202 His brother, sister-in-law and nephew.

203 His friend, Dean Daniel Keller of Youghal.

204 Anne Ryan was Canon Sheehan's house keeper. According to the Census of Population of Ireland (1911) she was born in County Limerick.

142. FROM: DONERAILE, CORK, 6 FEBRUARY 1906

Text: PAHRC/HJHP/SD/3, Manuscript Copy

My dear Canon,[205]

It was very kind and good of you to write to me, from your bed of sickness: and under an illness, that is generally so depressing, that one has only courage to sit still, and bear it. But I can hardly forgive you for having been so near us last Summer, and never paid us a visit. It is quite possible, that I was from home, as I generally go away for a fortnight after the Retreat, but this does not excuse you. I must say though, that, for your own pleasure, you were happy to have found such an entertaining and amiable host as Canon Higgins, who, as a raconteur, and general conversationalist, has no equal.[206]

I hope this letter will find you better, convalescent, if not quite well. If you come over this summer, I shall show you all the inmost creeks and recesses, and haunted spots, in and around Glenanaar.

I think you will read with interest the enclosed notices on a book that met with such a hostile reception at home [*Luke Delmege*].

Thanks for the glees. The energy of your English priests makes us quite ashamed.

I am, dear Canon, Yours very sincerely,
P.A. Sheehan, P.P.

143. FROM: DONERAILE, 7 APRIL 1906

Text: NLI/DP/MS 34, 169

Dear Lord Castletown,

I feel I must write to explain that it was through no lack of interest I was absent from Mr Ussher's lecture this evening. But, unfortunately for me, the hour co-incided with the hour (7 p.m.) when it is most incumbent on the priests to be present in the Church. And I, who am responsible for the order of things, must set the example.

205 Canon Dallow of Birkinhead.
206 Michael Higgins, parish priest of Castletownroche, Co. Cork.

I hope, however, to have the pleasure of reading Mr Ussher's lecture in print in the *Cork Archaeological Journal*[207] or elsewhere.

I am, dear Lord Castletown,

Very sincerely,
P.A. Sheehan, P.P.

144. FROM: THE SEAVIEW HOTEL, BALLYCOTTON, CO. CORK, 15 JULY 1906

Text: MS PA DON I/104; *Addressed:* Reverend Mother, Presentation Convent, Doneraile, Co. Cork; *Franked:* Edward VII, ½ d. green; *Postmark:* Midleton, 8 p.m., Jy. 15 06.

Forwarded papers by the post. All well. Place very useful and quiet. Only a few here. I hope all are well. Send me word: and particularly about Augustine's feast ceremony in Midleton on Monday 16th double jubilee. Invited. But prefer the rocks and cliffs.

P.A.S.

145. FROM: THE BAY VIEW HOTEL, BALLYCOTTON, CO. CORK, 23 AUGUST 1906

Text: MS PA DON I/105; *Addressed:* Sister M. Patrick, Presentation Convent, Midleton, Co. Cork; *Franked:* Edward VII, penny red; *Postmark:* Ballycotton Midleton, 5.45 p.m., Au. 23 06.

Dear Sr Patrick,[208]

I cannot have the pleasure of being present at the great ceremony tomorrow. I send you herewith my hearty congratulations on your profession.

May you wear the Black Veil many years; and may every year bring you graces and happiness.

Always sincerely,
P.A. Sheehan P.P.

---

207 *Journal of the Cork Historical and Archaeological Society* has been published since 1891.
208 Sr M. Patrick of the Presentation Convent, Midleton, Co. Cork.

146. FROM: DONERAILE, CO. CORK, 31 OCTOBER 1906

Text: PAHRC/HJHP/SD/4, Manuscript Copy

Dear Canon Dallow,

I am exceedingly obliged to you for sending me the copy of your very interesting memoir of the late Bishop.[209] He has been happy in having such a biographer as you.

It is a very touching story. The Bishop seems to have been, if not a rare (I hope not) at least an attractive personality. I like his reticence and his sincerity; and I am slightly astonished that he had not made more enemies than he seems to have done. It is just such a character as his, silent, reserved and just, that seems to attract most petulance and the hostility of others.

Elements of Character is now incorporated in a volume, just published by Longmans, London. Your idea is very good: but perhaps you would suggest it to the Catholic Truth Society, Dublin, to whom I gave license to print it.

I have not seen the Ruskin booklets: but I think I have most of his writings, and several *Analecta*. I am very much in sympathy with him; very little with the man, he, too humbly, designated as his master – Carlyle.

Need I say how pleased I shall be to see you, if ever accident bring you hither.

Very sincerely, my dear Canon Dallow,
P.A. Sheehan

147. FROM: DONERAILE, 7 NOVEMBER 1906

Text: MS IJPA J27/127/43

Dear Fr Russell,

I enclose a few specimen poems, rather for your inspection than in the hope of seeing them in print.

The Palace of Sleep is mystic: *The Lady Ida* too long, although I think it a sweet poem. *The Woman and Child* was put into type some years ago by Fr Glendon, of the *Rosary:*[210] but never saw the light.

---

209 William Vaughan (1814–1902), bishop of Plymouth 1855–1902.
210 *The Irish Rosary,* founded in 1897, was edited by the Irish Dominicans.

The sonnets you will like. All those poems are originals. I have kept no copies. Therefore, (you will understand) they are precious. Perhaps you will send me back, after perusal, whatever you will not print.

No fear of my getting "swelled-head". I am far too unpopular for that. And the Bishop, to keep me down, has sent me for the last eleven years a succession of curates, who did not exactly break my heart: but so well cauterized every little green sprout of pride and vanity, that they can never now reach a fatal harvest.[211] But, you are quite right, my dear Fr Russell. We are only safe the day after we are dead.

Perhaps you would send me Dr Tyrell's latest, if only in terrorem. I shall return it the same day.

Ever sincerely,
P.A. Sheehan

148. FROM: DONERAILE, CO. CORK, DECEMBER 1906

Text: PAHRC/HJHP/SD/5, Manuscript Copy

Dear Canon Dallow,

Even in the hurry and confusion of the Christmas season, I must send you a brief note of thanks for the *Ushaw Magazine*[212] and your little Carol leaflets which I have given the nuns here, in the hope that they may introduce them amongst the children.

I have looked over your article, but have not yet had the time to study it carefully. I shall keep it for the leisure time after Christmas. The whole number is interesting reading.

May I trouble you to send me a brief note to a query (suggested by the opening sentence in your article), whether in England it is regarded as a sin to participate with heretics in divinis – I mean attending Protestant services, acting as bridesmaid at a wedding etc. With us, it is a reseved sin: and I have some idea that it was held in England that the Natural Law, apart from Ecclesiastical legislation, forbids all communicatio cum

211 The senior curates were: Walter O'Brien (to 1906), Thomas Shinkwin (1906–1920). The junior curates were: Michael Madden (1895–1896), Maurice O'Callaghan (1896–1899), Timothy M. O'Callaghan (1899–1902), Patrick J. Leahy (1902–1904), Joseph Sexton (1904–1906), James Coghlan (1906–1908). Two further junior curates were appointed between 1908 and 1913: Stephen Wigmore (1908–1913) and Michael Rea (1913–1918).

212 Published from St Cuthbert's College, Ushaw, Durham from 1891.

hereticis in divinis. The question has been mooted here: and I am anxious to know what opinion is held amongst English priests on the matter.

Wishing you all the blessing of the holy season, and many more fruitful years in the ministry,

I am, dear Canon Dallow,

Yours sincerely,
P.A. Sheehan, P.P.

149. FROM: DONERAILE, 15 JANUARY 1907

Text: NLI/CP/MS 35,306

Dear Lord Castletown,

I have to thank you very much for the splendid fowl which has just come to hand.

I feel sure I am also indebted to your Lordship for the *Revue Blue*,[213] with the very generous article on *The Irish Clergy*.[214] But Mons. Firmin Roz makes me a Bishop, a calamity which has not yet overtaken me.

I understand that we may expect your Lordship and Lady Castletown very soon. The Gaels will be asking you for the Laundry for March 17th.

With all good wishes to your Lordship and Lady Castletown for the coming year,

I am, my Lord,

Yours sincerely,
P.A. Sheehan, P.P.

150. FROM: DONERAILE, 22 MAY 1907

Text: MS IJPA J27/127/44

Dear Fr Russell,

Imprimatur *Pallida Mors*. I have not returned proofs, as they need no correction.

---

213 *La Revue politique et littéraire* (1863–1939) was founded in opposition to the *Revue scientifique* or *Revue Rose*.

214 The article, entitled *Le Clergé Irlandais*, was published in *La Revue politique et littéraire*, Series 5, tome VI, n. 26 [29 December 1906], pp. 809–812.

As one who suffers much sometimes from bad writing, I am quite in accord with you on "the matter". I would go further and say that I think it quite impolite to inflict an illegible letter on one's friends. For, if the essence of politeness is to put others at their ease, and to save them trouble, surely the essence of impoliteness is to waste the valuable time of a correspondent, and put him through the painful ordeal of trying to decipher one's hieroglyphics. The worst offender I have met is Judge Holmes, son of the *Autocrat*; and the most beautiful penmanship comes from the hand of Dr William Barry, who, I grieve to say, has been lately dangerously ill. He solicits prayers, and you won't forget him.

Lisheen should appear in book form in October.[215] But I expect to have a second series of *Under the Cedars and the Stars* in the hands of the public before many weeks. I am trying to get in as much work as I can in the short time that is allowed me.

Ever sincerely,

dear Fr Russell,

P.A. Sheehan

151. FROM: THE BAY VIEW HOTEL, BALLYCOTTON, CO. CORK, 18 JULY 1907

Text: MS PA DON I/106

Dear Reverend Mother,[216]

May is to enter the home in Cork today.[217] The operation is on Saturday. The doctors have been putting off from time to time to the utter ruin of her nerves, and now comes the hot weather with all its dangers. She has an awful dread of chloroform. Her nervous system is shattered and she is simply killing herself about Jeff.[218] That young gentleman is thriving and quite a celebrity in and about Queenstown. Pray for May and get prayers said but keep the whole matter private. They wish it to be kept very secret.

---

215 *Lisheen* was published by Longmans, Green, London and New York in 1907. The holograph text of *Lisheen*, in two volumes, is conserved in Dublin: National Library of Ireland, MSS 4671–4672.

216 Mother Ita Ignatius O'Connell (1867–1950), Superioress 1906–1912.

217 His sister-in-law.

218 His nephew.

I return letter. It would be better in my absence to send it to the Mallow nuns, or one of the Mallow priests as probably it will entail some correspondence again.

I enclose a letter from Mrs Foster. Keep it until I return but if you decide on making the application let me know.

Weather intensely hot here. Far worse than wet or stormy weather for I cannot go out.

I have been thinking a good deal about poor Augustine.[219] The suffering must be very great now.

I hope all is well and that Noni and Masie and Chatterbox are in daily attendance.

Ever sincerely,
P.A. Sheehan

152. FROM: THE BAY VIEW HOTEL, BALLYCOTTON, CO. CORK, 19 JULY 1907

Text: MS PA DON I/107; *Addressed:* The Reverend Mother, Presentation Convent, Doneraile, Co. Cork; *Franked:* Edward VII, penny red; *Postmark:* Ballycotton Midleton, 5 45 PM, Jy 18 07.

Dear Reverend Mother,

May's operation takes place at 10 o'clock tomorrow (Saturday); she has been obliged to go to Cork every day this week to see Atkins. I was speaking to Dr Cremen here last night; and he assures me there is no danger whatsoever. May is very hopeful. She went to Mrs Goulding's last night. Keep praying for her.

Always etc.,
P.A. Sheehan

Would you tell Anne[220] to send my bath to John Hanlon's and have it painted in enamel (cream coloured) before I return home.

---

219 Sr Augustine Cronin (1864–1907). She died on 7 November 1907.
220 Anne Ryan, his housekeeper.

153. FROM: 2 NORWOOD VILLAS, RUSHBROOKE, QUEENSTOWN, CO. CORK, 21 JULY 1907[221]

Text: MS PA DON I/108

Dear Reverend Mother,

I came on here yesterday from Ballycotton, as I felt it was a critical time for Denis and May. The operation took place at 9.30 on Saturday; and was very successful. May had a frightful headache after the ether and also has much pain. To-day she is much better and cheerful. But no one can know what she suffered before she went to Cork by anticipation. I hope this operation is final; because nothing could induce her to go through the same again.

I had five good days at Ballycotton but the weather was not good for me, it was too hot. I was not sorry to have to leave. I shall remain here a few days and get home by the end of the week.

Poor Augustine must be suffering a martyrdom this weather.

Yours sincerely,
P.A. Sheehan

154. FROM: DONERAILE, 5 OCTOBER 1907

Text: Transcribed from David H. Burton, *Holmes-Sheehan Correspondence*, Fordham University Press, 1993.

Dear Judge Holmes,

I had followed you in spirit across the Atlantic, with all hopes that you would have a prosperous voyage; and I was much gratified to receive your letter and to learn that your passage, if dull, was quite uneventful in dangers. I am also greatly pleased to know that your domestics were gratified by the little gifts we were able to send them. I sincerely hope that this has been by no means your final visit to us; but that you will find time during the long vacation to run over again and give us the great pleasure of seeing you. For your little morning visits to me were gleams of sunshine across a grey and monotonous life; and I look back on them with pleasure, but also with regret that such experiences should be so transient. I think I mentioned to you that I felt my greatest want to be some intercourse with minds

221 His brother's residence in Queenstown (Cobh).

whose ideas would act as a stimulant to thought, by casting new lights on old subjects. And, although we agree to differ on many points, it was very refreshing to me to be brought face to face with original thinking on subjects that are of deepest interest to myself.

Lord Castletown has not yet returned. He has been very busy in Scotland and at a Pan-Celtic Congress, where the six Celtic Nations were represented, and which seemed to be most interesting from an international standpoint. I see that he is now engaged in the commission for the reafforestation of Ireland – an admirable idea, if our conservatism would enable us to carry it out. There is a great deal of promotion of Irish industries too, but the headway they are making is not apparent.

I don't like that last sentence in your letter about your feelings of "anxious uneasiness;" although I am quite certain from similar experiences that it is a passing sensation, probably the result of your sea-voyage. But I like very much your very kind and generous expressions of friendship, which I beg of you to believe, are most cordially reciprocated.

I am ordering my publishers to send you the copies of two new books of mine – *Lisheen* and *Parerga.*[222] This latter is the 2nd Series of *Under the Cedars and the Stars*.

Always faithfully,
P.A. Sheehan

155. FROM: DONERAILE, 9 NOVEMBER 1907

Text: MS PAHRC/HJHP/SH/45

Perhaps the following lines would suit your purpose:

Why did I write *Lisheen*?
To show the claims of brotherhood and kin;
the deep broad streams of love that flow
in peers' and peasants' hearts –
the sin of broken plighted vows – the Fate
that follows over land and sea –
on wheel and rudder those that flee

222 *Parerga* was published by Longmans, Green, London and New York in 1908. The holograph copy of *Parerga* is conserved in Dublin: National Library of Ireland, MSS 4686–4688.

The boundless bounds of the Estate
Of Right and Law inviolate!
If Nemesis relentless be,
And Fate has seals of certainty,
The spirit that has borne the test
Of Spirits ranks amongst the best –
The bravest who aspire to be
The Bayards of Humanity!

P.A. Sheehan
8 November 1907

156. FROM: DONERAILE, 14 NOVEMBER 1907[223]

Text: NLI/DP/ MS 34, 169

Dear Lord Castletown,

On last Saturday, we had the melancholy ceremony of the burial of one of our most gifted nuns at the convent here.[224] This is the eight interment in nine years; which is an alarming average in a community of 22 sisters.[225] The doctors are unanimous in tracing the mortality to the confined and limited space — which the nuns have to walk; and they suggested that the nuns should use as an occasional recreation-ground the large field in front of the convent, which they hold from your Lordship at present.

Would there be any objection to making a walk 5 or 6 feet wide at the northern end of the field overlooking the river; and to plant a light screen within the wall in Buttevant lane. This would secure privacy and at the same time give abundant room for healthy exercise.

The nuns would be only too glad to purchase this field altogether if your Lordship could see your way to sell it to them.

I was much touched by Birrell's speech in Dublin the other day when he said that, if his University Bill proved a failure, they would not hear of

223 A note in Lord Castletown's hand reads: "I should like a rough map showing where the Convent goes towards river in the glen so to speak".

224 A reference to the burial of Sr Augustine Cronin (1865–1907). Sr Augustine died on 7 November 1907.

225 Those of the community who died during this period were: Sr de Chantal Abbot (1823–1897), Mother Berchmans of Jesus Fitzpatrick (1850–1898), Sr Gertrude Myers (1824–1900), Sr Stanislaus McNamara (1871–1900), Sr Magdalen Vaughan (1882–1902), Sr Xavier Roche (1826–1904), Sr Augustine Cronin (1865–1907) and another who cannot be identified from available records.

him again. It seems such a horrible destiny that a man, animated with the best notions, and with such comprehensive intellect, should think himself almost doomed to failure. But this time, there appears every prospect of success.

I am, dear Lord Castletown,

Yours most sincerely,
P.A. Sheehan, P.P.

157. FROM: DONERAILE, 20 NOVEMBER 1907

Text: MS UCC U2/AP/178

My dear William,

I am ever so pleased to find that you like those lines. I enclose a copy corrected from the printers. There are only a few verbal alterations.

Wishing your Christmas no. every success,

I am always yours,
P.A. Sheehan, P.P.

158. FROM: DONERAILE, 29 NOVEMBER [1907]

Text: NLI/DP/MS 34, 169

Dear Lord Castletown,

I have to thank you for the brace of pheasants which you so kindly sent me last week. I also return *Kashmir,*[226] a very beautiful book, which I feared to retain any longer.

I read with much amusement your letter last week in the *Independent.*[227] Like the Guards at Waterloo, we are "all mixed up".

Hoping that your Lordship and Lady Castletown continue well.

I am,

Always sincerely,
P.A. Sheehan, P.P.

---

226 Major T.R. Swinburne, *Kashmir, a Holiday in the Happy Valley with Pen and Pencil,* Smith Elder, London 1907,

227 *Irish Daily Independent and Nation* was launched in 1900 by William Martin Murphy. It quickly displaced *The Freeman's Journal.*

159. FROM: DONERAILE, SUNDAY EVENING [1907][228]

Text: NLI/CP/MS 35, 306

Dear Lord Castletown,

I had a hurried visit from Colonel White[229] and Mr Philip Barry[230] this afternoon, and I quite approve of the resolutions which, I understand, were forwarded to your Lordship.

I have given the matter some consideration this evening, and I should like very much to see your Lordship before the memorial is typed and signed.

It would not suit any of us to risk defeat in this matter; and I fear the project is now beyond withdrawal. The rate is struck, the site selected and sanctioned, etc.; and if the matter is to be withdrawn, it must be by some means besides a memorial. But there are so many aspects of the question that I should have an interview with your Lordship to exchange views on the matter. In any case I think I would advise deferring the memorial until we had time to talk it over.

I am, dear Lord Castletown,

Very sincerely,
P.A. Sheehan, P.P.

160. FROM: DONERAILE, 10 MARCH [1908]

Text: MS IJPA J27/127/45

Dear Fr Russell,

I return proofs. I am pleased to know that you like the Lecture. I should wish it to be read in Maynooth. I am sure it will be read in America.

I see your order has sustained many severe losses this month. But it has noble substitutes. I have seldom read anything so convincing and eloquent as Fr Phelan's sermon on *Socialism* last Sunday in Cork at their mission in St Patrick's. It is really refreshing to find such a fine piece of thinking without a single tawdy purple patch of rhetoric.

---

228 A note in Lord Castletown's hand reads: "P.A. Sheehan, Doneraile, 1907".
229 Of Kilbyrne, Doneraile.
230 Of Ballyvonare, Doneraile.

I am out at the country stations every morning. It is trying, particularly when the roads are dangerous from frost; but I wouldn't miss them for anything. It is just such a pleasure to meet the people in their own homes.

Would there be any hope of realizing my foolish dream of creating a few well-read and cultivated circles in Ireland? I cannot bear to think that all our power is running to weed in angry political strife with so much personal acrimony. I am always dreaming of an Irish youth, silent, modest, reading much and talking little; and trying to bring into daily life some of the graces of civilization. But I am not hopeful. Everyone seems anxious to rush into print and speak dogmatically on every subject. Of course, infallibility is the privilege of youth; but what shall we do, when the new University turns out three or four thousand of such lay Popes?

I would be glad if you would look over the proofs again. Something may have escaped my notice.

Always sincerely,
P.A. Sheehan

161. FROM: DONERAILE, 27 APRIL [1908]

Text: MS IJPA J27/127/46

Dear Fr Russell,

I feel that I must thank you for the excellent notice of *Parerga* in the May *Monthly*; and also for the copy of *Booknotes* which you so kindly sent me. I think it is almost the first time that Mr Britten has said a kind thing about my books.

I had some scruples in writing at all about Shelly: lest I should be supposed to ignore his grave faults of character. But I have always regarded him as the "mad Shelley" of Eton and Oxford; and then, he had some fine qualities of mind and heart. I think it is almost certain that, if he had lived, he would have come around to the Church. The real beauty of Christianity, distorted and obscured by early education, was beginning to break on him.

I have no scruple about anything I have said about Shakespeare. I hardly ever like him. I sometimes loath him.

Ever sincerely,
P.A. Sheehan P.P.

162. FROM: THE BAY VIEW HOTEL, BALLYCOTTON, CO. CORK, AUGUST, [19]08

Text: MS PA DON I/109

Dear Reverend Mother,

I am nearly a week here; and have had a pleasant time – weather beautiful, and the hotel very comfortable. I wish Denis were here; but there is no chance of getting a room; as great numbers are sent away daily for want of accommodation. If all goes well, I shall put in my full time here.

A young teacher, Miss K. O'Shea, called on me yesterday, with her mother, to get Ballyvonare school. So Miss Murphy must have given out that she was resigning, altho' she has not sent her resignation to me. I informed Miss O'Shea that my own parishioner, Lizzie O'Connor, had a prior right to the school; and the assistantship at Skehanagh to Hannah Piggott. But this latter is very precarious and I could hardly advise Hannah to give [up] the <u>certainties</u> of England for the <u>chances</u> that the average would keep up in Skahanagh.

I hope you are keeping well. I have met only one or two persons here that I know.

Did Dr Maurice O'Reilly, CM, from Bathurst call at the convent? He sent me a telegram that he was going to Doneraile. He is an excellent priest and I hope he made your acquaintance.

My face is blistered from the Sun. I shall be as black as a "Darkey" when I return.

Always and sincerely,
P.A. Sheehan

163. FROM: THE BAY VIEW HOTEL, BALLYCOTTON, CO. CORK, 12 AUGUST, [1908]

Text: MS PA DON I/110

Dear Reverend Mother,

I received Miss Murphy's resignation this morning. It dates from September 30th. She was about to enter Bantry Convent, but the nuns at Castletown-Bere heard it, and persuaded her to remain with them.

I suppose Lizzie will accept Ballyvonare school; and I have written the Board[231] whether I can appoint Hannah to Skehanagh. It would mean £51 a year if the average keeps up.

Weather remains lovely here. The place is full, three occupying one room. Twenty were sent away from this hotel last week. I met Miss McGregor shivering on the cliffs last Sunday. Also, Miss Hanagan, formerly of Nolan's; and poor Mrs McLoughlin came up from Cloyne on Sunday and brought little Margurite to see me.

The time is passing so quickly here, although so quiet.

Ever

P.A. Sheehan, P.P.

164. FROM: THE BAY VIEW HOTEL, BALLYCOTTON, CO. CORK, 20 AUGUST 1908

Text: MS PA DON I/111

Dear Reverend Mother,

Many thanks for both letters received this morning. I think it all the better that Anne should leave. I have seen for some time that she was dissatisfied and unhappy; and inclined to find fault.

Don't you think that Mrs B would be embarrassing? It would be so hard to treat her as a servant and I am not sure she would be able to attend to the rougher work of the house – answer the door etc. I shall await your second letter to-morrow morning. I write now because I want Hannah Piggott to fill up the enclosed form and forward it immediately to the Board. If she is accepted, it will mean between Ciss and herself about £80 a year. I have signed it so it need only be filled up and forwarded.

After a period of unbroken sunshine we have had a bad day to-day. My present intention is to leave here next Wednesday or Thursday. If Denis and May return to Norwood, I shall go up there until Saturday.[232] If they have not returned, I shall go home direct on Thursday at the latest.

I have had several applications for Ballyvonare but answered all that I had a local claimant.

Let me have your own opinions about Mrs Beamish.

Always

P.A. Sheehan, P.P.

231 Board of National Education.

232 His brother and sister-in-law.

165. FROM: THE BAY VIEW HOTEL, BALLYCOTTON, CO. CORK, 21 AUGUST [1908]

Text: MS PA DON I/112

Dear Reverend Mother,

A priest recommended me to write to the Missies Russell, Killarney, who keep a training institute for servants. So I sent them a note this evening asking them to recommend a steady and confidential person. It may turn out well.

Yesterday was a cold wet day here – the first we had since I came. Today is beautiful again.

I think I mentioned I would leave here on Thursday and go straight home in case Denis is not back in Norwood. I shall regret leaving here. I have been very comfortable and have had three very happy weeks. It is not pleasant to face worries again.

Always,
P.A. Sheehan

166. FROM: THE BAY VIEW HOTEL, BALLYCOTTON, CO. CORK, 25 AUGUST [1908]

Text: MS PA DON I/113

Dear Reverend Mother,

I am glad to know that your little ceremony passed off successfully. I expect it is a relief to have it over.

The enclosed is the latest on the great question of a domestic. If I could wait it would be best; but of course I cannot. I feel very dubious about Mrs B. I cannot see how I could treat her as a servant. I should always feel constrained. We'll defer the matter until I return.

I leave here on Thursday morning. Would you ask Antony [sic] to tell Linane meet me at 4 o'clock in Mallow; and also to acquaint Anne that I shall be at home for tea on Thursday.

Jeff is after a slight operation for tonsillitis in Limerick;[233] and May has had very hard times.

Ever and sincerely,
P.A. Sheehan

233 His nephew.

167. FROM: DONERAILE, 11 SEPTEMBER 1908

Text: Transcribed from David H. Burton, *Holmes-Sheehan Correspondence*, Fordham University Press, 1993.

Dear Mr Holmes,

Yours is one out of two or three handwritings, which, when I recognize on an envelope, gives me a thrill of pleasure and compels me to leave my breakfast cool until I read it. The vast bulk of my correspondence I put aside until I have leisure; and some letters I should like to have the privilege of never opening. But, though I am always hoping that you will buy a typewriter – no, that's not true, for then I should miss the personality that shines through you letters – I always tear your envelope open, and I put you in my red arm chair and listen to your delightful monologue.

I have come up from the sea, where I spent three very happy weeks, my summer holidays, and where I saw sunsets and moonrises that would make a poet even of politicians. Of course, you haven't our glorious skies over there; and yet I can imagine from that little bit of description, which you allowed creep into your letter, that your woods and seashores must have an inexpressible charm for a mind that must be on the strain for eight months of the year. For if I am to judge by my own feelings, I think no mental effort uses up so much brain-power as the balancing of judgments, and the agony of making a right solution between conflicting arguments. I read some of your judgments lately in *The Literary Digest*; and I said what strenuous thinking that means. After all, the poets have the best of it. They touch the spring of their aeroplanes and are off into the empyrean.

The British Association have come by one. Lord Castletown had an idea of bringing some of the learned ones down here; but I think they were surfeited with Dublin hospitality. There seems to me to be some bathos in these scientists waltzing around a ball-room, or talking platitudes at a five o'clock tea. But I suppose Homer must nod, or go to sleep altogether. But there was not a single paper of even slight importance read. The scientific papers threw no light on the mystery of things; and your department of political economy was hardly touched.

How that terrible question of "socialism" is looming up! There is starvation amongst the workingmen of Glasgow, and riots, Prince Arthur[234] insulted, etc. I have just seen one word for democracy and the future in a volume I have just put down, where it is proven, that in your democratic

234 Prince Arthur, Duke of Connaught and Strathearn (1850–1942).

America with all its progressivism and levelling down, reverence for women is increasing. The thought had not struck me before.

Have you taken up as yet the great book I expect from you? With such a style as yours (although it could not be popular) and such ideas, you ought to give the world a memorable book.

I am just commencing in the *American Ecclesiastical Review* a story called *The Final Law*[235] in which I try to preach if I can not prove, that above the iron laws of the Universe there is a higher command; or, as Tennyson puts it: That Love is Nature's Final Law.

Always affectionately,
P.A. Sheehan

168. FROM: DONERAILE, 23 SEPTEMBER 1908

Text: MS PAHRC/HJHP/SH/46

Dear Dr Heuser,[236]

Your letter to hand. I should wish very much to meet your wishes in altering the title; but the one you suggest is somewhat cumbrous and too long; and, as I am sure to be carefully criticized here at home, I should not wish to put the feminine element too prominently forward; and it will reveal itself. I feel that a concrete title is best as you suggest. What would you think of:

The Blindness of Dr Grey.

It would apply to his physical and metaphorical infirmity,

Or:

Ward and Guardian.

I prefer the former. The latter, I think, has been used.

In suggesting to Longmans the sum of £3 per chapter (the additional £16 is their commission) I had in view the possibility of their taking over and utilizing your printing plates. Charles Longman thought that they would not suit the form of a novel. The arrangements for book-production are not yet complete; and I try and postpone the publication until the serial is finished by you. The publishers are always complaining about the

235 The novel would be published as *The Blindness of Dr Gray*. It had been serialized in *The Dolphin* in 1909. The manuscript is conserved in the papers of Fr Herman Heuser in the Philadelphia Archdiocesan Historical Research Centre. Some of the corrected proofs are conserved in the archive of the Presentation Sisters.

236 In 1905, Fr Heuser was awarded a Doctorate of Divinity, *honoris causa*.

enormous cost of American printing, altho' they could have printed *Parerga* in England. Could not you help them by offering *The Dolphin Press*? They cannot get better type or paper; and probably you could afford to give them plates cheaper than Cambridge University;[237] and it would help your magazine. It is only a suggestion; but if they can get an American edition printed at moderate charges, they will have no further reason to grumble at my royalties.

Ever sincerely,
P.A. Sheehan

169. FROM: DONERAILE, 24 OCTOBER 1908

Text: MS PAHRC/HJHP/SH/47

Dear Dr Heuser,

Some inquiries that have come to hand from London publishers lead me to express the hope that my new novel has been duly copyrighted in Washington and London, so that its rights would not be interfered with.

If you can keep the MSS intact for me, I should be much obliged.

Could you let me know what was the probable commercial value of the plates of *Under the Cedars and the Stars*, which you were kind enough to say were mine; but which the Bishop parted with to Brown and Nolan for £20, not knowing that they were my property. Has Benzinger taken them over? Or, are they still in your possession?

Many thanks for the grand set-off in the October No. I hope you and your readers will be much gratified.

Ever sincerely,
P.A. Sheehan, P.P.

170. FROM: DONERAILE, 13 NOVEMBER 1908

Text: MS PAHRC/HJHP/SH/48

Dear Dr Heuser,

I wrote, as you suggested, to Mr Longman; and he writes to say your request is reasonable; but that it is of so much importance that the book should be

237 University Press, Cambridge, U.S.A., printers of *Parerga*.

published in time for the Christmas market, it would be advisable to have it published in November 1909. It would injure the sale of the book, if its publication were delayed after Christmas. This would give you two months additional, and perhaps you could cram in 4 chapters in some of the last numbers.

I am greatly pleased to know that you would like to retain for yourself the MSS of *Dr Gray's Blindness*. By all means do so. I hope you have kept the other MSS also. But you must get the last 15 or 18 chapters typed in duplicate for me, because I must be able to place the entire book in the hands of publishers here and in America in the early Autumn. If necessary, I shall pay the expense of typing.

Messers. Longmans have not concluded any arrangements with me about book-publication. I think they are anxious to have it; but they seem to be waiting 'till they see how the book catches on in America.

Let me know if it pleases your readers from time to time.

Ever sincerely,
P.A. Sheehan, P.P.

171. FROM: DONERAILE, CO. CORK, 19 FEBRUARY 1909

Text: MS in Katherine Tynan Hinkson Papers, Morris Library, University of Southern Illinois, Carbondale, U.S.A.

Dear Mrs Hinkson,

Would you kindly let me know whether you find that the management of your literary arrangements has been carried out quite to your satisfaction by your Literary Agent, who, I see, quotes a letter from you in his circulars; and whether you would advise one who wishes to be saved from much correspondence and worry to entrust his affairs to the same firm?

I hope you are well and that your vast literary output does not make the call upon your physical energies which I, working within a narrower circle, sometimes feel.

I am, dear Mrs Hinkson,

Very sincerely,
P.A. Sheehan, P.P.
Doneraile.

172. FROM: THE ORMOND HOTEL, CLONMEL, CO. TIPPERARY, 5 MARCH 1909

Text: MS PA DON I/114; *Addressed:* The Reverend Mother, Presentation Convent, Doneraile, Co. Cork; *Franked:* Edward VII, penny red; *Postmark:* Clonmel 8.45 p.m., MR 15 09.

Dear Reverend Mother,

I came here in such a hurry that I hardly packed my valise; and my journey was made in a terrible state of depression such as I hope I shall never experience again. Thank God, I find things much better than I expected; and as yet no danger. Denis[238] has an attack of pneumonia in right lung, in front, and also at the base of lung behind. There appears to be an excellent Doctor in attendance and 2 skilled nurses. One great trouble is to keep the truth from him. I was so alarmed this morning that I wired May to send for Dr Graham of Limerick. He is coming on tonight.

Altogether, the symptoms are favourable but he is only in the beginning of his illness, and it will be tedious. So, you must get all the prayers you can said.

Please tell Fr Skinkwin[239] that he must manage the parish as well as he can for a few days, as I may be detained here. It is barely possible that I may go home tomorrow; but May is alone here, and a great deal depends on the verdict of Dr Graham tonight.

Always sincerely,
P.A. Sheehan, P.P.

173. FROM: THE ORMOND HOTEL, CLONMEL, CO. TIPPERARY, 16 MARCH 1909

Text: MS PA DON I/115; *Addressed:* The Reverend Mother, Presentation Convent, Doneraile, Co. Cork; *Franked:* Edward VII, penny red; *Postmark:* Clonmel 6.45 p.m., MR 15 09.

Dear Reverend Mother,

Today has passed very well; and our poor patient is somewhat better tonight, thank God! But all danger is not by any means passed; and you

238 His brother.

239 Fr Thomas Shinkwin, senior curate of Doneraile 1906–1920.

must continue your prayers. To-day, at his own request he had Confession and Holy Viaticum. This is an enormous relief to my own mind. I think he was running down lately in health; he then had an attack of influenza which he neglected with the present consequences. May is wonderful. She is up night and day; and if I did not know of old that she has great powers of endurance I should be alarmed. And her anxiety is very pitiful. Very often I see tears in her eyes; but she suppresses all that is in the sickroom.

Denis is calm and placid and not a bit disturbed, altho' he knows how serious his illness is.

I hope to be able to send you a good telegram in the morning.

Always sincerely,
P.A. Sheehan

174. Post Office Telegram from, Clonmel, Co. Tipperary, 17 March 1909

Text: MS PA DON I/116; Origin: Clonmel handed in at 10.51 a.m and delivered at 11.10 a.m.; *Addressed:* Reverend Mother, Convent, Doneraile.

"Restless night but holding his ground well Canon Sheehan"

175. from: The Ormond Hotel, Clonmel, Co. Tipperary, 17 March [1909]

Text: MS PA DON I/117; *Addressed:* The Reverend Mother, Presentation Convent, Doneraile, Co. Cork; *Franked:* Edward VII, penny red; *Postmark:* Clonmel 8.45 p.m., MR 17 09.

Dear Reverend Mother,

Denis had a restless night; and was weak and depressed all the morning; but pulled up a good deal during the day. The doctor says that if he can maintain his strength until Saturday, all will be well. Dr Graham is coming again tonight; and I have great faith in him, altho' everyone says that Dr Crean is a very clever and careful physician. Denis has the most perfect attendance and nursing night and day; and the hotel people are exceedingly kind. The proprietoress, Miss O'Keeffe, is an old Loreto Child at Fermoy.[240] There are no complications: it is all a question of maintaining his strength

240 Loretto Convent, Fermoy, Co. Cork.

until the crisis is passed. Of course you will keep besieging Heaven for his recovery. Poor May and myself are up and down in the scale of hope and despondency – sometimes quite sanguine, sometimes reverse. But May has been all her life a nurse, and is more or less used to it. But sometimes we have sad hours.

I think I must stay over Sunday here as I cannot leave, until his recovery is practically certain.

May sends you most grateful acknowledgements, she came down specially for the violets and shamrocks.

Always sincerely,
P.A. Sheehan

176. Post Office Telegram from, Clonmel, Co. Tipperary, 18 March 1909

Text: MS PA DON I/118; Origin: Clonmel handed in at 10.39 a.m and delivered at 11 a.m.; *Addressed:* Reverend Mother, The Convent, Doneraile.

"Very much better lung clearing doctors hopeful Canon Sheehan"

177. from: the Ormond Hotel, Clonmel, Co. Tipperary, 18 March [1909]

Text: MS PA DON I/119; *Addressed:* The Reverend Mother, Presentation Convent, Doneraile, Co. Cork. Post card.

Dear Reverend Mother,

This evening the doctor announced improvement – pulse and temperature lowered, spirits excellent and strength keeping up. I think he has almost turned the corner; but he will be extremely languid and weak.

I believe the lung is getting rapidly relined. The breaking up of the congestion has begun. St Joseph will bring us good news tomorrow.

Tell Sr Joseph[241] that I wish her a very happy feast; and keep up prayers for patient's strength.

Always sincerely,
P.A. Sheehan

241 Sr Joseph Guiney (1870–1942).

[178]. Post Office Telegram from, Clonmel, Co. Tipperary, 19 March 1909

Text: MS PA DON I/120; Origin: Clonmel handed in at 8.45 a.m. and delivered at 9.14 a.m.; *Addressed:* Canon Sheehan, Doneraile.

"Bad night I would like you to come May"

179. Post Office Telegram from, Clonmel, Co. Tipperary, 18 March 1909

Text: MS PA DON I/121; Origin: Clonmel handed in at 1.30 p.m. and delivered at 14.09 p.m.; *Addressed:* Reverend Mother, The Convent, Doneraile.

"Rather weak the crisis [torn edge] Doctor very hopeful Canon Sheehan"

180. Post Office Telegram from, Clonmel, Co. Tipperary, 19 March 1909

Text: MS PA DON I/122; Origin: Clonmel handed in at 7.40 p.m. and delivered at 8 p.m.; *Addressed:* Reverend Mother, The Convent, Doneraile.

"Everything hopeful and promising Canon Sheehan"

181. from: the Ormond Hotel, Clonmel, Co. Tipperary, 19 March [1909]

Text: MS PA DON I/123; *Addressed:* The Reverend Mother, The Convent, Doneraile, Co. Cork; *Franked:* Edward VII, penny red; *Postmark:* Clonmel 8.45 p.m., MR 19 09.

Dear Reverend Mother,

We had another anxious day here see-saw up and down. Denis was very weak about noon but pulled up in the evening. He is passing through the crisis – fever abated, pulse and temperature normal but great exhaustion. The Doctor was just here; and sees nothing to fear.

I think it will take him 6 months to recover. I was thinking of going home tomorrow, but that will depend on what the Doctor says in the morning. I cannot go until the danger is past.

Always,
P.A. Sheehan

182. FROM: THE ORMOND HOTEL, CLONMEL, CO. TIPPERARY, 20 MARCH [1909]

Text: MS PA DON I/124; *Addressed:* The Reverend Mother, The Convent, Doneraile, Co. Cork; *Franked:* Edward VII, two ½ d. green; *Postmark:* Clonmel 9.45 p.m., MR 20 09.

Dear Reverend Mother,

Denis is now convalescent. The crisis passed yesterday: and he mended rapidly to-day – so rapidly that if he continues at this rate he will, please God, be well soon. It is an enormous weight taken off our shoulders. Of course, now is the time for extreme care.

May is a marvel. I never saw such devotion and self-sacrifice in my life: and although she is suffering herself; she looks forward cheerfully to a month of continuous nursing.

If all goes well, I shall leave here at 8 a.m. (morning) o'clock on Monday and arrive at Mallow at 10 o'clock. Please tell Anne and also Linane.

Always etc.,
P.A. Sheehan

183. FROM: DONERAILE, 27 APRIL 1909

Text: MS PAHRC/HJHP/SH/49

Dear Dr Heuser,

In view of the controversy now proceeding in your pages re the use of the vernacular in the Liturgical Services of the Church, I send to you by this mail a little book, called *The Rebels of the Reformation*.[242] You will see how sturdily the "Western men" in Devon and Cornwall resisted any innovation.

242 London, 1909.

The author is a young London Journalist, who has strong leanings towards the Church.[243] The book would make excellent subject for an article, as it is otherwise deeply interesting.

Always sincerely,
P.A. Sheehan, P.P.

Fr O'Brien of the *S[acred] H[eart] Review* has begged a weekly letter from Ireland from me. I could send him some interesting papers from time to time; but I fear anything new appearing in a Boston journal would possibly hurt the popularity of *Dr Gray*. So I have put the question by for the present.

184. FROM: THE BAY VIEW HOTEL, BALLYCOTTON, CO. CORK, 4 JUNE 1909

Text: MS PA DON I/125; *Addressed:* The Reverend Mother, Presentation Convent, Doneraile, Co. Cork; *Franked:* Edward VII, penny red; *Postmark:* Ballycotton Midleton, 5.45 p.m., Jn 4 09.

Dear Reverend Mother,

Arrived here safely. Denis, Jeff and May came on on Thursday. Weather rough but fine. I hope Denis will be much improved here.

This is sad news from Mallow. I have written Mother Catherine this evening. I fear Sr Elizabeth has a poor chance.

In haste,
P.A. Sheehan

185. FROM: THE BAY VIEW HOTEL, BALLYCOTTON, CO. CORK, 6 JUNE [1909]

Text: MS PA DON I/126

Dear Reverend Mother,

I had a letter from Mother Catherine this morning. Reverend Mother had a narrow escape, and is not out of danger for the next four days. It appears

243 Wilkinson Sherren (1875–1953), born in Dorset, published several works including *A Rustic Dreamer and Other Stories* (1903), *The Chronicles of Berthold Darnley* (1907), *Two Girls and a Mannikin* (1911), *The Marriage Tie* (1914), as well as religious and hagiographical works. Cf. obituary in *The Catholic Herald* of 10 July 1953, p. 9.

that if the operation had been delayed for hours, the attack would have been fatal.

All well here. Weather cold, but bracing and very fine on the cliffs. Denis is already improved very much; and Jeff is also much better. He had developed a prodigious appetite.

Would you tell Anne to send on immediately a thick parcel of books that has been sent to Doneraile by Longmans and Co.. It is essential that I should have them soon.

Not a priest here but myself; but the hotel is full for the first two weeks in June.

I hope you are all keeping well. I wonder what can have happened poor Sr Elizabeth. I thought her very robust. Her brother will feel it very much.

Always sincerely,
P.A. Sheehan

186. FROM: THE BAY VIEW HOTEL, BALLYCOTTON, CO. CORK, 8 JUNE [1909]

Text: MS PA DON I/127

Dear Reverend Mother,

Many thanks for your own letter and enclosures which I return.

I am greatly pleased to learn that everything is going on well at home; and that Anne has some little enjoyment. She deserves it. She will send you up the *Am[erican] Ecc[lestical] Rev[iew]* if you like. I am busy preparing corrections and proofs for press as Messers Longmans wrote me for them.

The weather here is cold and bracing – exactly what suits me. But Denis took a slight chill two nights ago; and is afraid to go out. Up to then he was doing well. He is very nervous about himself; and I think this is retarding his perfect recovery. Dr Cremen has not helped him by insisting that he must go to St Moritz in the Alps. This is really quite unnecessary; but it has upset him a good deal.

Jeff is what is usually called "Trouble-the-House". He is the most restless being in the world. I gave him a penny yesterday to keep him quiet for 2 minutes at dinner. He succeeded: but it was an awful trial. He talks to everyone – English and Irish, gentle and simple, without exception; but he appears to have a great predilection for tradesmen, such as plumbers and [——]. Poor May. She rears him well. If he grows to manhood he ought to remember his mother. I never saw anything like her care.

I had a note from Mallow this morning. I think Mother Francis is all right.

Could you manage to have Denny plant nasturtiums in the two beds near the wall; and some sweet-pea. I think too the celery and Brussels sprouts should be put down now.

I enclose under another envelope some papers which perhaps Fr Shinkwin could see after.

Always sincerely,
P.A. Sheehan

187. FROM: THE BAY VIEW HOTEL, BALLYCOTTON, CO. CORK, 9 JUNE [1909]

Text: MS PA DON I/128

Dear Reverend Mother,

I suppose I gave you a fright last evening by my telegram: but the publishers want proofs of *Dr Gray* corrected at once: and I am sending on the whole parcel tomorrow. There should be another copy at my house and also one from Longmans. Anne could give one to you.

Denis's cold continues. He has remained within for today; but is out of bed. He is exceedingly nervous; and afraid of every puff of wind, and I am afraid he will hardly have the courage to stay here. I have suggested to him to go to Blarney until the weather becomes finer here. May and Jeff are well. The place suits them admirably.

Always etc.,
P.A. Sheehan

188. FROM: THE BAY VIEW HOTEL, BALLYCOTTON, CO. CORK, 13 JUNE [1909]

Text: MS PA DON I/129

Dear Reverend Mother,

They had packed all things on Friday to go away when luckily Dr Cremen came down, laughed at the cold, and directed them to stay, as the place had already improved Denis so much. So, here they remained. And yesterday suddenly burst into Summer. And today is heavenly. They are delighted now. The whole thing was pure nervousness. Then a D. Byrne from Cork, who had a frightful attack in May was ordered here and this has reassured Denis that he is in the right place. I am very glad for all their sakes, because it has done May and Jeff good also. The latter is developing prodigiously. He has not the reserve or shyness of his uncle. He makes up to everyone and chats away as if he knew them always. But he has a great contempt for anyone under a motor-car owner. These he respects.

I won't go back until 26th inst. Ask Fr Shinkwin to announce the examination of the children for 1st. Communion at Shanballymore, 11 o'clock, Sunday the 27th inst., and Doneraile after last Mass the same day.

I hope you will find W. Mitchell and Nellie and the ladies well.

Always,
P.A. Sheehan

189. FROM: BAY VIEW HOTEL, BALLYCOTTON, CO. CORK, 13 JUNE 1909

Text: Transcribed from David H. Burton, *Holmes-Sheehan Correspondence*, Fordham University Press, 1993.

My dear Judge Holmes,

I am here for a quiet holiday above the eternal sea – that same sea that washes the shores beneath your delightful villa. It needs no violent stretch of the imagination to picture us shaking hands across that little span of waters. But as fancy will not make things possible, I must only use the penny post to send you greetings, to hope that you keep well after this labouring session, and to thank you for the three printed copies of your legal decisions which duly came to hand, but which I have hitherto failed to acknowledge.

I was much interested in these judgments, although it is not easy for the lay mind to follow the intricacies of legal arguments; and the balancing of the three elements – justice, reason and precedent, which seems to me a most difficult task. I often wished that you could see a very remarkable treatise *De Legibus*, written by the Spanish Jesuit, Suarez, and in which lately I have been again interested as I have had occasion to refer to it in some writing. It is a ponderous folio volume of about 750 pages, double column, closely printed; but it is a masterpiece of close, consecutive reasoning, and as such, it is a monument of industry and intellectual power. It has never been translated into English; and like so many other vast treasures, it lies locked up in medieval, but correct, Latin. I often wonder, why legalists have not heard of the book. They would burn Coke upon Lyttelton and all other commentators.

This is an antique, out of this world, Keltic and fishy village, just enlivened by the presence of half a dozen Londoners, who come over here from the smoke and fog of Babylon, to inhale some sweet air, and to exercise man's great privilege of destruction by killing all the fish they can, out upon the deep seas. It is not for food they kill but for "sport" – to be able to say in a London club: "I killed a skate, weighing 125 pounds, and several hundred congar eels". It reminds me of Teufelsdrockh's Epitaph on Count Zachdarm in *Sartor: Quinquies mille Perdices Plumbo confecit.*

I hope the water will waft you to Doneraile in the Autumn.

Always most sincerely,

my dear Judge,

P.A. Sheehan

190. FROM: THE BAY VIEW HOTEL, BALLYCOTTON, CO. CORK, 17 JUNE [1909]

Text: MS PA DON I/130

Dear Reverend Mother,

I have sent the parcel duly. It will be of use in case this very hot weather continues. It is mid-Summer here, with a nice cool breeze from the North. The hotel is very quiet, except for Jeff who strives to keep everyone lively.

I am not surprised that M. Cuinan is back. She can keep her place.

I find I shall have to return on Friday the 25th inst. I must call at Mallow to see Reverend Mother. I think Denis is quite well; but Dr Cremen is very cautious about asserting his convalescence.

Always,

P.A. Sheehan

191. FROM: DONERAILE, CO. CORK, 28 JULY [1909]

Text: MS PAHRC/HJHP/SP/1

Dear Fr Phelan,

Many thanks for your letter of this morning. I had two telegrams from Lismore[244] on June 19th to the same effect. It is altogether a graceful compliment from priests, who have never known me; and I appreciate it highly. But it is a thing that must not be. The Holy See is too wise to send out to a young and expanding diocese an old man of 58, with as many infirmities as holy Job, and who would probably, if he were sent, join the hosts of Pharaoh in the Red Sea.

I am ever so pleased that your book is doing so well. It seems to augur a new awakening. The words of Franzalin have been haunting me by reason of the sad contrast between the Irish College of today with 35 students and the other College on which their respective Bishops are lavishing such care, sparing nothing by way of equipment and increasing every year the number of students.

I was once at — and have pleasant memories of the Sisterhood and the out-of-the-world, old-world little hamlet.

Ever sincerely,

My dear Fr Phelan,
P.A. Sheehan

192. FROM: DONERAILE, CO. CORK, 31 AUGUST 1909

Text: Transcribed from David H. Burton, *Holmes-Sheehan Correspondence*, Fordham University Press, 1993.

My dear Judge Holmes,

If you were now in Washington, gowned and ermined, and trying to maintain judicial equanimity in an atmosphere of 94 degrees or so, I would not inflict a letter on you. But, seeing that you are happily in undress, and with no responsibility beyond the ordinary human duty of killing time, and strolling on pebbly beaches, and driving through fragrant pine-woods, I can

244 The provision to the diocese of Lismore in New South Wales arose in 1909 with the death of Bishop Jeremiah Doyle. Canon Sheehan was proposed by the clergy for the Episcopal succession of that diocese but asked not to be taken into consideration for appointment.

forgo what is to me a very great pleasure indeed, – namely, to congratulate you on the distinction lately conferred on you by the Oxford Dons.

The fact has raised these latter gentlemen somewhat in my esteem, because it seems to indicate that they have departed from what has been a religious tradition in the British mind, that everything American is very "young" and immature, and still under the benevolent patronage of the mother country. Only quite lately in *The Times Literary Supplement*,[245] some letters of Swinburne's were published, in which he speaks in a very patronizing manner of your Emerson; and again, quite lately, I have been reading the letters of Coventry Patmore in which he ridicules the idea that Longfellow could be considered a poet. And I send you herewith a copy of the supplement (Times) in which you will notice a certain tone of British condescension towards American litterateurs, whilst accepting the world's verdict on the *Autocrat*. When, therefore, Oxford found *you* out, I am beginning to respect the English intellect a little, and to think that in their own elephantine manner, they are being purred into line with the thinkers of other nations.

Only yesterday, your name turned up in Doneraile Park. Lady Castletown mentioned that you had been over; but I think they regretted they had not seen you, or that you were unable to visit. Lord and Lady Castletown were much pleased with the Oxford affair.

To drop down to my humble self, I am sure you will be interested to hear that some good priests out in Australia want me to travel 12,000 miles, and to spend the rest of my life with a mitre (far weightier in every way than your wig) governing an immense diocese under a tropical sun. Of course, Rome is too wise to listen to such suggestions; and I have been selfish enough to use all the machinery I could avail of, to prevent the possibility of such a thing. So I take it as a pretty French compliment and nothing more. But these are the little accidents of life.

I do hope the Centenary celebrations of your revered father will be the success every lover of his books and gentle character expects.

The leaves are beginning to turn here; and our Indian summer is commencing. I suppose you will soon be in the Forum again.

Always most sincerely,
P.A. Sheehan

245 *The Times Literary Supplement* appeared as a supplement to *The Times* in 1902. It became a separate publication in 1914.

193. FROM: DONERAILE, 27 OCTOBER 1909

Text: PAHRC/HJHP/SL/3, Manuscript Copy

Dear Mr Lysaght,

I was greatly pleased to hear from you and to know that you contemplate returning to the old land again. I belong to the Thomas Davis school of politics, which would band all Irishmen in one common phalanx for the betterment of our common country, and I hope these ideas, now repudiated, may yet prevail ... But Ireland has changed a good deal ... Fr Finlay and Sir Horace Plunkett would be almost alarmed to find how far they have made the fine old Irish people a "commercial" nation. You are doing well in giving us another volume of poetry. I do not know any poems that appeal to me so strongly in their melancholy music as yours. That opening poem about the *Camaraderie* of the "failures" haunts one.

You won't think me impertinent if I say that the less agnostic your future volume is, the greater chance it has of success with the public. Swinburne owes his failure in catching the "aura" of popularity to his earlier poems, altho' he practically repudiated them, and almost apologised for them; and Tennyson owed a great part of his success to the fact that he gave a doubting and anxious world some little substitute for lost faith. The world can never do without religion. In Art, Literature, even in Science, it is always predominant.

Yours etc.
P.A. Sheehan

194. FROM: DONERAILE, 4 NOVEMBER 1909

Text: MS IJPA J27/127/47

Dear Fr Russell,

I am sorry to say that I have seen but one copy of *America*;[246] but that gave me a good idea of what was in store for the reading public of the States.

I have a good deal of manuscript on hands; but nothing of the kind you require. Two years ago, Fr [Ambrose] Coleman, O.P. pressed me very hard

246 *America* was founded in 1909 in New York by the Jesuits as a national weekly magazine on Catholic issues and American political and cultural life.

for some material for the *Rosary*. But I see from the tone of such magazines that, such as I should wish to help, somehow or other, the matter which I could submit, would not be suitable, nor acceptable.

America must remain my happy hunting ground; as Germany is my great Patroness and defender.

But you are not to be pitied. I imagine you suffer from the embarrassment of selecting from the pile of valuable papers which reach you from all the young aspirants of Dublin and elsewhere. What will it be when our National University is in full swing?

Always sincerely,
P.A. Sheehan

195. FROM: DONERAILE, 9 NOVEMBER 1909

Text: MS NLI/DP/34,169

Dear Lord Castletown,

From the circumstances mentioned in your letter, I think your correspondent must be the Rev. Canon Wigmore, P.P. Bathview, Mallow. He writes most illegibly; but you may be able to decipher his signature from this.

I am,

Always sincerely,
P.A. Sheehan, P.P.

196. FROM: THE BAY VIEW HOTEL, BALLYCOTTON, CO. CORK, 9 JUNE 1910

Text: MS PA DON I/131; *Addressed:* The Reverend Mother, Presentation Convent, Doneraile, Co. Cork; *Franked:* Edward VII, penny red; *Postmark:* Ballycotton Midleton, 5.45 p.m., Jn 9 10; verso, Buttevant 2.30 a.m. Jn 10 10.

Dear Reverend Mother,

Got here all right on Monday afternoon. Yesterday we had a heavy fog and intense heat. To-day Summer has suddenly burst on us: and this place is delightful. Only 9 or 10 people here; and perfect quiet. I shall enjoy my stay here, I think, more than ever.

There is a parcel of *Irish Rosary*[247] magazines at the railway station for the past 10 days, sent there by mistake. Perhaps you could ask James Cleary to bring them to you. You can dispose as you please of them, keeping one for me. I think they will send on some more by P[arcel] Post.

This is Columba's feast.[248] I have not forgotten.

Always,
P.A. Sheehan

197. FROM: THE BAY VIEW HOTEL, BALLYCOTTON, CO. CORK, 10 JUNE 1910

Text: MS PA DON I/132

Dear Reverend Mother,

I have read over your letter carefully; and although there seems to be a chance of something advantageous to the Convent, the risks are also very great. I fear this poor lady would tire of conventual life; and then the subsequent dangers of trouble arising must be considered. Of course, you must write to the Bishop at once – and give him all the particulars. If the offer were made to myself personally, I should decline it; but then you have to consult the welfare of the community.

I was greatly pleased to see the appointment on the paper. I hope he will keep all right. It is a nice thing for him. It is very good of him to take up the Church job under such circumstances.

If you got the bundle of *Irish Rosaries* from the station, cut out the pages of *The Semator* from one copy; and send it on to me. Dispose of the rest as you please.

The weather is so delightful and things are so pleasant here, that I am almost afraid something will turn up to break them. But it is to be anticipate.

Give enclosed paper to Fr Shinkwin.

Always sincerely,
P.A. Sheehan

---

247 *The Irish Rosary*, founded in April, 1897, as a small magazine, edited by the Irish Dominicans, was enlarged to eighty pages in 1901, and its scope widened. Father Ambrose Coleman, O.P., who became editor in 1903, added a certain journalistic tone to it, thus making it bright and up-to-date. In 1910 the editor was Father Finnbar Ryan, O.P. Among its contributors are many able Dominican writers, well-known laymen like Professor Stockley, Dr Fitzpatrick, R.F. O'Connor, Shane Leslie, Jane Martyn, S.M. Lyne, Sister Gertrude, and Nora O'Mahony.

248 Sr Columba of the Five Wounds Sheehan, (1869–1918), his cousin.

198. FROM: THE BAY VIEW HOTEL, BALLYCOTTON, CO. CORK, 13 JUNE 1910

Text: MS PA DON I/134

Dear Reverend Mother,

I return Ned's [struck out and overwritten with Kattie's] letter; and am glad to hear that May is out of danger. Ned ought to represent matters to the Mallow Guardians. It is too bad that they should be exposed to such danger.

The weather continues delightful here. Yesterday there was an invasion of Cork people who came down on the steamer *Audiz,* and the place was in commotion for about 2 hours. Today we are more tranquil than ever.

There are two parcels of *Irish Rosary* sent out from Dublin – one, 6 copies, was sent by rail; the other, 2 copies were sent by Post. If they reach your hands, keep two copies for me for reference purposes. The rest you can dispose of.

I would want about a dozen clean collars towards the end of the week. Tell Anne to send them to me.

There are plenty of them in the drawers.

Always sincerely,
P.A. Sheehan

199. FROM: THE BAY VIEW HOTEL, BALLYCOTTON, CO. CORK, TUESDAY, [14 JUNE 1910]

Text: MS PA DON I/133. Personal stationary.

Dear Reverend Mother,

I return Bishop's letters lest they should be lost here. Keep them carefully.

The whole thing is strange and mysterious enough; it is marvelous how these Irish exiles cling to the memories and the old associations.

Weather continuing fine.

Everything here peaceful and restful.

Always,
P.A. Sheehan

200. FROM: THE BAY VIEW HOTEL, BALLYCOTTON, CO. CORK, 19 JUNE 1910

Text: MS PA DON I/135; *Addressed:* The Reverend Mother, Presentation Convent, Doneraile, Co. Cork; *Franked:* Edward VII, penny red; *Postmark:* Ballycotton Midleton, 5.45 p.m., Jn 18 10.

Dear Reverend Mother,

The collars came quite safely; and I think I shall have enough of everything to last until I return; which will probably be on 30th inst. for the retreat commences the following week. The weather here continues very fine, brilliant sunshine, and cool breezes from the sea. And hardly any visitors. I have the place practically to myself.

There was 1st Communion of the children this morning here. The children are much bigger and more advanced than ours. But look very poor, and altogether there is an anaemic look about them, as if they had not sufficient, or only unhealthy, food.

I had a wire from Denis yesterday that they were coming on here on Tuesday; but this morning a letter came that they have changed their minds and are going on to Blarney on Tuesday. I fear May is not at all well.

I was very sad about Nellie O'Connor. It must have been a dangerous disease.

It is a great comfort to know that the Church is repaired: it will be a relief against the Winter.

I hope McCarthy will make your affairs with your visitors all right so that no trouble can ensue after. It was a wise thought to get a — solicitor.

There was a rumour here that Fr Horgan of Killeagh was about to resign; that Fr Maurice O'Callaghan would be appointed Adm[inistrator] with right of succession; and that Fr Rea from here would go as Adm[inistrator] to Fermoy. But I don't think Fr Horgan will resign.

Get the 1st. no. of the *Cork Free Press*[249] and read the leading article *A Forecast and a Review.*[250] I think it has caused a sensation in Cork.

Always sincerely,
P.A. Sheehan

---

249 Based in Cork, the *Cork Free Press* was a nationalist newspaper which circulated primarily in Munster. Published daily from June 1910 until 1915, and weekly in 1915–16, it circulated from 11 June 1910 to 9 December 1916. It was the third of three newspapers founded and published by William O'Brien MP. It was the newspaper of the *All-for-Ireland League* (1909–1918).

250 This was written by Canon Sheehan.

201. FROM: THE BAY VIEW HOTEL, BALLYCOTTON, CO. CORK, 20 JUNE [1910]

Text: MS PA DON I/136.

Dear Reverend Mother,

I wrote to W. Mitchell a week ago to alter the vestment press in the sacristy to suit the new vestments; and also, to see after the flooring in the hall, and the wainscoting in the lavatory at Bridge House. He wrote promising that both would be looked after during the week. Perhaps he is engaged at the sacristy. It would be no harm if Anne would see him when passing the door (always for the mid-day post) and tell him that I shall be home next week. I wrote you on Saturday that I should be home on the 30th, the day after the holiday.[251] The weather here has become cooler; but as yet there has been no rain. There are only one or two persons staying here. The place is as quiet as Melleray,[252] except on Sundays, when a crowd of trippers come down from Cork and elsewhere; and remain the day.

The wiring that is required in the Church is not <u>in the sacristy</u> but in the round ventilators on the roof of the Church just above the sacristy, where the swallows enter. Con should get it through the ceiling from the organ gallery, and work along the roof to the West end where the ventilator is.

I do hope Wm. Mitchell will finish the job in the sacristy and house before I return. It is such a bother to have tradesmen knocking around.

Always sincerely,
P.A. Sheehan

[Note written along the right margin of the first page: *I suppose Fr Hennessey sent you a copy, like enclosed*]

202. FROM: THE BAY VIEW HOTEL, BALLYCOTTON, CO. CORK, 21 JUNE [1910]

Text: MS PA DON I/137; *Addressed:* The Reverend Mother, Presentation Convent, Doneraile, Co. Cork; *Franked:* Edward VII, 3 penny reds; *Postmark:* Ballycotton Midleton, Jn 21 10; verso, Buttevant 2.30 a.m. Jn 22 10.

---

251 In 1910, the solemnity of Sts Peter and Paul (29 June) was a holiday of obligation requiring attendance at Mass.

252 Founded in 1833, Mount Melleray is a Cistercian abbey located near Cappaquin, Co. Waterford.

Dear Reverend Mother,

The enclosed cheque for £ 5–4–6 came to hand this morning from Sam Sheehan. I haven't Fr James O'Connell's address; and it would be too much to wait 'till I return, so I have enclosed it and would ask you to forward it with list of Mallow subscribers to Fr James's address.

We had a thunderstorm here last evening and a heavy down-pour of rain. To-day is beautifully fine. I hope Mr Mitchell will finish the Bridge House before I return.

Always sincerely,
P.A. Sheehan

203. FROM: BAY VIEW HOTEL, BALLYCOTTON[253]

Text: MS PA DON I/190; 23 June [1910]

Dear Reverend Mother,
It will be for the Bishop to decide in what securities the money will be invested; but there are few now that can pay 4%. I think the donor's wish to have her name inserted is very reasonable. There can be no reason now why the money should not be withdrawn; and reinvested, when you have got the Bishop's opinion as to the best securities.

Weather continuing fine here. I have been most fortunate. I am somewhat uneasy about May. They were to reach Blarney on Tuesday and Denis promised to write at once; but there has been no word since. He is horribly careless about writing. Poor May was suffering severely from headache in Cloverfield.[254] They are very anxious to leave Queenstown as the climate is much against her.

Thanks for forwarding cheque to Fr James. He is much distressed at the death of an old and faithful housekeeper and he has asked for prayers.

Always sincerely,
P.A. Sheehan, P.P.

253 This letter is out of chronological sequence in the series of the Presentation Convent archive.
254 Cloverfield, Co. Limerick, his sister-in-law's home.

204. FROM: DONERAILE, CO. CORK, 26 AUGUST 1910

Text: Transcribed from David H. Burton, *Holmes-Sheehan Correspondence*, Fordham University Press, 1993.

Dear Dr Holmes,

You are very much on my mind these last few weeks, probably because of the Autumn holidays or perhaps it was a presentiment of your letter for which I was craving. The great want of my life is lack of intellectual intercourse; and your letters are a stimulus that drives me from the superficialities of daily life into depths of thought where I have no temptation otherwise to plunge.

I think Fr Benson's forecast of the future of the Church in America is not altogether chimerical, although probably his reasons for thinking so are quite different from mine. Whether America is yet in its adolescence, or whether it be the result of climatic conditions, there is a certain buoyancy and delightful optimism in the character of the nation that is very much akin to the Catholic spirit. And there is also depth of feeling and generosity which the older nations have long since cast aside in favour of the "critical spirit". All this tells in favour of the Church; and I think if some great thinker could reveal the inner serenity, and sense of security, with the occasional raptures that belong to certain choice spirits, particularly in our cloistered communities, half of America would rush away from the fever of modern life, like the anchorites of old, and bury themselves in monasteries.

Would you be surprised to hear that in what you say about "intellect", you come very near the dogmatic teaching of the Church, especially as revealed in the late Papal Encyclical against *Modernism* – one of the most remarkable documents that has been issued by the Holy See? It is a condemnation of "emotionalism" or "intuitionalism", as the sole motive of faith. The Church takes its stand upon reason as the solid foundation on which the Faith rests. Hence its approval of the Thomistic philosophy, which rests entirely on the syllogism, a view accepted by John Stuart Mill. But, as you say, intellect has its limitations, which we are all painfully conscious of; and, therefore, if we are to reach Truth, there must be some other avenue. This we call faith. For after all, if Intellect is the supreme and final Judge of Truth, the question at once arises, whose Intellect? Or what condition of Intellect? Is it the intellect of one solitary thinker, like Aristotle, or the common intellect of the "man in the street"? or is it the intellect of an Aristotle or a Bacon in his youth; or in his manhood, or in his old age?

I have just been reading *The Autobiography of Herbert Spencer.*[255] He appears to have modified, at the age of 60 or 70, half his dogmatic teachings as a young man. Age, experience, illness, imperfect circulation of the blood in the arteries of the brain, impure blood from hepatic troubles – all these were elements that modified half his conceptions during life. What then? Well, it follows that if we accept "intellect" alone as the norm and standard of truth, we drift at once into the belief that all knowledge is relative, and there is no absolute truth. That won't do! And it is here the intense logical consistency of Catholic teaching comes in. The Absolute Mind alone can discern Absolute Truth. The moment you speak of limitations, or say "we cannot know", you admit that. Therefore, what we can know about the Universe, is just what reason verifies and what Absolute Truth has chosen to reveal.

Why do I underline that word? Because, such is the pride of human intellect, that what we are really in revolt against is – the Reticence of God. We forget our place in the Universe, because we have never got rid of that Geocentric Theory which makes the little microbe, man, the apex of the Universe. We have to be humble, if we are to aspire; and we have to accept with thankfulness the little and yet great deal, that the Absolute Mind has chosen to reveal. We, Catholics, believe that that revelation has been made to the Church; and it is the only Church in Christendom which asserts that and speaks with authority. You think that therefore the Church is bound to coerce and persecute. Certainly not. First, because to coerce conscience by punishment is totally opposed to the spirit of the Church on the sole ground that is a fundamental principle of Catholic theology that "the end can never justify the means". You will lift your eyebrows at this; and say: What about the *Provincial Letters* and *Jesuitism* and all that? But, I am only stating the literal truth, no matter how Catholic doctrine has been twisted and abused by men. There is no more fundamental principle in all Catholic ethical teaching, so much so as that one of the most familiar questions in our daily catechizing of children, and in our Sunday preaching is: "If by one lie you could liberate your father from prison, or release all the souls that suffer in Purgatory, would you be justified in uttering it?"

And the answer is: "No. No object, however holy, can justify a thing that is evil in itself".

255 Published by Williams and Norgate, London 1904.

I know you will not urge medieval persecutions which we all condemn and deplore. The ages were barbarous; and then heresy was a political crime, a kind of treason – felony when the Church was identified with the State; and when heresy was productive of many social evils. No one finds fault with the Versaillais troops for shooting down the Communists who set Paris on fire.

Besides, the spirit of our age will not tolerate persecution, altho' the *Kulturkampf* of Bismarck is rather recent. Advanced education will kill all that.

I send a little volume on the attitude of the Church towards animals. You will see how hopelessly wrong Pierre Loti[256] is! Have you seen Huysmans's *En Route*? The story of a swineherd Simeon is unique – a mixture of ecstatic rapture and daily and hourly contact with animals that makes me sick. But it is "Catholicity" undoubtedly, in one aspect, though it is an aspect that does not appeal to me.

I am in thorough sympathy with you in your conviction of the sacredness of human liberty. It seems to me a kind of sacrilege to trespass on the Holy of Holies – the human conscience. Hence I have been for the last few months here in Ireland in a state of silent fury against the insolent domination of the Irish Parliamentary Party and their attempt to stamp out all political freedom. At last, I was forced to speak, and I send you two articles on our political situation, and in favour of a new movement to establish political liberty and break down the barriers between Protestants and Catholics in this country. But, whilst I would resent any political attempt to interfere with my principles or convictions in political and social matters, or to restrict my freedom in any way, whenever the Eternal speaks (and every day I am becoming more overwhelmed with a sense of His Omnipresence) either through direct inspiration or through the Vicariate He has established on this little planet of ours, I am a little child; or as Pasteur[257] said: "I have the faith of a Breton peasant; and if I live much longer I shall have the faith of a Breton peasant's wife".[258]

---

256 Pseudonym for Julien Viaud (1850–1923), French naval officer, novelist and member of the Académie Française.

257 Louis Pasteur (1822–1895), French chemist and microbiologist. He treated the 4th Viscount Doneraile for rabies but without success.

258 The accuracy of the quotation is contested. It first appeared in *Semaine religieuse … du diocèse de Versailles*, 6 October 1895, p. 153.

You will smile at all this. No matter. You will see what Dante thinks. I know from what you have said that you have seen the glories of the *Paradiso*.

We have had disastrous weather here. Eternal rain. Not a glimpse of sunshine any day; but sheets of rain. The harvest is ruined.

The Castletowns are here. Lady Castletown is only recovering from a serious operation on the eyes; and Lord Castletown is not so robust as usual.

The infirmities of age are creeping down on myself and I am becoming more home-tied every day, working on and trying to get in as much useful travail as I can before the night falls. It would be the rarest of all pleasures to see you; but you are right to economise your strength, and yield to the physical inertia which your mental expenditure induces.

With all respect for my co-religionists, I do most sincerely wish that my next letter shall be addressed to the Lord Chief Justice of the States.

Ever sincerely, my dear Dr Holmes,
P.A. Sheehan

205. FROM: DONERAILE, 29 SEPTEMBER 1910

Text: MS IJPA J27/127/48

Dear Fr Russell,

As we say down south: "You have always the pleasant word!" and your kind remarks about the *Semator* came in very pleasantly just now, when Fr Coleman has decided to suspend, or rather, terminate the series in his magazine. You will see by the enclosed letter that the serial is not popular with his readers; and he seems to think that the *Irish Rosary* is in jeopardy, if it is continued.

I confess I foresaw all this; and that it was with much reluctance, and only at his repeated solicitations, I placed the MSS in his hands. I gave him abundant time to read over the MSS carefully before finally accepting it. Not that I have any blame to him. As he rightly says, the interests of the magazine should not be imperilled. One good effect follows – that I can bring out the book now at Christmas or the New Year, instead of postponing publication to midsummer. There are 37 sessions in all; only 18 have appeared.

I am quite incorrigible about such words as "morn", and "pearl". Miss Emery pointed out the misdemeanour before. It is the "Cork accent", which rattles and rolls the "rs".

I have just had a cordial invitation from Dr Maurice F. Egan to the American Legation at Copenhagen! And it costs me infinite effort to go outside my parish even for a day.

You say: How many minds I have influenced already ! I hope for good; because as the night draws on, we are thrown ever more inward and inward in self-examination; and I can only say that my intentions were always upright and sincere, in trying to lift the minds of man to higher levels of thought, through the medium of literature. How far I have succeeded, cannot yet be known.

I am, dear Fr Russell,

Ever sincerely,
P.A. Sheehan, P.P.

206. FROM: DONERAILE, CO. CORK, 1 NOVEMBER 1910

Text: PAHRC/HJHP/SD/6, Manuscript Copy

Dear Canon Dallow,

Very many thanks for this delightful and edifying story. I have an old partiality for monks, and I delight in reading about them. Everything that touches the cloister is dear to me, and hence, I read your little story with great pleasure. I feel also that it will be popular, and will be widely read in Ireland.

I am not too much surprised that it was refused in America: and yet it is in these types of sanctity, formed on the Divine Model, that the too materialized modern world needs so badly. I hope you will give us a few more monastic Idylls like this. They are little sermons, that go deep down into human hearts.

I am, dear Canon Dallow,

Very sincerely,
P.A. Sheehan

207. FROM: DONERAILE, 3 JANUARY 1911

Text: MS IJPA J27/127/49

(Arrived 4 January)
Dear Fr Russell,

I enclose my annual tribute (7/–).

I am very busy correcting final proofs of *The Intellectuals*[259] the name (under Mr Longman's wish) under which *The Sunetoi* is to appear at the end of the month. It should form a handsome volume.

Do you [know] anything of a writer named William Smith, the author of *Thorndale*,[260] and a book called *Gravenhurst*.[261] I found a review of *Thorndale* many years ago in *The Critical Essays of a Country Parson*,[262] and I procured the book immediately after. It has been a favourite volume of mine; but on account of some skepticism that was incidentally introduced; I forbore mentioning the book in any of my writings. But I am anxious to know something of the author. I wrote to Blackwood, his publisher, but they referred me to the National Library in Dublin. Once I came across the name merely in the *Life of G. Eliot*; but I can get no further information. Yet I think he must have been a singular man; and in some way, his name is associated in my mind with his sister's: William and May Smith.

With all good wishes for the eventful year that is stretching out before us.

I am, dear Fr Russell,

Always sincerely,
P.A. Sheehan

208. FROM: DONERAILE, CO. CORK, FEBRUARY 1911

Text: PAHRC/HJHP/SH/7, Manuscript Copy

Dear Canon Dallow,

I have waited a few days, to try if I could recall the author of the wise saying in your letter, but I cannot remember having seen the expression,

259 Published by Longmans, Green in 1911. Holograph text of *The Sunetoi* is conserved in Dublin: National Library of Ireland, MSS 4681–4683.

260 *Thorndale, or the Conflict of Opinions*, published by Blackwood, Edinburgh and London 1858.

261 *Gravenhurst, or Thoughts on Good and Evil*, published by Blackwood, Edinburgh and London 1857.

262 Andrew Kennedy Hutchison Boyd (1825–1899), *The Critical Essays of a Country Parson*, Longman, Green, Longman, Roberts & Green, London 1865.

("The greatness of a Nation depends upon the Education of its Children") although it seems to me familiar. At any rate it is pithy and a wise saying, which any worthy author might be proud to acknowledge.

The little magazine (*Quarterly Review* of Boys' refuge Industrial School, Liverpool), considering its object is very good, and I am sure must do a great deal of effective work amongst your boy-waifs and strays.

I am, dear Canon,

Very sincerely,
P.A. Sheehan, P.P.

209. FROM: DONERAILE, CO. CORK, 25 MARCH 1911

Text: Transcribed from David H. Burton, *Holmes-Sheehan Correspondence*, Fordham University Press, 1993.

Dear Dr Holmes,

I hardly expected that you would find time from your judicial work to cast your eyes over *The Intellectuals* and I am greatly pleased that you did not dislike the book. It would be too much that you should give it the "Index" *Approbatur*! Because I know that you think in a complex and involved manner, whereas this book had to deal with platitudes, and I am afraid in a way too transcendental for the multitude, and not academic enough for the truly learned. I intended it to be an *Eirenicon* between the rather furious parties into which Irish life is divided; but here again I am not over-sanguine, because the book will not be read except by a few, whose tastes and sympathies have already placed them beyond the zones of political antagonism. It is an unhappy and distracted country and the one thing that hitherto saved it – a certain kind of Celtic idealism – has now given way before the advances of materialism.

The Castletown affair was very tragic. Lady Castletown has undergone a painful operation for the eyes in London; and was partially relieved. They had returned here, and then the crash came. So unconscious was Lady Castletown that any danger impended, she spent £400 in erecting a new Hall in the village. Her grief was pitiable; and so was Lord Castletown's remorse. He had sold out all the purchased estates; and had speculated wildly (so it was said) in foreign investments, which proved useless. Receivers were at once sent down here to take charge of everything. Lord Castletown is at

Granston;[263] Lady Castletown in London. I understand they are allowed £2000 each per annum; and the latest news is, that the estate was not so involved as was first supposed; and that possibly, they may be able to return at no very distant date. Meanwhile, Sir John Arnott,[264] who has rented the place for the last few years during the hunting months, has now taken over the Court for 12 months. One of the sad things connected with the affair was the destruction of the entire herd of deer in the Park. During the autumn, all day long we heard the crack of rifles in the Park. They wrapped the venison in the hides and sent all along to the London market. The one agreeable feature was the universal sympathy awakened for Lord and Lady Castletown, especially for the latter. It was very touching.

I must not fail to congratulate you on your new degrees. The two leading universities of the world have now said: Well done. It is a fine verdict on your three score years and ten.

I suppose you will run over for the Coronation in June.[265] If you can get the glitter out of your eyes and submit to a little Irish greyness and boredom, there is one at least who will be more pleased at seeing you again than you can well imagine. I am just entering my 60th year; but I have no long lease on life. I am only anxious to get in as much work as I can before the night falls.

I am, dear Dr Holmes,

Always affectionately,
P.A. Sheehan

I am taking a liberty in sending you by Book Post this evening my copy of *Dante* – the companion of my holidays. I have unfortunately made pencil marks here and there; they will only amuse you. It is a pretty portable edition; and perhaps it has not reached your side of the Atlantic. Don't trouble to acknowledge; but keep it in *pignum amicitiae.*

263 Queen's County or Co. Laois.

264 Sir John Alexander Arnott, 2nd Baronet (1853–1940). The Baronetcy of Arnott of Woodlands St Anne in Shandon in the County of Cork, is a title in the Baronetage of the United Kingdom. It was created on 12 February 1896 for the Irish entrepreneur and philanthropist John Arnott who had substantial commercial interests in Cork and Dublin, among them Cash's stores in Cork, The Irish Times, the Passage Docks Shipbuilding Company, the Bristol General Steam Navigation Company, and Arnott's Brewery in Cork. See also note 198.

265 The coronation of King George V took place at Westminster Abbey on 22 June 1911.

210. FROM: DONERAILE, CO. CORK, 4 AUGUST 1911

Text: Transcribed from David H. Burton, *Holmes-Sheehan Correspondence*, Fordham University Press, 1993.

Dear Dr Holmes,

I received your Harvard speech and the kind words accompanying it. It has one fault. It is too brief; it compresses too much into a narrow space. But perhaps I am judging rashly of Harvard intellects. Such an address should be diluted into twenty pages over here, before it could be fully grasped. I underline the following for future reference:

1. "For I own that I am apt to wonder whether I do not dream that I have lived".
2. "The 20th never wrote about itself to the newspapers".
3. "To hammer out as a compact and solid piece of work as one can, to try to make it first rate, and to leave it unadvertised".
4. "Life is painting a picture, not doing a sum".
5. "In the very heart of it there rises a mystical spiritual tone, that gives meaning to the whole".
6. "Our only but wholly adequate significance is as parts of the unimaginable whole".
7. "While we think we are egotists, we are living to ends outside ourselves".

How cordially I can agree with all this – and yet with what different eyes we look at the same thing and draw such different conclusions. I perceive this is what you mean when you say, Life is painting a picture. But I won't accept that. It sounds too like the subjective Idealism of Fichte.[266] There must be objective truth somewhere; and all questions in religion and metaphysics run to this: where is objective truth to be found?

Now this little crossing of swords is all your fault. You achieve in your brief lines, what I have always been anxious to achieve in larger spaces, i.e., you provoke controversy. The best compliment that can be paid to an author is to challenge him; and I want to know what are "the ends outside ourselves". I could never appreciate Tennyson.

There lives more faith in honest doubt

266 Johann Gottlieb Fichte (1762–1814), one of the seminal figures of German idealism, which developed from the theoretical and ethical writings of Immanuel Kant. He was one of the fathers of German nationalism and taught at the universities of Jena and Berlin.

Believe me than in half the creeds.

for:

And one far-off divine event
To which the whole creation moves.
What is? What is? What is?

There! You have stirred up the Celt.

You will have received *The Queen's Fillet*[267] by this time. I think I have been impartial. But nothing can convince me to adopt the new theory that Robespierre's[268] atrocities may be condoned because he was *just about* to do better things.

I have been reading again all about Beverly Farms,[269] north side of Massachusetts Bay; the villas perched on cliffs, or nesting by the shore; the broad beach; and the man who carries with him everywhere three wounds suffered in his country's service, and *"unadvertised"*. They are not the least factors in the profound esteem and affection of your Irish friend. You will have noticed how tenderly I have handled Tallyrand – because he put France before the world.

Always affectionately,
My dear Dr Holmes,
P.A. Sheehan

211. FROM: DONERAILE, 29 AUGUST 1911

Text: MS IJPA J27/127/50

Dear Fr Russell,

Many thanks for special copy of the *Irish Monthly*, for your own gracious critique, and for the extracts of notes from the reviews. They have all been singularly, I might say, surprisingly favourable; and the Americans are even more generous than the English. In a fortnight after publication, 1500 copies of the 6/– edition; and 1110 copies of the Colonial Edition had been sold. So everything looks well for the book.

I dare say Hiliare Belloc will differ from the estimate of the leading characters. I think he adopts the Carlylean view that the Revolution was

267 Published by Longmans, Green, London and New York 1911.

268 Maximilien François Marie Isidore de Robespierre (1758–1794), a lawyer and one of the most influential figures in the French Revolution. He was guillotined on 28 July 1794.

269 The summer home of Oliver Wendell Holmes, Jr., 868 Hale Street, Beverly Farms.

"a truth clad in hell-fire", and this is partly correct; but how, under any circumstances its excesses can be condoned is to me inexplicable.

I think I have been fairly impartial all round. I have not spared the noblesse, nor the Jacobin, nor the Bourbon, in trying to exemplify my two favourite theories:

That injustice begets injustice;

That fear has been the cause of the world's greatest crimes.

Always sincerely,

P.A. Sheehan, P.P.

212. FROM: DONERAILE, 8 SEPTEMBER 1911

Text: MS IJPA J27/127/51

Dear Fr Russell,

I am afraid you will not find these *Memoirs* too entertaining; but there are a few interesting episodes here and there.

They are not intended for print at any time; I wrote them about eight years ago just to preserve them for my own amusement. There is another fasciculus dealing with my life in Doneraile and as an author; but it is not complete.

Mrs Thornton's death was very sad. I never saw her; I understood she led a solitary life at Ardmore (in the Summer) and seldom saw even her own friends. (She was very unhappy in her marriage).

If you are not ambitious enough to reach the century, you will surely surmount the last fence, marked 90.

Always sincerely,

P.A. Sheehan

213. FROM: DONERAILE, 13 OCTOBER 1911

Text: MS PAHRC/HJHP/SH/50

Dear Dr Heuser,

I have got some idea that I am somewhat in your debt for the *American Ecclesiastical Review* etc.

If you would kindly let me know the amount I shall send you a Bank Order.

I hope you are keeping very well; and that the *Review* is prospering.

Very sincerely,
P.A. Sheehan, P.P.

214. FROM: DONERAILE, 28 NOVEMBER 1911

Text: MS IJPA J27/127/52

Dear Fr Russell,

I enclose my annual tribute to *Irish Monthly*. I hope you keep well.

I noticed a remark of yours at some meeting in Dublin to the effect that Protestant reviewers of *The Queen's Fillet* seemed more generous than the Catholics. That is so. I have seen above 100 cuttings; and, I think, all are kind but three – two of which are *The Dublin Review* and the *Catholic World*. But I have no reason to be dissatisfied.

I don't get the *Irish Ecclesiastical Record*, so I don't know what it has said.

Dr Barry was anxious to come down here on a short visit, when he was lately in Dublin; but, unfortunately, I was not in a position to receive him. He is one for whom I have the greatest admiration. I think he is a great power. I hope Dublin received him well. I have been reading his *Heralds of Revolt*.[270] Some of the papers I do not care for; but some are of great excellence, especially that of *John Inglesant*,[271] a book that has completely fallen out of notice.

I have a new novel completed; it deals with socialism in Ireland and many other matters; but I am holding it in reserve.

Always sincerely,
P.A. Sheehan, P.P.

270 William Francis Barry (1849–1930), *Heralds of Revolt: Studies of Modern Literature and Dogma*, London 1904.

271 Joseph Henry Shorthouse (1834–1903), *John Inglesant: A Romance*, London 1881.

[215]. FROM: MAY SHEEHAN, SEAFIELD, QUEENSTOWN, CO. CORK, TUESDAY, [11 JUNE 1912]

Text: MS PA DON I/138; *Addressed:* Presentation Convent, Doneraile, Co. Cork; *Franked:* George V, penny red; *Postmark:* Queenstown, Jn 11 1912; verso, Buttevant 2.30 a.m. Jn 12 12.

Ever dearest Ita,

You must think me a cruel, heartless wretch to have written to Reverend Mother[272] as I did on Saturday last.

Well dearest, I did it for two reasons principally: To ease both our minds with regard to the "second opinion" as I could see how very anxious you were on that point, and secondly for Denis' sake – to spare him answering many questions which would be most painful to him with regard to our dear Father Pat. Even to me he (Denis) does not care to discuss poor Fr Pat's case. It seems to grieve him too much to talk about his illness and so I had to read between the lines. He writes me daily news about our darling invalid and I shall just tell you what he writes in this day's letter to try and console my feelings: We must only endure what it may please God to do now and Patrick is quite happy and resigned. It is good to be with him![273]

I am so happy to think he likes the nun – and that she is so attentive and kind. Denis tells me of your and Rev. Sr Mary's repeated acts of thoughtfulness for our dear Fr Pat in sending down jelly, carrots etc. which he likes and is able to take and retain. I understand from Denis' letter that poor Fr Pat is resting in bed since Saturday and has not been down stairs. But his news is cheering. He says Fr Pat had a good night and a good day – though sick since Saturday evening. He had trout for dinner and was taking his carrot and chicken jelly.

As Reverend Mother says in her very nice letter to me (which I was so pleased to get) that: "The Sacred Heart is more powerful than all the Doctors". There is great hope that prayers (intense prayers) will do Fr Pat a lot of good – and that it may be God's will to spare him to us yet for many long years.

I always looked upon our darling Fr Pat as one quite apart from all other priests; I felt a certain reverence for him and everything belonging to him

272 Mother Alphonsus O'Keeffe (1852–1938), Superioress 1912–1918.

273 In June 1912, Canon Sheehan's health seriously deteriorated as the cancer with which he was diagnosed in September 1910 entered its final phase.

that I could not feel for any other priest. He seems to me to be a perfect saint. He seems at all times to care so little for life and its pleasures though anxious that others should enjoy themselves as much as possible. He only wanted his books, his garden and God's sea. (How he loved to penetrate into the deep blue sea and how he used to enjoy his visits to Ballycotton for the sake of the sea alone.

Ita darling, I must go now and attend to baby[274] so good bye and we must only hope, hope the best and pray with all our fervour for his recovery.

May

Please give my affectionate love to Reverend Mother and thank her for her nice letter.

[216]. FROM: MAY SHEEHAN, SEAFIELD, QUEENSTOWN, CO. CORK, FRIDAY MORNING, [14 JUNE 1912]

Text: MS PA DON I/139

Ever dearest Ita,

I have your two dear letters to acknowledge. Your first crossed with mine to you some days before. I really feared you would never care for me again after telling you how seriously ill our dear Fr Pat is – but you are a brave soul; you who have suffered so much yourself, took it in the proper spirit and how you are unselfish enough to do your utmost to cheer up others, and so make us resigned to God's Holy Will. This also is the dear invalid's wish and, is he not showing us this good example. As Denis tells me he is so happy and so resigned that it is good to be with him. This news consoled me more than anything else. The daily reports have been very satisfactory since Sunday – but this morning's news, both from Denis and your dear self brought me sad news. I fear he must be very weak indeed after the straining with the sickness during the night and through the day. Ita, dearest, I quiet agree with your views about our dear one's sickness and share your feeling entirely in the matter. Like you, I have seen so much of my dear one's last illnesses and nursed them to the end (Father, mother and sister) and I have witnessed such suffering that I prayed to God to take them out of pain

274 Eva Sheehan, born March 1911.

quickly. I think it miraculous that our darling Fr Pat is spared pain – as suffering from an internal complaint, such as tumour, nearly always means great and very severe pain and God is so good to him, his only trouble being great weakness.

You were his great favourite, he gave you his confidence far more than he ever did to me – but it is only right he should, you were his cousin and just like a sister to him and he always spoke of you in such terms to me. Of course he took an affectionate interest in all the Sisters and was devoted to the Convent, but you and Reverend Mother (whom he thinks so very highly of) were his favourites.

Ita, dearest, do not trouble to write to me. I know your hands are full, and Denis is very good – he tells me everything (the smallest details) about Fr Pat – he knows I am so full of anxiety and would not be satisfied otherwise.

I think it would be wise for you and Reverend Mother to give him to understand that you look upon the illness as most serious. You cannot but think otherwise from the daily reports you have and he will be spared thus of breaking the news to you. He does not care to enlighten you so far as he sees you so hopeful – that is his — .

We are both thankful to God that he is spared pain and may God grant that his illness may continue free from pain and suffering. This helps us to be so resigned to God's Holy Will and to leave everything in His hands.

Do encourage Denis to get Fr Pat's consent to a second nurse. It is very hard on Anne and Bridget to look after the house – callers, etc. and nurse the invalid as well.

Please give my affectionate love and thanks to dear Reverend Mother. She wrote me such a very nice letter which I am glad to read many times over. It helps me to bear up and be brave. I have such a very bad week (just a week to-day since I saw him!) and he has been in my thoughts both night and day – it is difficult to suffer in silence. Of course I don't give my confidence to anyone here. I keep awake through the night for many hours thinking of him, going over his life since I first met him nearly twelve years ago now. I am feeling much happier about him to-day. Somehow I am more resigned.

With dearest love to yourself and Reverend Mother.

Affectionately,

May

[217]. FROM: DENIS BERNARD SHEEHAN AT DONERAILE, CO. CORK, 22 JUNE 1912

Text: MS PA DON I/140; marked Private.

My dear Ita,

I am taking the Canon up to Cork today by Dr Cremen's and Dr O'Connell's directions, as he is not improving here. I wished to bring him home with me but they think it better to have him under Dr Cremen's care in the South Infirmary for a week or so to put him right before coming out with me. The Sisters of Mercy have charge and he will have a fine bright room there, and good medical attendance and nursing, so it is the best thing to do at present. May is most anxious to have him at home.

He did not like the idea at first, but as his stomach is still so troublesome he thinks it wiser to take the doctors' advice and try to get better. We will go in the motor brougham.

I shall let you know how he gets on from time to time and I may have to come down here a few times to get things for him, and I shall see you.

You must excuse me for not calling up these days past. I had to give the Sister some time to get a breath of air in the garden. She is very good, very kind and very attentive to him and he likes her immensely, though he says nothing.

Tell Rev. Mother.

Yours sincerely
D.B. Sheehan

[218]. FROM: MAY SHEEHAN, SEAFIELD, QUEENSTOWN, CO. CORK, 24 JUNE 1912

Text: MS PA DON I/141; *Addressed:* Rev. Mother Ita, Presentation Convent, Doneraile, Co. Cork; *Franked:* George V, penny red; *Postmark:* Queenstown, 8.15 p.m., Jn 24 1912; verso, Buttevant 2.30 a.m. Jn 25 12.

Ever dearest Ita,

Denis and Geoff have just come back from Cork and have brought good news. Our dear Fr Pat continues well and is retaining his food. He has not been sick once since his arrival and he is taking twice as much food as he did when in Doneraile. He gets Bergin's pasteurized milk and chicken broth and delicious China tea and toast (to use his own words, and — — served). He is very comfortable and happy and is in good spirits. He asked Denis to get him some books to read – so you may judge from that that he is feeling better.

He is up in his room (Denis says it is such a comfortable bright room with three windows) and a beautiful look out to the green.

I hope to see him tomorrow or Wednesday. He had a grand refreshing sleep of two hours this afternoon (between Denis' visits) he did not sleep well last night though. Denis paid him a second visit last night and was up with him until 9 o'c and left him in a very happy mood. He was actually laughing, as Denis told me.

Ever dearest, we have every reason to be cheerful and hopeful. Prayer as Reverend Mother says is doing wonders already for him.

Keep what I told you yesterday about the doctors private.

Love to self and Reverend Mother,

Yours fondly,
May

[219]. FROM: MAY SHEEHAN, SEAFIELD, QUEENSTOWN, CO. CORK, SUNDAY EVENING [23 JUNE 1912].

Text: MS PA DON I/142; *Addressed:* Rev. Mother Ita, Presentation Convent, Doneraile, Co. Cork; *Franked:* George V, penny red; *Postmark:* Queenstown, 8.15 p.m., Jn 23 1912.

Ever dearest Ita,

Your letter this morning brought tears to my eyes – you do write so expressively. Well. There is good news for you – our dear Fr Pat is now so much better. Already he is wonderfully well and delighted with himself.

Both Doctors Cremen and Atkins examined him this morning and told him he would be well and up and out of the South Infirmary in four or five weeks at most. So now your pious prayers have already worked wonders for the dear invalid.

I have heard it reported that Fr Pat has cancer. Such is not the case. He is suffering from an internal tumor but it is not malignant and is not the cause of his present illness (though Dr O'Connell was under the opinion all along that it was). Cremen and Atkins say it is his bladder and stomach etc. that are out of order and this trouble can be remedied.

Cheer up dearest.

Note along the margin reads: Excuse paper – I am out of paper. Keep what I have told you private except from Reverend Mother. Love to all. Will write you daily.

Yours ever,
May

Note in pencil on the back: Assistant Inspector 11 years, Bank cashier in Don.

[220]. FROM: DENIS BERNARD SHEEHAN, SUNDAY [23 JUNE 1912]

Text: MS PA DON I/143; *Addressed:* Sister Ita, Presentation Convent, Doneraile; *Franked:* George V, penny red; *Postmark:* Queenstown, 8.45 p.m., Jn 23 1912.

My dear Ita,

We had an awful time over the motor. He would not allow me to tell you and in fact I had to force him to go and he would not decide until Friday when I rushed up to Cork to arrange and I got a wire then saying he got sick again and could not go. However, he was better yesterday morning and I wired for the motor brougham but it was gone and could get no car until 5 p.m.. We started at once and the car broke down halfway to Mallow. I need not say what a state I was in thinking we would be stuck there.

After some time, the man got us on again and we reached Mallow at 7 p.m. and waited at Dr O'Connell's until the 8.15 p.m. train to Cork and arrived at the Infirmary at 9.30 p.m. and in bed at 10 p.m. Such a day, but strange to say, he bore it very well.

He has a lovely room, sunny and bright. Sisters very kind. Dr Cremen and Dr Atkins to take care of him.

I saw him today. He was up sitting before the fire and brighter than I saw him since I came to Doneraile. Did not sleep well the first night but not tired and very happy there. Every comfort of course and the doctors say they expect him to improve rapidly now and get rid of the sickness etc, etc but don't know what may be behind all this. However, they say not to be alarmed about him and after 4 weeks of good treatment all distressing symptoms will cease. Only that I forced Cremen on him unawares he would never consent to see him. What a pity he allowed all these weeks and months indeed go by and see no good doctor, but there you know him as well as I do and we must only hope that we will have him out again in a few weeks. He asked me to let you and Reverend Mother know that he was very comfortable.

Yours,
D.B. Sheehan

221. FROM: THE SOUTH INFIRMARY, CORK, SATURDAY, 6 JULY [1912]

Text: MS PA DON I/144; *Addressed:* Sister M. Ita, Presentation Convent, Doneraile, Co. Cork; *Franked:* George V, penny red; *Postmark:* Cork, 10 p.m., Jy 6 1912.

Dear M. Ita,

I have been allowed up yesterday for some hours; and I take the opportunity of sending you the first bulletin of my "progress" towards recovery. I say "progress" because I am very far from being out of the woods as yet. I am astonishingly weak in physical strength; and very much emaciated; but I suppose that will disappear.

With one or two little daily experiences of what is meant by physical pain, I am having a life of luxurious idleness; for I cannot describe the attention and care of everyone here from Mother Albeus (who is a very remarkable woman) down to the nurses, who do not know what to do for me. Their skill, their promptness, and their solicitude, are beyond praise. The doctors are equally kind. Dr Cremen has been watching me anxiously and Dr Atkins is the kindest old fellow in the world, except when he hurts, when I draw in my breath and say: Suf[fering] J[esus], I have never said: Damn, even once.

A good many people call but I cannot see them because my head aches from talking. Denis comes up every day for a couple of hours. I don't feel the time at all lonely, except on a few occasions when I was in much agony. I lie down all day long, reading a little, praying a little – too little; and watching the wind tossing a big lime tree outside my window. But I look forward with a kind of terror to the future – beginning a weary life again; and regretting, if it had been God's holy will, that I did not pass away. No man was ever so eager to live, as I was, and am, to die. I think the wish is increased by the amount of human suffering I hear of here. The whole world seems to be diseased. But we must struggle on until the night falls.

I wish George would send up to the Convent all the peas in my garden. It is a poor recompense for all your kindness. Thank Martha and Veronica[275] for me for their dainty cake and Anthony[276] for the fruit and flowers. I was sorry I could not see Bridget.[277] She is one of those I would have wished to speak to.

The Bishop called twice and I had a good long talk with Canon Morrissey yesterday. We have both passed through the same Purgatory; but he suffered more than I.

I am off to bed again at 5 p.m. so must wind up – Remembrance to all the sisters and much gratitude towards yourself,

Always sincerely,
P.A. Sheehan

Would you get Anne to send a box of the youngest peas to May at Seafield, Queenstown.

222. FROM: THE SOUTH INFIRMARY, CORK, 13 JULY 1912

Text: MS PA DON I/145; *Addressed:* Sister M. Ita, Presentation Convent, Doneraile, Co. Cork; *Franked:* no stamp.

Dear M. Ita,

I received your welcome note this morning: and was greatly pleased at the cordial reception Fr Petrowski received. I did not know that Denis had written; and I was afraid you would all take him for a commercial traveller and send him away. He appears to be a kind-hearted, generous man, full of faith and great enthusiasm about the "Isle of Saints". He is thrown altogether in Chicago amongst his own people (Ruthenians) and hence speaks English imperfectly.

I am doing very well (D.G.). The doctors seem to see a marked improvement to-day; but, whilst my days and nights are placid, and go

275 Sr Martha Conway (1851–1929) and Sr Veronica Conway (1851–1940).
276 Sr Anthony Keneally (1878–1948).
277 Mother Bridget Kearney (1851–1915), Superioress 1897–1900.

painless, I have to face two very bad half-hours morning and night. Dr Atkins is away in Dublin with his boy, who has undergone an operation for appendicitis; but the house surgeon has done his work well. There are 93 patients in the house this week. Nurses and all continue their kind ministrations; life would be almost too luxurious but for the morning and evening martyrdom.

I told Denis to forward to Columba a letter from Nella Harold announcing her forthcoming marriage. Would you ask Columba to write explaining that I am too unwell to do so; and send my kindest congratulations.

I suppose the doctors here will patch up some way this old wretched body of mine; and send me adrift on the world again; but I do not think I can ever hope to be anything more than an invalid again.

William O'Brien, who is in Blarney, is calling in to see me tomorrow.

I am anxious to know how Fr Phelan got on in Fermoy at the retreat. I felt pretty sure that it was successful; but with priests no one can tell.

A young priest, Dr Ahern, says Mass here sometimes. He says he called upon you all in Doneraile. I am greatly pleased to hear that there is such a good supply of priests for the Sunday Masses.

Kindest remembrance to all the community.

As ever,
P.A. Sheehan

223. FROM: THE SOUTH INFIRMARY, CORK, SATURDAY, 27 JULY 1912

Text: MS PA DON I/146; *Addressed:* Mother M. Ita, Presentation Convent, Doneraile, Co. Cork; *Franked:* George V, penny red. *Postmark:* Cork, 9.30 p.m., Jy 27 1912 – new cancellation system.

(I have lost all count of time and don't know the day of the month)
Dear M. Ita,

Many thanks for all your letters. They are a great boon and pleasure. Today, I have been out of bed for some hours; and am easier and happier than before. I had some very bad days this week; but I have been very well today and the operations have been painless. General health excellent; can eat almost too well; but it will be some time I think before I can stand at the Altar. The weather has been very depressing. The nurses are not tired of me yet; but continue their assiduous attentions. Sr Albeus comes in twice a day; and is most kind.

I see few visitors. Today I had five – amongst them a Monsignor from Minnesota and a Miss Flush from Boston – a very holy soul, whom I could not refuse to see, as she had letters of introduction from friends at the other side. I was very glad to see Bridget.[278] Did she tell you that she brought me the most delicious peas I ever ate. Miss Flush sent up some beautiful flowers from the Victoria Hotel.

I am glad to hear that all is going well at home; and I would like Fr Ben. Kenealy[279] to be told how much I appreciate his kindness in saying a Novena of Masses for me.

Dean Keller was here today for half an hour. He is quite alarmed at all the preparations that are being made for his Jubilee. He was to see Fr Moore, OP, who is hopelessly paralysed at Clifden under the care of the Good Shepherds. I also had a visit from Reverend Mother Magdalene (Josephine Barry) who is now in charge of St Raphael's asylum for the blind.

I think it better not to send on the down quilt. I have a superabundance of bed clothes.

I suppose I shall survive this attack; so direct all your prayers to one object – that I may not be a confirmed invalid for life, and a burden to others. This is what I dread most.

Kindest and most affectionate regards to all the nuns. I hope you will have a fine vacation and many sunny days in Glenanaar.[280]

Always etc.,
P.A. Sheehan

224. FROM: THE SOUTH INFIRMARY, CORK, WEDNESDAY, [7 AUGUST 1912].

Text: MS PA DON I/147; *Addressed:* Mother M. Ita, Presentation Convent, Doneraile, Co. Cork; *Franked:* George V, 2 half penny green. *Postmark:* Queenstown, 8.15 p.m., Au 7 1912.

Dear M. Ita,

Very many thanks for your kind letter of Monday; and for the box of fruit and flowers which reached me yesterday afternoon.

278 Mother Bridget Kearney (1851–1915), Superioress 1897–1900.

279 Fr Keneally was born in 1876, ordained in 1901, served on the mission in Glasgow before returning to Cloyne. He died parish priest of Inniscarra in 1961.

280 This Glenanaar was a rustic retreat which Canon Sheehan had built for the nuns in the convent garden.

I am greatly gratified that Anne was so pleased with her visit. The hat was a wonder; but she looked remarkably well. Canon Michael O'Hea was here this morning; and Reverend Mother and M. Augustine on Saturday. They are greatly distressed about Sr Dominic who is in a critical condition after two operations. There were symptoms of heart failure yesterday: but an injection of strychnine made it all right.

As for myself, I am free from all pain; can eat well, sleep well, and the doctors seem pleased; but I cannot see any progress towards recovery. I am still quite emaciated; and consequently weak. The doctors say "Time" and "Patience"; but I am afraid the time will be long, and my patience exhausted. Still, I am not in the least depressed and the days seem to fly by like an express train. The nurses and doctors are not tired of me yet; but continue as assiduous and attentive as ever. If I could get out into the air I would probably improve, but it would be suicide in this awful weather.

This letter may find you on retreat. I take it for granted that Fr Bourke will sleep at Bridge House.

Sister Albeus is in Bantry. She sends me an occasional post card. Sister Benignus is very attentive and sympathetic. They are all dreadfully over worked here. There never were so many patients in the house at this time of year and the accident in Lombardstown[281] has sent in six more.

Pray for me during your retreat. I need it because I cannot do much praying myself.

Always sincerely,
P.A. Sheehan

225. FROM: THE SOUTH INFIRMARY, CORK, FRIDAY, [16 AUGUST 1912]

Text: MS PA DON I/148; *Addressed:* Mother M. Ita, Presentation Convent, Doneraile, Co. Cork; *Franked:* George V, penny red. *Postmark:* Cork, 10 p.m., Au 16 1912; Buttevant, 10.50 a.m. Au 17 1912.

Dear M. Ita,

281 An excursion train from Killarney to Dublin, consisting of an engine and six vehicles with 200 passengers, was derailed at 8.50 p.m on 5 August 1912 while entering the goods loop of the Great Southern and Western Railway station at Lombardstown, Co. Cork. The accident caused 96 injuries and 1 fatality. A report on the accident, compiled by Lt. Colonel P.G. von Donop and published by the Board of Trade on 1 January 1913, found that the accident was primarily due to driver error and excessive speed, as well as to inadequate track layout at Lombardstown station.

I am pleased to hear you have had a pleasant and profitable retreat. It is only what I expected from Fr Bourke. Your holidays now commence and I hope they will be pleasant in weather otherwise.

After two or three days spent out of doors, my temperature ran up to 101; Dr Cremen got alarmed, thought I had taken a chill and I have been a prisoner these last few days.

My own opinion is that there was no chill; but I probably remained out too long; and a very little exertion fatigues me still. But I don't mind being indoors. I have no pain whatsoever; and so long as I have a book, I don't feel the time passing. Talking to visitors who are strangers distresses me very much, for I am still weak. I have no idea how it will end. The doctors are hopeful; but I cannot see that I am gaining ground. All are agreed that I must have patience; and I have. It is wonderful how rapidly the days fly by. I shall be 8 weeks here tomorrow. There is a complication of — which makes recovery slow; and the weather is very much against me.

I hope by this time Philomena[282] has passed the crisis of her attack. She has recovered so rapidly before that there is every hope she will recover now.

Of course, this is the place for diseases; but one gets appalled at the frightful maladies that afflict people. There appears to be no end to them, and one worse than another. There is hardly a day but an operation for appendicitis takes place.

I hope something will turn up in Doneraile to let Fr Shinkwin away for a brief holiday in Lisdoonvarna.

I am writing under some disadvantage and must bring this to a speedy conclusion.

Ever sincerely,
P.A. Sheehan

P.S. Thank Annie[283] for the beautiful box of grapes, they were delicious and I enjoyed them very much.

226. FROM: THE SOUTH INFIRMARY, CORK, 20 AUGUST 1912

Text: MS PA DON I/149; *Addressed:* Mother M. Ita, Presentation Convent, Doneraile, Co. Cork; *Franked:* George V, penny red. *Postmark:* Cork, 9.30 p.m., Au 16 1912.

282 Sr Philomena Lane (1869–1917).
283 His housekeeper.

Dear M. Ita,

The grapes, Martha's[284] cake and peaches came to hand today in excellent condition. I hope to have some of Sister Martha's cake just now for tea.

Of course Mrs Heffernan[285] will go to Bridge House. I am only sorry the children are not with her; it would be such a pleasure to you.

I had visits today from Canon O'Callaghan, P.P. of Kildorrey and Dr Beecher of Maynooth.

I have been out for an hour or two; but they are as tender about me here as if I were made of salt, like Lot's wife. They are very nervous about my taking a chill; of course it would throw me back and I should go over the same process again. As it is, I feel I am not gaining much ground. It gives me enough to do to walk across the grounds and there sink into a chair. Even the process of dressing and undressing fatigues me; but Dr Cremen says "patience", "patience" and all will be well. You know that unlike most cases, I have a complication of disorders – a general strike of the whole system.

The enclosed paper will interest you. Doneraile has done well, Liscarroll is nowhere.

I hope you are all enjoying your holidays. As the cat is away, I dare say you will have 6 weeks this year.

Kindest remembrance to Reverend Mother[286] and Community.

Always etc.,
P.A. Sheehan

Geoff has been very bad. Temperature 104.5; but was better last night.

[227]. FROM: THE SOUTH INFIRMARY, CORK, 20 AUGUST 1912

Text: MS PA DON I/150 ; fragment of a letter to Mother Ita O'Connell written on the headed notepaper of the South Charitable Infirmary and County Hospital, Cork City, 20 August 1912.[287]

284 Sr Martha Conway (1851–1929).

285 Ellen O'Connell, Mother Ita Ignatius' eldest sister, born 7 November 1858, married to Michael Heffernan of Kidderminster. Their daughter, Ita Heffernan (1892–1962), entered the Presentation Convent, Doneraile, in 1916, taking the religious name of Imelda of the Sacred Heart.

286 Mother Alphonsus O'Keeffe (1852–1938) returned to the office of Superioress 1912–1918 in succession to Mother Ita O'Connell (1867–1950).

287 This letter was written by a nun in the community at the South Infirmary, possibly Sr Benignus.

Dearest Mother M. Ita,

Sister M. Francis seems to have raised your hopes of the Canon's "home coming" very soon – well, you see his is an especial case and needs the doctor's attention twice daily. He has said just now he is "absolutely a prisoner" on that account, then the weather is so uncertain he cannot go out – it is too cold to sit down if he has not strength enough to keep moving. I wished very much that he would have a bath chair and allow himself to be wheeled out when the day permitted as it would protect him from the damp and save the fatigue of walking in but he did not take kindly to the suggestion – I ventured to say it to Dr Cremen and he agreed with me that it would be a good idea. About the *Sanatogen*[288] – he has a great objection to it on the grounds that it is made out of rather objectionable materials apart from the odour – of course, I did not mention it to him today but when I did speak of it to nurse O'Sullivan, she seemed terrified lest it would cause vomiting again and that would be serious. He likes wild fowl and relished the grouse you sent him. We got some today when I discovered that poor Mr Sheehan has not been here for a week – the Canon seemed anxious about him, and the boy "Geoff" has influenza, and they have no nurse for the baby yet and that worries him too – I am very, very, sorry for him – he is particularly tried, but all great men are – and he is a great man. (It sounds very cheeky of me to give an opinion of Canon Sheehan, but I cannot help it). No – I did not give him your second last message. I feared it would be too presumptuous for the "likes of me". It should be Mother Mary Ita for that. It is a great privilege to be even on the outside of the crowd where he is concerned.

Dr Beecher of Maynooth is with him now – the day is too uncertain to go out. The sponge cake and peaches came all right – I wish he could be at home with all his own surroundings and have the few advantages the South Infirmary affords too, if God does not will to free him from the necessity he has of them. We would never know his real worth without this trial – "only suffering can elicit the perfume of the soul" they say and he is getting his share.

Sister Albeus is returning from the Bantry breezes and seems much improved by the rest and change. We let her know how our beloved patient is sometimes. I shall tell you if the *Sanatogen* is a success. We have two nuns

288 A tonic wine which is a preparation of casein and sodium glycerophosphate.

from Castletownbere staying with us since last Friday. They have a protégée of the Canon's with them whom he inquired about and got very good news of a Miss Murphy (Sister M. Finn-barr). Remember me affectionately to Sister M. Cregan tho' she must be too young to know me personally.

228. FROM: THE SOUTH INFIRMARY, CORK, FRIDAY, [16 AUGUST 1912]

Text: MS PA DON I/151; *Addressed:* Mother M. Ita, Presentation Convent, Doneraile, Co. Cork; *Franked:* George V, penny red. *Postmark:* Cork, 9.30 p.m., Au 29 1912.

Dear M. Ita,

You get so many accounts both personally and by post, of my poor self, that I have very little to tell, except to thank you for those magnificent plums and peaches which you were kind enough to send me. I was able to send a few plums to May[289]. It is the only fruit she cares for. She has had such worry about the baby[290] – such sleepless nights etc., that the doctor is quite apprehensive about her health. But she has got an excellent nurse now. If she remains, it will be a great relief.

I am much the same as I have been for some weeks. I cannot see any hope of immediate recovery; but I keep on doing what I am told. The drives you suggest are quite impossible just yet, partly owing to the weather, and partly to the nature of my maladies which are numerous and complicated.

I get out of the bed every day, sometimes at 12; sometimes at 2 p.m.; have dinner at 2.30; cross over to the convent, about the width of your garden: and remain in the community room till 6 p.m. writing letters, reading my office etc. By the way, could you manage to send me the *Pars Autumnalis* of the Breviary and the Latin *Ordo*. They are both on the ledge of my bookcase in my dining-room.

I have tea at 7 p.m.; and get to bed at 8 p.m. where I read a little, pray a little, until the doctors come; and get to sleep generally about 10.30. I feel very much that I cannot say Mass; but I cannot leave the room until the doctors come in the morning; and I could not fast as yet. There is a good deal of hemorrhage; and it is debilitating.

Mrs Sheehan, Doneraile, Jack and Denis, called to see me this morning. Denis is going to Irish College, Paris. Mrs Fagan called also, but at a most awkward time, and Sister Benignus could not let her see me. She cried a

289 His sister-in-law.
290 Eva Sheehan born in March 1911.

good deal; and I have been thinking since how disappointed she will be, if she hears that Mrs Sheehan was allowed to see me – But the truth is, I do not care to see any visitors. It excites jealousy and does no good.

Strange to say, altho' I have occasionally some moments of depression, I never feel lonely and the days pass by more swiftly than when I was at work. It is the uncertainty of the future that tells on me. I feel that I am a chronic invalid; and that my work is done. But I take each day as it comes. Yet, I must come to some decision soon.

Canon Morrissey[291] caught pneumonia at Sr Dominic's funeral, and has been somewhat unwell. He is a dear, kind, affectionate friend – the one man in whom I place all my confidence.

As to our political differences in Doneraile, I never changed even for a moment my feelings towards those who differ from me. They had as much right to their opinions, as I have to mine, and I never thought less of them because they acted independently.

I hope Philomena [is] continuing well. If Mrs Heffernan calls, I have left word that I shall see her.

Always sincerely,
P.A. Sheehan

229. FROM: THE SOUTH INFIRMARY, CORK, 30 AUGUST 1912

Text: MS PA DON I/152; *Addressed:* Mother M. Ita, Presentation Convent, Doneraile, Co. Cork; *Franked:* George V, penny red. *Postmark:* Cork, 9.30 p.m., Au 30 1912; Buttevant 10.15 Au 31.

Dear M. Ita,

I return paper duly signed. Mrs Heffernan has just been here, looking as bright and youthful as ever. I hope she will have a pleasant time in Doneraile; and that Anne will make her perfectly comfortable. Fr Morton[292] was here at the same time; so it was a pleasure to see old friends meeting.

Today is fine; but breezy. I am writing in the Convent reception room in front of a blazing fire.

Always etc.
P.A. Sheehan

291 Parish priest of Banteer, Co. Cork.

292 Fr Edmond Morton, born Freemount, Co. Cork, educated in Paris, served as curate with Canon Sheehan in Mallow, parish priest of Ballyhea, Co. Cork (1902–1931).

230. FROM: THE SOUTH INFIRMARY, CORK, 9 SEPTEMBER 1912

Text: MS PA DON I/153; *Addressed:* Mother M. Ita, Presentation Convent, Doneraile, Co. Cork. *Marked:* Private and Confidential.

Dear M. Ita,

I had a bad set back last week – a feverish attack, temperature 102.8 etc. It vanished after 3 days, but left me very weak. Today, I have spent hours in the sunshine, and feel better. Fr Madden is just after leaving me after a long talk. He had been to Exeter and Plymouth, and seen many of my old friends. May brought up the baby last Saturday morning under adverse circumstances. Baby screamed without intermission in the train; in the car coming over; up the lift and all the way home. She treated me to one or two yells; but to the astonished eyes of everyone, submitted to be kissed without a murmur. She is a splendid child; no more like me than a canary is like a crow. To my eyes, she resembles Maggie (Sr Augustine)[293] the same eyes, the same eyes etc; Jeff has been poorly again. Denis is taking him to Blarney tomorrow.

For the present, I have put aside the idea of resigning the parish, altho' between rent and rates and Fr Ashlin's stipend my receipts will be small. But I have been recommended to close up the house, and not to be under a double expense of keeping house in Doneraile and paying here. What would you think of it? From all that I can hear my sojourn here will be a prolonged one, if ever I leave it. I was thinking of discharging George immediately – the garden is of no gain to me; and then after a few weeks, I could close up the house and give the keys to Anthony and perhaps his wife or himself could open up the windows and let the air in sometimes. Let me know what you think of it: the expenses here between the doctors (2) and the house will be great but altho' I had given away nearly all that I possessed, I was prudent enough to keep some reserve, as will enable me to pay my way to the end. Of course, if I resigned the Bishop would keep for me some place to lay my head, that is, if ever I should leave here and be able to resume work. Dr Cremen thinks I shall not be able to do so. Canon Morrissey is coming up on Thursday to talk it over.

---

293 His sister, Margaret Sheehan, in religion Sr Augustine of the Mercy Convent, Mallow, Co. Cork. She died on 7 November 1868.

I am grateful to hear that Mrs Murphy and Sarah[294] are not resentful. Dr Hegarty was a bit alarmed about the 103 temperature and afraid of the least excitement.

Of course Fr Somer will stay at Bridge House. Remember me kindly to him.

Always sincerely,
P.A. Sheehan

I should be pleased if you would send up some of my books in my name to Sister Albeus for Thursday next.[295] There are plenty of copies in my library. The autograph does not matter.

231. FROM: THE SOUTH INFIRMARY, CORK, 11 SEPTEMBER 1912

Text: MS PA DON I/154; *Addressed:* Mother M. Ita, Presentation Convent, Doneraile, Co. Cork; *Franked:* George V, penny red. *Postmark:* Cork, 9.30 p.m., 11 Sep 1912.

Dear M. Ita,

I think your suggestions are all good, only in order to square matters, I would like if you would arrange with Anne and George to terminate their engagement with me on September 30th. This day closes the quarter; and I want to wind up my affairs on that day by paying off the servants, and the bills that are due about town. Anne, then, could retain her room at her own expense if she likes; until she gets a suitable situation.

It is possible that the Bishop when he returns home may wish to appoint a new P.P. but that remains to be seen. Distribute and dispose of the fruit and vegetables as you suggest in your letter. There are also some bundles of old clothes in the house, which Anne wished to give to the little Sisters of the Poor.

I was quite sure I had paid James Kearney for the range but of course it is parochial property and must be paid out of parochial funds.

Fr James O'Connell and Anthony were here today. Anthony left all your messages.

---

294 Cf. letter 228 and letter 239.

295 The 12 September, feast day of St Ailbe, patron of the diocese of Emly, and of Sister Albeus.

I was very sorry to hear of Arthur O'Leary's death. He was one of the old generation whom I esteemed so much. I would have written to Jack to express my sympathy with the family; but the news came rather later.

I am changing into another room this week. It will be more comfortable than the present one; and I shall have greater privacy. I think it will also be less expensive. I suppose I shall have to spend the Winter here.

I enclose Money order for £14–2–0.

I cannot realize that I am an incurable patient in a public hospital. Everything has been made so easy for me; and above all, I have the Supreme grace from Our Lord to accept it all as something that should have happened; and without one shade of lowliness or depression, even when I see the doctors in their toggery and trollies carrying in poor patients to the operating room.

I seem to have been born to it.

Always etc.
P.A. Sheehan

232. FROM: THE SOUTH INFIRMARY, CORK, 11 SEPTEMBER 1912

Text: MS PA DON I/155; *Addressed:* Mother M. Ita, Presentation Convent, Doneraile, Co. Cork; *Franked:* George V, penny red. *Postmark:* Cork, 9.30 p.m., 16 Sep 1912.

Dear M. Ita,

I have changed into the smaller room today. It has been newly painted and looks more like a little drawing-room than a bedroom. I think I shall be comfortable there. One of my nurses who has been particularly attentive to me goes on holidays today. She will spend time in the neighbourhood of Mallow; and may visit Doneraile. I need not bespeak for her your usual kindness. Her name is Miss Sullivan; and her quiet, watchful ways have contributed not a little to my comfort here.

Dr O'Connell called on Friday and urged me strongly to go home. This disquiets me a good deal; because it seems to imply that I ought to be out and at work. I consulted Dr Cremen in the evening. He said it would be absolutely suicidal. He dreads complications setting in such as septicaemia; that is a kind of blood poisoning from the absorption of blood and toxin. I have had two minor attacks already, in which there was much fever. He also evidently dreads obstruction, which would necessitate an operation; and he says if taken suddenly ill at home, I may find it impossible to get a room here again; as they are nearly always full. I have to look forward therefore to a prolonged stay here, as far as I can see. The haemorrhages continue. There is no stopping them, and they are weakening. I get up early now; and I have dispensed with barber and the nurses' ablutions. I remain 3 or 4 hours in the Sun; then dine and go to the Convent to write letters etc. Some days I have visitors. Yesterday, William and Mrs O'Brien called and remained for an hour. Matt Burke also called and several priests.

I would wish that all lamps etc. would be disposed of. My only apprehension is, lest my black clothes in the 2 wardrobes and chest of drawers, soutanes, coats etc., should get mildewed or moth-eaten. I may require them yet. But there are old garments and a good deal of rubbish which should be got rid of.

At the end of the month I will get all my passbooks made up, and send cheques for the amount.

Denis and Jeff are at Blarney, enjoying it very much.

Anne packed in a whole lot of old towels in my port-manteau which are quite useless to me, as everything is supplied. I forgot to send them back. The only thing I would require here would be my Winter flannels; but I think I must get them here, as probably the old ones are shrunken.

May Sheahan has just called on her way to Youghal looking well and strong.

Always etc.
P.A. Sheehan

Many thanks for the grouse, or grouses which were very welcome.

233. FROM: THE SOUTH INFIRMARY, CORK, 23 SEPTEMBER 1912

Text: MS PA DON I/156; *Addressed:* Mother M. Ita, Presentation Convent, Doneraile, Co. Cork; *Franked:* George V, 2 halfpenny green. *Postmark:* Cork, 9.30 p.m., 23 Sep 1912.

Dear Mother Ita,

Many thanks for your letters and your description of the reception. I was about to write a note of congratulations to Sr Benignus; but some visitors took up the necessary time. Would you kindly say so to her; and tell her I hope to be at her profession.[296]

Your are taking too much trouble about these plants, which are not worth selling. The chrysanthemums are, I believe, a good lot; and I should be pleased if they could be added to your conservatory. The only other thing to be considered are the begonia bulbs which Anthony could probably house against the Winter.

Keep the receipt for the range for the present.

I had a visit from Fr Maurice O'Connell.[297] He had come up with his mother from Lacka to see the doctor. Happily, there is nothing seriously wrong. He told me that Sister de Pazzi had died in Mitchelstown. Would you convey my sympathy to Sister Teresa as nicely as you can.

I think I would want a pair of boots. The present ones are giving way. If any of the old ones at Bridge House are not good enough to send on, William Murphy of the Monster House could send me on a pair. He knows my size. I think I can manage about everything else, at least for a time.

I have a very pleasant daily visit from Fr O'Reilly, SJ, who is concluding a retreat near here at the Convent of Marie Réparatrice. He was with Fr Russell just before he died.[298]

(Private)

Everything as usual here; but just now there is some friction owing to the fact that the house surgeon, who has to relieve me morning and evening, goes out nearly every night and remains out to 11 or 11.30 and I have to wait sleepless from 8 o'clock till he returns. The nurses, Sister Albeus and Benignus are very angry over the matter; and so are the nurses. The matter was reported to Dr Cremen and he left orders which were disregarded. Sister Albeus is taking up the matter hotly today. It is a pity; because in every other way, I am a spoiled priest. But this neglect is serious.

I have seen Dean Flynn only once. He is leaving for Queenstown tomorrow.

I have not been permitted to leave my room today, temperature gone up to 99.2. You can see how carefully I am watched.

Ever sincerely,
P.A. Sheehan

296 Sr Benignus Martin (1893–1983) was received into the community of St Joseph's Presentation Convent, Doneraile, in 1912. She made final profession in 1914.

297 Fr Maurice O'Connell, a native of Castlemagner. He served as a chaplain to the forces during the First World War. He was parish priest of Doneraile 1941–1958.

298 Fr Matthew Russell, SJ, (1834–1912), editor of the Irish Monthly died on 12 September 1912.

234. FROM: THE SOUTH INFIRMARY, CORK, 26 SEPTEMBER 1912

Text: MS PA DON I/157; *Addressed:* Mother M. Ita, Presentation Convent, Doneraile, Co. Cork; *Franked:* George V, penny red. *Postmark:* Cork, 9.30 p.m., 26 Sep 1912.

Dear Mother Ita,

I received your letter today. Do not send up my winter flannels yet. They would only be an encumbrance in my room, where the space is very limited. I can get them later on, if necessary. But the boots may be sent.

When Annie's time of service expires, it would be well I think, to lock up the house having shuttered all the windows, and let the keys be brought up to the convent.

The inconvenience I alluded to in my last letter has almost ceased. Things have taken a better turn. I am much undecided about my future; and can only leave it in God's hands to dispose of it. Fr O'Reilly is quite sure the Little Flower of Jesus[299] will effect a permanent cure for me. He is going tomorrow. I shall miss him.

If you could get Anne to have all my passbooks made up to September 30th and also Anne's own account, and George's, I would send you cheques for all. Of course, you need not send the passbooks – only specify the account.

The weather has been awfully cold here, yet I manage to get across to the convent twice a day and write and read as I please.

Denis is urging me strongly to resign Doneraile and go and live with them. But I am not inclined that way at present.

Always sincerely,
P.A. Sheehan

235. FROM: THE SOUTH INFIRMARY, CORK, 2 OCTOBER 1912

Text: MS PA DON I/158.

Dear M. Ita,

I enclose two cheques – one from my own account (£32–18–5) and one from Church account (£8–1–5). When you have paid and got receipts, you

299 Saint Thérèse of Lisieux (1873–1897), or Saint Thérèse of the Child Jesus and the Holy Face, born Marie-Françoise-Thérèse Martin, beatified in 1923, canonized in 1925, co-patroness of the missions 1927, co-patroness of France 1944, and declared thirty third doctor of the Church in 1997.

can keep the passbooks etc. till I return. But I am afraid I am giving you great trouble.

Tell M. O'Shea to give shrine money to Fr Shinkwin to lodge in No. 2 account at the bank.

I think if Reverend Mother[300] would give Fr Shinkwin one pound for Shanballymore poor, the rest might be kept by the convent for distribution among the poor of Doneraile.

I have got an idea (it may be only a suspicion) that Dr Atkins' advice was inspired and suggested by the only person here who is tired of me. But, in any case, he makes light of many things which Dr Cremen would look upon as serious. His work is altogether surgical; and he does not view things as a medical man would. Of course I am very anxious to get back to the privacy and solitude of my own house; but I can see clearly that I must resume parochial duty if I go back; and I don't feel equal to that at present. There is a steady improvement in general health; and I must not get thrown back if I can.

I suppose Anne would be impossible as future housekeeper and in any case, she cannot wait.

I have just had a visit from Mrs Eaton and Reverend Mother of the Sisters of Charity. Mrs Eaton was superioress of the hospice in Dublin when William O'Brien's mother was dying there. She is a fast friend of William and Mrs O'Brien.

Many thanks for the fruit which came safely yesterday. I share with my nurses and they are so grateful.

Always etc.
P.A. Sheehan

5 p.m.
What about Church account for electric light? Did Mitchell furnish it?
I have just heard that 2 Doneraile nuns called, but couldn't wait; and I was enjoying my siesta, and the nurse would not disturb me.
[Attached bill]

Amount of Bills:	£25–3–8
Anne's wages:	£3–13–3
George's:	£ 2–2–0
	£32–18–11
Retreat Expenses:	£8–1–5
Total:	£41–0–4

300 Mother Alphonsus O'Keeffe (1852–1938).

236. FROM: THE SOUTH INFIRMARY, CORK, 5 OCTOBER 1912

Text: MS PA DON I/159; *Addressed:* Mother M. Ita, Presentation Convent, Doneraile, Co. Cork; *Franked:* George V, penny red. *Postmark:* Cork, 9.30 p.m., 5 Oct 1912.
(The night caps would not be of any use to me here)

Dear M. Ita,

Thanks for letter and enclosures which I return. I had a visit from Dr O'Connell, Minnie and Norah on Thursday. The doctor urged me strongly to go home. He thinks I would do better than here. I consulted Dr Cremen that evening. He said it would be disastrous, I should be so far from medical help, if required; and probably I would drift back into the same pitiable state again.

I think there is some reason in his view. I am anxious to get home, and I cannot see any marked improvement in my condition. I have got very little help from medical science. There were three maladies, all of them incurable from the beginning.

Things have much improved with the house surgeon. I am able to keep myself now; and at night I can manage with the aid of a student. This has relieved him a good deal; and he has more liberty.

The wall paper in the dining room is in a bad condition. I think it would be a good opportunity to get it repapered or better still, painted in distemper: a dado in oils up to four or five feet, and the upper part in distemper, divided into panels, like your community room. Let me know what your think of it; and whether the time is opportune.

I am not sleeping well. There is a kind of feverish heat, which makes me toss about till 3 or 4 in the morning when I get some sleep. I suppose it is part and parcel of the same illness.

Everyone continues kind and obliging here. Denis is in Tralee. May has influenza again but slightly.

I feel quite relieved that all my debts are paid, except the Doctors' and the Hospital, which will be considerable.

Always sincerely,
P.A. Sheehan, P.P.

237. FROM: SOUTH INFIRMARY, CORK, 6 OCTOBER 1912

Text: Transcribed from David H. Burton, *Holmes-Sheehan Correspondence*, Fordham University Press, 1993.

Dear Judge Holmes,

My brother forwarded your last kind letter of inquiry to me; and, altho' not convalescent (for that would imply recovery, and recovery with me is out of the question), I am able to satisfy one desire, that of letting you know how grateful I am for all your solicitous inquiring. Two years ago a Dublin surgeon diagnosed some internal trouble, and left no hope of cure;[301] but I went on working until a sudden collapse came in June, which brought me to the gates of death. To my intense disgust and regret, the doctors pulled me back from the "eternal rest" to face the world as a chronic invalid. I have hopes of leaving here, and perhaps of resuming some parochial work; but life for me is henceforth to be carried on on a broken wing. Fortunately, I have no pain; and no depression of spirits whatsoever. But I wish I had been at rest.

The words "regret and disgust" may surprise you; but I am pretty well tired of this curious drama of earthly life, and would be glad of a change of scene. All my dark views of this poor diseased humanity of ours have been more or less deepened by the scenes I have witnessed here; for altho' I am cut away from the main body of patients, I cannot help coming across sometimes some poor fellow being rolled in on a trolley to the operation theatre; and I cannot help hearing talking of gruesome things which they have witnessed amongst a hundred patients. The bright spot in all this mystery of human suffering is the faith and patience of the afflicted; and the almost superlative kindness of the nurses and some of the doctors. I think women are nearer to heaven than we are. At least, their love and kindness under the most revolting conditions seem a foreshadowing of that Providence that counts the sparrow on the housetops and numbers the hair on our heads. And just as war, hideous at it is, develops all the latent good in our race, so suffering (and it seems universal) seems to call forth all that is divine within us. Someone has said that the invention of the Lucifer-match was the greatest achievement of the 19th century. I am of opinion

301 Sir Charles Bent Ball made the diagnosis in September 1910. See letter 249 of 12 November 1912.

that the match must yield its place of precedence to the establishment of trained and skilled nurses.

I hope you keep well. I am sure you are working hard as ever. Your remarks in your letter of 5th July as to the attitude of the working man toward the capitalist, viewing life spectacularly, and not rationally, have often occurred to me. The vast body of the people have yet to learn what are the real constituents of human happiness; and alas! The whole tendency of modern thought and action is to intensify that universal and ruinous theory that all things have to be measured by their money value, and there is no other. If ever the masses came to understand that money is the meanest and most powerless factor in creating human happiness; and that all the great and good things of life are unpurchasable, things might swing around to an equilibrium. But the brown-stone mansion seems such a contrast with the tenement house that reason has no place there.

I shall probably be retained here for some time longer. It would be a great pleasure to hear from you, if your time permits. Meanwhile keep me in your memory. Your friendship is one of the sheet-anchors of life.

Ever affectionately,

dear Dr Holmes,

P.A. Sheehan

238. FROM: THE SOUTH INFIRMARY, CORK, 7 OCTOBER 1912

Text: MS PA DON I/160

Dear M. Ita,

I have just had a deep hour's sleep in my armchair. I had a bad night, and wanted rest. I was sitting down after dinner to a good sleep, when a visitor came who remained for three quarters of an hour. But I secured the hour's rest all the same.

Now for the items:

1. Don't send flannels until I write.
2. There must be no question of that £200 which I gave the convent. I have enough altho' I have sacrificed a good deal; but in some way or other, my little store has not run too far.

3. Would you ask Anthony to see J. O'Hanlon about painting my dining room. The furniture need not be removed. The bookcases alone would need to be drawn out from the wall; and I think they could manage that without opening them.

What you say about Dr Cremen is correct. I made a mistake in questioning Atkins and Dr O'Connell. If left to himself, he may order me out after a few weeks. I think he dislikes suggestions.

I asked for my account here after I was here 3 months; but they put me off, saying there was plenty of time.

What a lucky fellow Pat Joe was to seek his future in America. He has got a splendid chance now; and perhaps under a new sky, his very faults may turn to virtues.

Don't write about that £200 any more. What I gave, I gave; and will not touch it.

Always sincerely,
P.A. Sheehan

239. FROM: [THE] S[OUTH] I[NFIRMARY], CORK, 12 OCTOBER [1912]

Text: MS in the possession of the Very Reverend Canon Casey, Parish Priest of Mallow.

My dear Sarah,[302]

I was greatly pleased to learn by your letter that you had made your First Holy Communion and that you and all the children were going to H[oly]. Communion regularly. I am very thankful for all your prayers and I hope they may do me some good. So I hope you will continue them and get all your class to do the same. You will all be so big when I return that I must learn your names all over again. Give my love to all the children.

Yours sincerely.
P.A. Sheehan

302 Cf. letter 230.

240. FROM: THE SOUTH INFIRMARY, CORK, 13 OCTOBER 1912

Text: MS PA DON I/161

Dear M. Ita,

Many thanks for the pheasant that came yesterday, and which probably I will have for dinner today.

What you say about the dining room makes me believe it will be well if J.J. O'Hanlon puts it in hands at once. The estimate is moderate. I am bewildered by all the pretty colours, and must leave the selection to yourself. The dado should be deep colour to conceal the damp; such as 47 or 56. I notice that the painters here have given up stencilling. They use now (particularly under the cornice) strips of wall-paper of various designs about a foot deep. They look very nice and break the monotony of the colouring. I hope they won't dislocate the bookcases.

I am holding my own pretty well, quite able to hold myself now. I had an ugly purple rash on the skin these last few days; but I had an oatmeal bath last night; and it has disappeared almost entirely.

I did apply for my account but was put off. I dare say it will be high; and so will the doctors' bills. I do not care, if only I were done with them. I shall not be surprised if Dr Cremen sends me home soon; altho' he is very apprehensive and the fact that there is no medical help in Doneraile weighs very much with him, in case any emergency should arise. So we must keep on hoping and praying.

Always etc.
P.A. Sheehan

241. FROM: THE SOUTH INFIRMARY, CORK, 13 OCTOBER 1912

Text: MS PA DON I/162. A post card.

I find that the *Magnificat* and *Ave Maria* are forwarded here, altho' I left instructions at the post office that they were to be sent to the convent.

P.A.S.

The decorated paper over the dado should be about 6 inches deep; and the frieze under the cornice about 18 inches.

242. FROM: THE SOUTH INFIRMARY, CORK, 16 OCTOBER 1912

Text: MS PA DON I/163; *Addressed:* Mother M. Ita, Presentation Convent, Doneraile, Co. Cork; *Franked:* George V, 2 halfpenny green. *Postmark:* Cork, 9.30 p.m., 16 Oct 1912.

Dear M. Ita,

It is quite possible that I exaggerate the importance of the Bishop's remark but it showed that he must have been thinking about matters, whoever or whatever put it into his mind. I can only wait events; and hence, as the preparations for painting the dining-room are gone so far, it would be as well to continue the work, and you can instruct J. O'Hanlon accordingly.

I have just had a visit from Dr Madden. He says he has secured a housekeeper for me who was lately with Miss. Davis. Of course I have made no arrangements.

Dr Mannix[303] is coming to Queenstown next Monday. There will be a banquet on Tuesday, and on Wednesday the Bishop leaves for Rome.

I am suffering lately from insomnia. I get no sleep until 3 or 4 o'clock in the morning; and the night after the Bishop left I counted all the hours until breakfast. This is part of the malady, which I think is growing worse.

I had your pheasant for dinner today.

I enclose salary papers. The others I have sent on to Fr Shinkwin.

Always etc.
P.A. Sheehan

243. FROM: SOUTH INFIRMARY, CORK, 16 OCTOBER 1912

Text: Transcribed from David H. Burton, *Holmes-Sheehan Correspondence*, Fordham University Press, 1993.

Dear Dr Holmes,

I wrote you a few days ago; and the infliction of this second letter is due partly to the superabundant leisure I have at present; but principally to my desire to tell you how pleased I am at the compliments that have lately been paid you. Dear old St Paul tells us: "Rejoice with them that rejoice", and to

303 Daniel Mannix (1864–1963), former president of Maynooth, recently consecrated Coadjutor to Archbishop Carr of Melbourne. See footnote 173.

me, it is far the greater pleasure to be able to congratulate my friends than to receive congratulations for myself. The compliment of the President is worth noting; but, of the many others, I sh'd prefer the reception you had at the College, when your degree was conferred. There is a spontaneity in the enthusiasm of the young that makes it very valuable; and you have now not only academic honours; but this unique distinction that you are the only septuagenarian that ever lived who would say that the young lads of the present day are quite equal, if not superior, to our own contemporaries. For myself I am always the laudatory *temporis acti*; I think the world, at least this little section, that makes so much noise in the world, is much degenerated. I hope no whispers of envy will follow these acclamations; for there is a truth in the old saying: *Laudatur, et alget*. There is only one matter which to me is unforgivable in your fine career – that you have not written some great book on history or political economy. I have always thought you could do so as well as Bryce or Lecky; and I should like future generations to know you, even as you are known to your contemporaries. I think mysticism is not your line. I remember you had no sympathy with Emerson; and not much with Carlyle. But you could direct this very special and erratic generation on your own lines. And, considering the stirring days of your youth, your Memoirs would be very valuable to the future.

I am pulling along like a bird with a broken wing; when Death looks in through one window; the doctors order him off, altho' I should like to open the door to him; and then he hovers around trying to get them off their guard. Some day he will succeed.

I have just had a letter from Lady Castletown. Lord Castletown is much better. They leave for London at the end of the month.

Always affectionately
and sincerely,
P.A. Sheehan

244. FROM: THE SOUTH INFIRMARY, CORK, 22 OCTOBER 1912

Text: MS PA DON I/164; *Addressed:* Mother M. Ita, Presentation Convent, Doneraile, Co. Cork; *Franked:* George V, penny red. *Postmark:* Cork, 9.30 p.m., 22 Oct 1912.

Dear M. Ita,

Everything much as usual here. No great pain; but general inconvenience from hemorrhages etc.

I had a visit from Archbishop Mannix yesterday. He was on his way to Queenstown where the Bishop has a big banquet in his honour. The whole Chapter will be there; some celebrities as well. The Archbishop was exceedingly kind and nice, laid aside all dignity, and was very cheerful. He looks a little worn and fatigued and no wonder.

Dr Madden was with him. He is the one priest who has been most assiduous in calling on me, and he is now trying to persuade me to spend some days with him when I am moving homeward. Another priest who was very kind, was Fr Green of Castlemagner, altho' I never exchanged 10 words with him. He appears to have had an old *gradh* for me.

I am now troubled a good deal by insomnia. After lying down, my feet etc. become burning hot; and I get no peace until about 3 o'clock in the morning. I thought it might be the strychnine which I am taking, but it all proceeds from this fibroid tumour, the centre and source of all my troubles. However, I manage to get a good hour's sleep after dinner every day in my chair, except when visitors call.

Denis was here today on his way home from Tralee, where he has been these three weeks.

I hope you all keep well, I think the Archbishop will visit the convent soon.

Always etc.
P.A. Sheehan

245. FROM: THE SOUTH INFIRMARY, CORK, 28 OCTOBER 1912

Text: MS PA DON I/165; *Addressed:* Mother M. Ita, Presentation Convent, Doneraile, Co. Cork; *Franked:* George V, penny red. *Postmark:* Cork, 10 p.m., 28 Oct 1912.

Dear M. Ita,

I gave Denis today a copy of *Miriam Lucas*[304] to forward to you tonight; so that you will have it with this letter. It is a small acknowledgement for all

304 Published by Longmans, Green, London and New York 1912. A holograph fair copy of *Miriam Lucas* is conserved in Dublin: National Library of Ireland, MSS 4690–4692.

the trouble you have taken with an old derelict of a priest; but you will take the will for the deed. I don't suppose you will bother reading it; but keep it for my sake.

Denis returned from Tralee last Wednesday: and has had rough times since he came back – up every night till 3 am minding the baby so as to give May some chance of having a little sleep. They cannot get a nurse and May is completely worn out. Unlike all other babies, this young lady suffers from insomnia like her uncle – sleeps two hours only, then tosses off every shred of clothing and amuses herself marching around her cot singing away and talking to herself. Denis goes to Waterford tomorrow; a new nurse comes today; so I hope all will be well.

I slept somewhat better last night; but I have to get up 8 or 9 times every night and this prevents anything like deep wholesome sleep.

I cannot see my way to going against Dr Cremen's advice. There is no doubt whatever that this rectal malady is not improving, and it is of this he is afraid. Sometimes, I have a great desire to go out when feelings of depression come down, especially on Sunday evenings; but then I argue that I cannot under any circumstances have the care and attention at home that I have here. However, there is nothing for me but to wait. Some day, Our Lord will open up a way for me and solve all doubtings. But it does sting me to be told: You are looking so well, you ought to be at home! Conscience strikes in here with its blows. I can only fall back on the fact that I am a confirmed invalid; and that however long or short I live, there is no prospect of ultimate recovery.

I got the albums from Miss O'Sullivan; wrote some lines on each with my autograph; and am only waiting until some Doneraile friend calls to send them back.

When the painting is finished, I shall send you a cheque for the amount. J. O'Hanlon has an unhappy habit of keeping bills hanging over; and I want to keep out of debt.

I hope you all keep well; let me know how the children got on with Fr O'Keeffe.

Always sincerely,
P.A. Sheehan

Burn the enclosed when you have read it.

246. FROM: THE SOUTH INFIRMARY, CORK, 1 NOVEMBER 1912

Text: MS PA DON I/166; *Addressed:* Mother M. Ita, Presentation Convent, Doneraile, Co. Cork; *Franked:* George V, penny red. *Postmark:* Cork, 2.30 a.m., 2 Nov 1912.

Dear M. Ita,

I have just been reminded that I never acknowledged receipt of the tea-cakes, fruit (peaches and grapes) which you were good enough to send me. The reminder came in the shape of a very plump pheasant, which I had today for dinner, I demurred being Friday, but the nurses were better theologians than I, and they insisted that meat was allowed all over the world today.[305]

I had a most enjoyable visit from the rector of the Irish College last evening. He remained three or four hours; and we talked about everything under the Sun. He is one of the very few with whom I feel altogether comfortable and safe.[306]

There is a young priest here also (a patient) – Fr O'Brien, chaplain to St Angela's, a very intelligent and entertaining young priest. I think Katie Moriarty is in service there. I met her in the hall. She had come to inquire for him.

I have been wondering whether Fr Shinkwin managed to have a Solemn Requiem Mass tomorrow. You put me at ease about Shanballymore but I would be pleased to hear that the High Mass was kept up, altho' it makes but little difference to the Holy souls.

William O'Brien gave me a tremendous puff on Tuesday's paper. I suppose you saw it.

I have not replied to any of your suggestions about Miss Bell, altho' she is just the person, whom I should like to see around my house. But everything is so uncertain, that I cannot make any engagement. Dr Cremen makes no sign. He sees me about thrice a week for a few seconds but never touches on the question of my going home. Although, I have found the doctors very helpless.

Always etc.
P.A. Sheehan

305 The Solemnity of all Saints, falling on 1 November, relieves the Friday obligation to abstain from meat.

306 Monsignor Michael O'Riordan (1857–1919), born Feenagh, Co. Limerick; educated at the Propaganda College, Rome; ordained in 1883; rector of the Irish College Rome 1905–1919.

247. FROM: THE SOUTH INFIRMARY, CORK, 4 NOVEMBER 1912

Text: MS PA DON I/167

Dear M. Ita,

Very many thanks for the loaves and fruit which James Kearney brought today. I sent back the books after looking through them. I reserve the pleasure of reading them when I return. The buildings and illustrations are so fine that I fear they might be injured here, as my bedroom is small, and there is but little accommodation for books.

I enclose a cheque for J.J. O'Hanlon. He is a good poor fellow; but through all his tears and lamentations I think he manages his business well.

Fr O'Brien, who was here for the last fortnight and a Capuchin lay-brother who was starving himself to death, left here today. The place is becoming lonely and depressing; but I must not complain. And I have an abundance of books from John Horgan, St Marie of the Isles Library etc.

Sleep somewhat better last night. The night before I never closed my eyes. I suffer from dry intense heat altho' the temperature is normal. It is only in the cool of the morning I can sleep; and then there is an invasion of doctors, nurses etc. which banishes it.

Today is very gloomy and wet; and the spirits go down accordingly. It is not a cheerful place.

Dr O'Connell was very kind and did not press matters. He knows I am not free to act in this matter. I dare say Dr Cremen, if left alone, may suggest something. He has a curious habit of opposing every suggestion that does not emanate from himself. He has countermanded all of Dr Atkin's orders; and then proposed them himself. I must say I have derived little or no benefit from medical advice since I came here.

Denis is in Waterford. He can at least sleep, which he couldn't do at home. May had to send away two nurses this week – one had a rash on her neck and face; the second had a kind of epileptic fit the morning after she arrived.

I am glad things are so well at Knockane.[307] There is a big flock now.

Ever sincerely,
P.A. Sheehan

---

307 Knockane, Ballyclough, Co. Cork, the paternal home of Mother Ita O'Connell.

248. FROM: THE SOUTH INFIRMARY, CORK, 1 NOVEMBER 1912

Text: MS PA DON I/168; *Addressed:* Mother M. Ita, Presentation Convent, Doneraile, Co. Cork; *Franked:* George V, penny red. *Postmark:* Cork, 9.30, 8 Nov 1912.

Dear M. Ita,

The turkey came to hand by this morning's post. I suppose it will be reserved for Sunday's dinner.

I had a visit from Dr Cremen today. He is relenting a little; would see no objection to my going to Queenstown, or any place within easy distance from Cork; but Doneraile is so very remote; and then, if I needed a room here again, it might be impossible to get one. However, he is inclined, I think, to let me go; and probably will come to some definitive conclusion very soon.

Meanwhile, my many maladies are rather increasing than otherwise; and this insomnia is growing upon me. I am getting some remedies tonight; and perhaps they may make the inconveniences more easy to bear.

By all means get rid of the lawnmower, if you can. It is of little use to anyone.

The coat you speak of was sent to me by Denis some time ago. I never wore it, nor did he; but if it isn't too much moth eaten, I may find use of it about the garden later on.

I was half afraid Fr O'Keeffe would be inclined to be exacting this time on account of the Bishop's remarks at the last visitation.

I hope you are all keeping well. Kindest regards to Reverend Mother and community.

Always sincerely,
P.A. Sheehan

Private

It is a little waste to send me your dainties, such as pheasants, turkeys etc., for I see them only once.

At home they would make dinners for a week. But here they think I am too grand to see a fowl a second time. But I am sure they are well disposed of amongst the poor patients.

249. FROM: THE SOUTH INFIRMARY, CORK, 12 NOVEMBER 1912

Text: MS PA DON I/169; *Addressed:* Mother M. Ita, Presentation Convent, Doneraile, Co. Cork; *Franked:* George V, 2 halfpenny green. *Postmark:* Cork, 9.30 a.m., 8 Nov 1912.

Dear M. Ita,

Very many thanks for the papers and tea-cakes which John O'Hanlon brought today. The cakes would make anyone wish for home. I wonder does Sister Martha keep to her old recipe and discard these modern ideas.

John looks well and apparently is keeping steady. He sees a great many things in Bridge House which he would like to set right with paint and brush, if he were allowed. Amongst others, he tells me that nearly all the glass in the conservatory is broken, and that the rain is coming down in torrents. I gave him no order until Anthony should see the place and report to me. But he tells me unblushingly that they have not replaced the bookcases or pictures in the dining-room; but that they are all pell-mell on the floor.

I suppose Jeff[308] has sent you some experiments he has been making with me on the camera. They are ugly and good. If he has not sent them, I shall send you the two he has given me, as I have no use for them.

I had a succession of visitors today. The Sisters of Charity from the Incurable Hospital come every week – Mrs Eaton, William O'Brien's friend, being always one. They help to make the hours pass pleasantly.

I don't know if you remember a hurried visit I paid to Dublin in September 1910. That was memorable in many ways and it was then I received my death sentence from the leading surgeon in Ireland. I could not have spoken of it because it would only entail additional suffering on myself and others. These two years were a time of trial; but strange to say, I never minded, until the new development set in, which drove me here.[309]

Yesterday, I had a little setback, which showed me what might possibly be, if I were not careful. I had a good deal of pain yesterday and during the night; but today (D.G.) I am better. The weather is bitterly cold; but I don't stay out. And at night, I am too warm until the cool hours of the morning arrive.

---

308 His nephew.

309 See letter 237 of 6 October 1912.

Let me know if the Winter flannels are presentable. What I could wear at home, I could not wear here; and I can get a set from the Arcade.

Ever sincerely.
P.A. Sheehan

Ned Flannery[310] was here a few days ago.

250. FROM: THE SOUTH INFIRMARY, CORK, 14 NOVEMBER 1912

Text: MS PA DON I/170

Dear M. Ita,

Don't send the flannels etc. until I write for them. I do not feel the cold as yet. The great heat continues at night; and I sleep well only towards morning. Appetite good, although the nurses complain that I am not taking enough to equalize the waste etc.

I had a long talk with Dr Cremen today. He agreed there were pros and cons, for and against my going home; but he assented to my going, laying down however so many regulations that he has quite unnerved me about going. He is very farseeing; and he dreads seeing me again in the condition in which he found me. I must, he says, have a Bon Secours sister; and on the first setback I must make for Cork again etc.

As to Miss Bell, I cannot come to a decision. If I were able to return at once, I would say engage her. But I doubt if she understands how much of an invalid I am, and, for her own sake, I think she is making too great a sacrifice in throwing up £25 a year in a permanent situation for such a precarious situation as mine. However, if Miss Bell can wait, all the better.

Always etc.
P.A. Sheehan

251. FROM: THE SOUTH INFIRMARY, CORK, 18 NOVEMBER 1912

Text: MS PA DON I/171; *Addressed:* Mother M. Ita, Presentation Convent, Doneraile, Co. Cork; *Franked:* George V, penny red. *Postmark:* Cork, 9.30, 18 Nov 1912.

310 Mother Ita's brother-in-law of Churchtown, Co. Cork, married to her elder sister, Catherine Mary O'Connell, born 2 February 1865.

Dear M. Ita,

Many thanks for your letter of this morning. Denis closes his audit at Waterford this week; and when he returns, I shall very probably make immediate arrangements to get home some time next week. I had a long talk with Sr Albeus to-day and she is anxious I should have a change, as the insomnia is growing upon me. She assures me that she will make arrangements for me here; in case I should have to return. I propose taking Miss O'Sullivan with me; and if Miss Bell were there before her, she could in a week teach her everything necessary to be known. All this is subject of course to the supposition that I get no setback.

I must have some assurance however that there will be no demonstrations in Doneraile. I want to slip home as quietly as possible. If I were returning in good health, and able to resume my work, I would not so much mind. But I am a confirmed invalid and only stretching out a miserable existence with care. My appearance deceives people for I flush up so easily; but I am in very low water, and for that reason I hate the thought of having to face demonstrations of any kind. I want quietness and peace. Nothing else. Bands and bonfires and illuminations would be intensely disagreeable.

Of course, I shall keep you acquainted of all my designs during the week.

Eve sincerely,
P.A. Sheehan

- A book from London and a roll of manuscript from Dublin were forwarded to Doneraile. Would you ask J. Pratt to forward them here?
- It would be well to keep my homecoming as private as possible.

252. FROM: THE SOUTH INFIRMARY, CORK, 22 NOVEMBER 1912

Text: MS PA DON I/172; *Addressed:* Mother M. Ita, Presentation Convent, Doneraile, Co. Cork; *Franked:* George V, penny red. *Postmark:* Cork, 9.30, 22 Nov 1912.

Dear M. Ita,

I hope you all had a happy feast day yesterday.[311] There were great celebrations at the South Presentation Convent in this vicinity. All the city clergy appear to have been there.

311 Feast of the Presentation of the Blessed Virgin Mary, patronal feast of the Presentation Order.

Denis comes home tomorrow (Sat.) to make arrangements for next week, which I will keep you informed with. I am afraid the journey will try me somewhat; but I must get away. This insomnia is growing on me.

A nurse from here would be indispensable for a fortnight or so. Miss O'Sullivan is very quiet; and I think would be a help to the housekeeping etc. She could dine with me at 2 every day. I must follow the hospital regime as far as I can.

If Miss Bell cannot come, perhaps you would write to Fr Madden about the housekeeper he spoke of to me. Miss Bell would require a second female help, I think, as she has not been used to the drudging of a large house and had always two servants to help.

I am greatly pleased to hear that I can slip home unobserved and without any demonstrations. It would be very unsuitable in my condition.

I shall write again the moment we arrange matters. I wonder if the latch key I left in my vest pocket and the book of instruction are safe?

Always sincerely,
P.A. Sheehan

253. FROM: THE SOUTH INFIRMARY, CORK, SATURDAY EVENING [23 NOVEMBER 1912]

Text: MS PA DON I/173

Dear M. Ita,

Our present arrangements are to leave here next Monday (the 25th) by the 3.30 p.m. reaching Mallow at four p.m. Denis and Miss O'Sullivan will be with me. A short visit to the doctor at Mallow. We should reach Doneraile about 5.30 p.m. I hope you will not consider the notice too short; but as I am to go at all, I am impatient to go at once. If there is any difficulty in Doneraile, you could let me know by Monday's post.

I had intended at first to send Denis and the nurse in advance; but I think it as well we should all go together.

Bridget could have a flitch of bacon from Gallagher's or M. Murphy's, and the other appliances, including meat for the week.

Always sincerely,
P.A. Sheehan

254. FROM: THE SOUTH INFIRMARY, CORK, 24 NOVEMBER 1912

Text: MS PA DON I/174; *Addressed:* Mother M. Ita, Presentation Convent, Doneraile, Co. Cork; *Franked:* George V, penny red. *Postmark:* Cork, 2.30 a.m., 25 Nov 1912.

Dear M. Ita,

Sister Albeus has arranged that Miss O'Sullivan shall go on tomorrow (Monday) in advance of the 12 train from Cork, taking most of our luggage with her. Would you send a car to meet her at Buttevant about 1.20; and I will ask her call at the convent at once; and perhaps you could have a chop for her, so as to spare Bridget.

Denis and I dine here and go to Mallow by 3.30. We should arrive in Doneraile at 5.30.

I think Miss O'Sullivan will be a help to Bridget rather than a burden. She can dine every day with us a 2 p.m.

I shall take the Bishop's room for the present and Denis takes mine. Miss O'Sullivan can have the other spare bedroom.

I shall be very happy to be at home. Dr Atkins is delighted that I am going out.

Always sincerely,
P.A. Sheehan

255. FROM: DONERAILE, CO. CORK, 2 DECEMBER 1912

Text: Transcribed from David H. Burton, *Holmes-Sheehan Correspondence*, Fordham University Press, 1993.

Dear Dr Holmes,

Just at this moment, sitting at "my ain fire", your letter was put into my hands. I have two or more correspondents whose handwriting on the envelope gives me cold chills all over; and a few, which I open with anticipation of pleasure. Amongst these latter, yours holds first place; and I always open your letter with the exclamation: "Not Forgotten!".

I made a dash for liberty last Monday week. One of the doctors was holding out against me to the last; but he was finally persuaded that hospital life was not good from my standpoint; and so I packed up, and got back once more amongst my books and papers, and the kind faces of friends.

All here have been exceedingly kind without distinction of class or creed; and altho' I begged and prayed that there should be no demonstrations, I am afraid I shall have to face the band and illuminations tomorrow night. Poor people! They insisted on it; and it would be churlish to refuse any little testimony of their affection.

I do not know what you will think of *Miriam Lucas*. It carries out my pet theory that there is an equilibrium in human life – some compensation or balance that, in the end, makes the poor somewhat nearer to real happiness than the rich. I have seen both sides of the big question; and so far as mere happiness is concerned, I think on the whole the poor have the best of it, at least in this Ireland of ours. I am never tired of quoting a story by A[nthony] K[ennedy] H[utchinson] B[oyd] (*The Country Parson)* in one of his books – the Grampian shepherd, coming home after a day's honest work, and declaring, after he had changed his boots, and swallowed a wholesome supper, and taken up *Chamber's Journal*:[312] "I do not envy the Duke of Buccleuch"; and, as a contrast, the monomaniac in his ducal mansion above the Thames, shouting impatiently: "Oh, that river, that river, always rolling and rolling, and never rolling away!"

I see that the *New York Herald* and another American paper hint that in the 3rd. book of *Miriam Lucas* I write "in complete ignorance of the conditions of life in New York". I should like to know where the picture fails. It is not flattering, but I wrote after making careful inquiries amongst friends who have visited from time to time. But I perceive that nations have nerves as well as individuals; and altho' I thought we Irish had a double dose of them, I perceive that the malady is universal.

Don't speak of death. Death is not for you for many years to come. I wish the President would make you Ambassador at St James's, or at Paris. But I suppose a Democratic Government will keep the plums for its own. I believe this party politics is the one great curse of mankind. It has paralysed everything here; and stifles all genius and original talent. And I suspect it is the same the wide world over.

If too early to wish you happy Xmas, it is never premature to wish you every blessing, temporal and spiritual.

Always affectionately,
P.A. Sheehan

312 *Chambers's Edinburgh Journal* was founded in Edinburgh by William Chambers in 1832 and covered topics such as history, religion, language, and science. The title changed to *Chambers's Journal of Popular Literature, Science, and Arts* in 1854 and to *Chambers's Journal* in 1897. It continued in publication up to 1956.

256. FROM: DONERAILE, 7 DECEMBER 1912

Text: NLI/CP/MS 35,306

Dear Lord Castletown,

How am I to thank you for your kind and sympathetic letter of December 4? It is so like you – always considerate and anxious about others.

I made a dash for freedom a fortnight ago, having overcome the fears and scruples of one doctor, who was holding out against the others. The change from the monotony and rather gruesome surroundings of hospital life to the freedom of home has been already beneficial. The people have been so kind as to make me ashamed of my incompetence and backwardness.[313]

It will be a great pleasure to see you and Lady Castletown in February. Kindly give my regards to her Ladyship and Mrs Wingfield.[314]

And believe me to be always,

My dear Lord Castletown,

Sincerely and affectionately,

P.A. Sheehan, P.P.

257. FROM: DONERAILE, CO. CORK, 8 JANUARY 1913

Text: MS PAHRC/HJHP/SP/2

Dear Fr Phelan,

I received a half dozen copies of *The Austral Light*[315] a few days ago; and I have been since trying to compose my nerves so that I could frame my expression of gratitude to you in somewhat moderate terms. Let me say at once then, that I feel deeply indebted to you for such kind words about myself and my books. They are all the more valuable as coming from your pen on the principle that it is the highest distinction:

Laudari a Laudato.

And also because such an expression of opinion is rather a rare experience of mine; for on the whole, I have not received much favour from the Catholic Press. The very book (*The Queen's Fillet*), which you appreciate so highly, received but scant, and decidedly unfavourable notice from two

313 A reference to his decision to leave the South Infirmary in Cork City after five months in hospital.
314 Lord Castletown's sister.
315 Published in Melbourne 1892–1920.

such Catholic journals as the *Month*[316] and the *Catholic World*.[317] This is all the more strange, because the entire secular press of the world wrote kindly of the book. But it is useless to dwell on these things, except to emphasise one's appreciation of a Catholic critic like yourself.

I think you acted the part of the *Advocatus Diaboli* also with gentleness and discretion. *Glenanaar* is more a favourite than you think. It is generally coupled with Kickham's *Knocknagow*.[318] And it is not *Geoffrey Austin*, so much as its sequel *The Triumph of Failure* that remains a favourite book of mine. It is somewhat overladen with philosophy; but it is a good psychological study; and I have been told that it effected a great deal of good in the German Universities. I do not think I have written anything equal to the apostrophe, commencing: p. 333 –

"I know Thee, Alpha and Omega – the beginning and the end" etc.

And the chapter:

"From my cell" page 371.

Have you noticed too, that altho' I plunge all my heroes and heroines in a sea of affliction, I make them come out triumphant in the end. Per aspera ad astra.

Enough of myself! I am delighted to hear that you are going to America next year. Remember you'll have to economise your strength by learning to say No! over there; for there will be infinite calls for sermons, lectures, etc. But we shall have time to talk all that over before you go.

Accept the most grateful thanks for your kindness – all the greater because unsolicited and unexpected.

Always sincerely,

My dear Fr Phelan,

P.A. Sheehan, P.P.

258. FROM: DONERAILE, CO. CORK, 20 JANUARY 1913

Text: Transcribed from David H. Burton, *Holmes-Sheehan Correspondence*, Fordham University Press, 1993.

316 Published by the English Province of the Society of Jesus 1864–2001.
317 Published in Washington by the Paulist Fathers from 1865.
318 Published in 1873.

My dear Dr Holmes,

A sentence in your last letter (dated, to my shame, Dec. 15th, 1912) makes me half timid in writing to you. I pictured you to myself, as all day long in a stuffy court, listening to evidence and appeal, the harangues of barristers making special pleas, the testimony of witnesses more or less credible; and then enduring that most severe of all moral strains, the balancing of data and arguments and the forming of a conscientious judgment on knotty and difficult points of fact and law; and I said: Is it right or fair that after such a day's work, that Judge Holmes should sit down and write a long and interesting letter to an old parish priest in a remote Irish village, instead of burying himself in an armchair and giving his mind every repose? And I resolved that I should write and write regularly in order to keep up a chain correspondence that is so precious, that he must only write during vacation terms, when he has abundant leisure. Yet, I want you to understand that in a pretty extensive correspondence, there is only one address that makes me jump, and that is your handwriting. Let me add, that I think I have received all your letters. They are carefully filed and kept to be disposed at your pleasure when I shall have gone.

There was another remark in your last letter, that showed how deeply interested you are in your great profession, altho' it depressed me somewhat to reflect how difficult it is to secure a great position as a jurist. Probably I am speaking from inexperience, because so few, so very few legal men have left a permanent reputation behind them in these countries. The great English judges are hardly dead when they are forgotten; and what is more strange, whilst this generation reads with some pleasure great judicial charges of a hundred years ago, no one cares about contemporaries. Lord Russell became famous for his splendid cross-examinations and final address in the Parnell trial; but no one minded him as Chief Justice. Our Chief Justice (Palles) is known in legal circles as a profound student of law; but his reputation is limited to the Law Courts in Dublin.[319] But I suppose all this is true of every profession. Is it the general levelling up or the general levelling down of this Democratic age that makes remarkable men almost impossible? And nothing has astonished me more than the manner in which obscure and partly illiterate men in the States, such as Lincoln and Grant, etc., developed such tremendous powers and became

319 The Rt. Hon. Christopher Palles (1831–1920), Chief Baron of the Exchequer, often referred to as "the greatest of Irish judges".

"leaders of men". I have just been reading W[inston] Churchill's *Crisis*[320] and got a larger idea of these men than ever before. I can forgive Walt Whitman a good deal for "Captain! Oh, my Captain!".

There I have scarcely left space to wish you a most prosperous and happy New Year, full of good, noble work, and rich in all manner of blessings.

Always sincerely,

my dear Dr Holmes,
P.A. Sheehan

259. FROM: DONERAILE, CO. CORK, 25 FEBRUARY 1913

Text: Transcribed from David H. Burton, *Holmes-Sheehan Correspondence*, Fordham University Press, 1993.

Dear Dr Holmes,

I was just about to write to you to ask the favour of a newspaper cutting of your speech in New York, when the coveted article reached my hands. It is just what I expected – terse with thought. Your auditors if they followed you with intelligent interest, must have carefully abstained from champagne. But then you must know that you have spoken not a speech but a book.

A kind friend was good enough to pay me the compliment lately of saying (he is an organist) that my books are like Wagneric music – they must be read three or four times before one can understand them. However accurate that may be, I can say it truly of your speech. As I went over and over the sentences I said – that idea needs pages to develop. There is a tremendous truth hidden away in the chrysalis of a few words. I notice the same circumstances in all your speeches. How absolutely original they must have sounded at the banquet; and what a dainty morceau they must be to the studious epicure of the library. I like too the glints of poetry here and there; and if I can not share in your sunny optimism (because I think it is the individual and not nations, or races, we have to study that develop) at least it is charming to hear the Alpine shepherds calling each other across their desolate valleys.

My health continues poor enough, days of relief alternating with days of pain and discomfort. I find a consolation in thinking how much worse

320 The American novelist Winston Churchill (1871–1947). *The Crisis* was published by Macmillan in 1901.

I might be; and contrasting my infirmities with those of others. "It is a sad world, my merry masters".

I find I gave some offence in New York in Book III of *Miriam Lucas*. Yet I can not perceive that I said anything but what may be said of all great cities. But I notice how sensitive are whole nations, as well as individuals. My books have never caught on in France because I have written somewhat enthusiastically about Germany; but in the Fatherland and especially Austro-Hungary, these books are great favourites. I think it was the curious remark made by Whistler, or some other artist, that modern New York with its skyscrapers resembled nothing so much as a canyon in the Sierras that set the teeth of my American friends on edge. I should not like to be thought capable of wilful offence there; because, like many other authors, it was to American appreciation that was mainly due the success of my books.

Adieu! All blessing by with you.

Thanks for all your letters which came in quick and welcome succession; and which must have consumed much of your precious time.

Your name turned up a few days ago, when Lord and Lady Castletown called here. Her Ladyship was wondering whether you would pay the Green Isle a visit this year. We are in the throes of expectation about the Home Rule Bill.[321] It will be the best think for England; the worst thing for Ireland since the Act of Union.[322]

Prospere procedet.

Always affectionately,
P.A. Sheehan

260. FROM: DONERAILE, CO. CORK, 3 APRIL 1913

Text: MS PAHRC/HJHP/SG/1

Dear Lady Gilbert,

I have to thank you very much for your most kind letter of March 31st.

---

321 The Government of Ireland Act 1914 (4 & 5 Geo. 5 c. 90), received royal assent on 14 September 1914. However, with impending war, it was formally suspended and never implemented, being superceeded by the Government of Ireland Act of 1920.

322 Two complimentary acts, The Union with Ireland Act 1800 (39 & 40 Geo. 3 c. 67), of the Parliament of Great Britain, and The Act of Union (Ireland) 1800 (40 Geo. 3 c. 38), of the Parliament of Ireland for the unification of the Kingdom of Great Britain and the Kingdom of Ireland.

I am much better in health since I came home, and found myself able to take part in the ordinary work of the parish. It is a wholesome distraction, and acts as a kind of tonic, keeping the mind from dwelling too much on physical disabilities. But I shall always be an invalid, just struggling along, and consoling myself with the reflection that it is God's Holy Will, and the cross might have been much heavier than it is.

I am quite sure you have no need to —— our generation, for I know no author who has given the reading public such a splendid output of genuine literature as yourself. I do not think this has been adequately recognized; for somehow Catholic editors and Magazines are rather too economical of praise, particularly in the case of recognised authors, which, by a singular inconsistency, they are constantly clamouring for good Catholic literature as an antidote to the poisonous productions of the English Press. I think our good Fr Russell[323] alluded to this in a speech he delivered some months ago. But the world goes on — ; and one who has the vocation of the pen must keep on ever mindful, and duly striving to get in a great life's work before the night falls.

I am not now writing. I am too weak to attempt anything now. But I have a novel completed for the press;[324] but I think it advisable to defer its publication until the Autumn of the year. But I scribble away a little now and again, just for amusement and to while away a lonely hour. This habit of writing is a wonderful anodyne. Apart from the question of success or failure, it is in itself a reward for the little labour involved.

I am, dear Lady Gilbert,

Yours most sincerely,
P.A. Sheehan, P.P.[325]

I have just opened the April *I[rish] Monthly* at your poem in the current chapter of your novel. It is a marvellous piece of work. I cannot remember

323 Editor of the *Irish Monthly*.

324 *The Graves at Kilmorna*. A holograph copy of *The Graves at Kilmorna*, in seven notebooks, and dated March 31, 1912, is conserved in Dublin: National Library of Ireland, MSS 4693–4695.

325 A note to Fr Herman Heuser, in the hand of Mother Ita O'Connell, is written on the verso of the third page: "Lady Gilbert has been very ill, hence delay in sending papers. I hope it will reach you safely. No time for more today. One of our sisters is very ill. Shall write very soon. It is quite possible that I may have a little blotter for my wee nephew. His Daddy was most anxious to know how our dear Canon looked as a young priest. Very much better than as we knew him. I hope you got Fr Burton's little sketch of Maynooth days. I must stop, our poor sister is very weak and we cannot let her alone. Mr Galbally will remember the young nun who was in consumption. Best wishes. M. Ita".

anything of yours that rivals it. If Yeats or Synge had written that poem we would never hear the end of it.

261. FROM: DONERAILE, CO. CORK, 12 MAY 1913

Text: MS PA DON I/175

Dear Reverend Mother,[326]

Very many thanks for your kind offer. Fr Shinkwin wished to take over the responsibility also. But it would never do. The trouble will be almost entirely with the servants; and I shall have nothing to do, but look on. Mary and Bridget will give a helping hand; and I shall have only a few to dine both days.

I hope the procession was a success. I am weather-bound. There is no stirring about.

Always sincerely,
P.A. Sheehan

262. FROM: NO ADDRESS

Text: MS PA DON I/176

14 June 1913

1. These deposits to be retained by M. Ita O'Connell until after my decease.
2. The deposit (£150) to be then invested; and the interest to be applied to the establishment of a perpetual monthly Mass for the repose of my soul, to be celebrated in the chapel of the Presentation Convent, Doneraile, the honorarium to be fixed by the Bishop.
3. The deposit (£100) is a free gift to M. Ita O'Connell, to be applied after my death, according to her own wishes.

P.A. Sheehan, P.P.
Doneraile

---

326 Mother Alphonsus O'Keeffe (1852–1938).

263. FROM: DONERAILE, CO. CORK, 21 JUNE 1913

Text: Transcribed from David H. Burton, *Holmes-Sheehan Correspondence*, Fordham University Press, 1993.

Dear Dr Holmes,

It was only yesterday that Lord Castletown told me you were in London, and that they were expecting you this month or next. This is a delightful piece of news, I am distinctly of the opinion that your visit to the Castletowns would not only be a pleasure to them; but would raise Lord Castletown's spirits a good deal. He is much improved; and I am sure if his solitude were broken by a visit from you, it would help him much. I think they have none, or very few visitors just now, and we have Irish weather, variable, but charming.

Need I say what a ray of sunshine your visit will cast over a broken life like mine?

Always affectionately and
Sincerely,
P.A. Sheehan

264. FROM: NO ADDRESS.

Text: MS PA DON I/177; 7 July 1913

Dear M. Ita,

The truss is working fairly well.

I am rather sorry that Dr Cremen has been approached about the matter. He has a horror of all kinds of anaesthetics; and would very probably interdict the use of the sup. altogether.

I have already declined the offer of Lord Castletown to put down sand in front of my door; and if you value my peace of mind, you will at once write to Dick O'Brien not to send sand here. I should only have to send his men back again. The inconvenience is very little and I want to avoid attracting public attention above all things and people making talk. I want privacy, privacy, privacy if only I can get it.

Whether it was the cassara on some fruit I took, I suffered a good deal yesterday and last night. The symptoms are mitigated today.

Always etc.
P.A. Sheehan, P.P.

265. FROM: NO ADDRESS.

Text: MS PA DON I/177

Dear M. Ita,

I had a fairly good night; but felt so tired and fatigued this morning that I could not get up. The liver trouble is persistent after dinner; but seems less at night. I find the 1/5 gr. suppositories the best. I have none remaining.

Denis can come if he likes on Saturday. If writing to him, say that the parcel about which May inquires did not reach here.

I enclose D. O'Sullivan's prescription – book 151; no. 571–2.

Pleased to hear that everything is doing well.

Always sincerely,
P.A. Sheehan

266. FROM: NO ADDRESS.

Text: MS PA DON I/179

Dear M. Ita,
The medicine came all right this morning; but I have not used it yet. It is, I think, a preparation of petroleum. The other has been very troublesome all day. I feel the heat very much these last two days; but there is some appearance of a change.

Always sincerely,
P.A. Sheehan

267. FROM: NO ADDRESS.

Text: MS PA DON I/180. A card.

Dear M. Ita,

Quite unable to go out today. Stomach upset and much languor and debility. Medicine came from Hannigan's – bisumuth (salicylate) and chlorodine; not to be used after more than 3 times in 24 hours.

Brandy came this morning. I fear I shall make little use of it. It is too heating.

Always sincerely,
P.A.S.

268. FROM: NO ADDRESS.

Text: MS PA DON I/181; dated 17 September 1913 in the hand of Mother Ita O'Connell.

Dear M. Ita,

The 4 gr. of cassara had no effect hitherto. I am trying another tonight. I had a very bad night up to 2 p.m. (sic) Then I had a little sleep and rest from pain till morning. I had to take another supp. The pain in the hip, knee and foot is very great sometimes and there is a great numbness.

I don't think I need anything at present. The only sup. I would require would be some more ½ gm. I must conquer the great pain at any cost. I think it is sciatica or rheumatic gout.

I am afraid I cannot see you for some days.

Always sincerely,
P.A. Sheehan

[In pencil on the margin, in the hand of Mother Ita O'Connell]: This is his last letter excepting the ones asking for the nurse.

269. FROM: NO ADDRESS.

Text: MS PA DON I/182; 19 September 1913. In pencil.

Did Dr speak of coming over today. Am in great pain and would require a nurse at once.

P.A. Sheehan

270. FROM: NO ADDRESS.

Text: MS PA DON I/183; 18 September [1913]. In pencil.

Very bad night. Excessive pain in hip and leg. Must see Dr O'Connell today. Mention sciatica and rheumatism. Bring the remedies from Mallow.

P.A. Sheehan

271. FROM: NO ADDRESS.

Text: MS PA DON I/184; no date.

Dear M. Ita,

I had hope of seeing you today but I had to stay at home.
You see I am now on liquid diet; and I think it best.

Always,
P.A.S.

272. FROM: NO ADDRESS.

Text: MS PA DON I/185; two postcards, no date.

Dear M. Ita,

The inscription is really beautiful and quite worthy of the book. Send on tonight.

I had an excellent day yesterday; a poor night. Until just now, I have been fairly well; but the pains have come back.

The trusses I fear are useless; so I am sending them back also.

Always sincerely,
P.A. Sheehan

[On second card]
Conium ointment Dr Whitla's Formula.

273. FROM: NO ADDRESS.

Text: MS PA DON I/186; Monday, no date.

Dear M. Ita,

I had two very poor nights, sleepless from pain, whether sciatica or rheumatism I am not sure. I am fairly fine from it during the day; but it attacks me at night. I blame the Oxo for it. I was always warned against these rich soups. So, farewell Oxo.

I am just as well pleased that our American friends took their leave. It is all curiosity.

William and Mrs O'Brien and Mrs Eaton (Sister of Charity) are expected here now. They may visit the convent. If so, be particularly kind to Mrs Eaton. She was very good to me in Cork.

I am taking some salicylate of soda to keep down the feverish symptoms in the blood. Clearly, nothing but the lightest things suit me.

I had a most unpleasant interview with the Byblox people on Friday, and wrote Mildred that I would not interfere further.

Always sincerely,
P.A. Sheehan

274. FROM: NO ADDRESS.

Text: MS PA DON I/187; Sunday evening, no date.

My dear M. Ita,

I have had a very bad time, night and day, since Friday afternoon, I cannot account for it, unless it be the potatoes which may be indigestible. I am leaving them off today, except twice a week. I was quite unable to say Mass this morning; and all remedies were of no avail.

William and Mrs O'Brien are coming today at 3.30. I am sorry the Sisters cannot see them.

I hope everything is going well. I enclose a few pages which perhaps Fr Phelan could develop in his own words, and thus enlarge the pamphlet, altho' I fear that too much honour has been done my critics already, by such a castigation as Fr Phelan's.

Perhaps the choir would sing the Hymn to the Sacred Heart for Fr Phelan; and he could judge if it were fit for the public.

Always sincerely,
P.A. Sheehan

[275]. FROM: DONERAILE, CO. CORK.

Text: MS PA DON I/188; a card, no date.

My dear M. Ita,

Failing rapidly but no pain, thanks be to God. It is as you said, he would be spared pain in the end – Fr Shinkwin is most of the day with him and consoling and comforting him.

He said only last night to me of Fr Shinkwin's goodness, and he could not ever forget him, and that I must remember him.

Ever yours,
Denis.

Could you put flannel lining over the other in this vest? I am sending by Anthony.

[276]. FROM: DONERAILE, CO. CORK.

Text: MS PA DON I/189; a card, no date.

Dear Ita,

I returned from Cork about 5 p.m. Excuse me not going up. P. is very weak tonight, but has hardly any pain. He spoke a while with me and asked me to tell you how thankful he is to you for all you have done for him.

I hope to see you tomorrow

Denis.

277. FROM: DONERAILE, CO. CORK.

Text: MS PA DON I/192; no date.

Dear Reverend Mother,

Would you kindly enclose this little pamphlet to Fr Somer with *Parerga.* The letter I wrote this morning was to spare you trouble.

And in writing to Mr Hodkinson,[327] do not state any price for painting the chapel; leave that to be determined.

Yours,
P.A. Sheehan

327 James Hodkinson & Sons Ecclesiastical Decorators, Henry Street, Limerick. The Decoration of the Chapel was estimated for in 1916 and again in 1919, when the decoration was to be "artistically carried out in approved style" for the sum then of £600 – which suggests that the Chapel must have been very elaborately decorated. This work was eventually carried out by Louis Hodkinson. James Hodkinson had previously decorated the Chapel in the 1880s together with a small mortuary chapel in the convent grave yard. The chapel was last decorated by Hodkinson's in 1960.

278. FROM: DONERAILE, CO. CORK.

Text: MS PA DON I/193; no date.

My dear Ita,

With all good wishes for you feast day, I send you *The Perfect Woman*,[328] you'll recognize yourself in every page; but how did the authoress come to know you? Come home quick! After the experience of the Kanturk nuns on Sunday night with the burglar, we'll want your cool nerves here. Otherwise, the convent bell will be going all night. Tell Evangelist[329] I'm examining her class to-day for premiums. All here expect the best – Nora Murphy.

Always and affectionately,
P.A. Sheehan

I wouldn't write the above, only I'm in good spirits at last about you.

279. FROM: DONERAILE, CO. CORK.

Text: MS PA DON I/194; a card, no date.

Dear Reverend Mother,

I am almost sure Dr Cotter is at home. He does not go away until September.

Ask M. Alphonsus[330] to send me the ½ year cheque as we make up accounts tomorrow; and Sister Dympna[331] to send me the genders of the Irish words: *caoine, banshee* and *ceol.*

Always sincerely,
P.A. Sheehan

---

328 Emily Mary Shapcote (1828–1909), *Mary: The Perfect Woman*, Manresa Press, Roehampton 1903. An American edition was published by the Dolphin Press in 1904.

329 Sr Evangelist Daly (1868–1942).

330 Mother Alphonsus O'Keeffe (1852–1938).

331 Sr Dympna Whelan (1879–1919). See footnote 182.

280. FROM: DONERAILE, CO. CORK.

Text: MS PA DON I/195; a card, no date.

Dear M. Ita,

I have just remembered that these candles have been blessed and therefore cannot be sold; and I feel otherwise that it would be wrong not to devote them to the purpose for which they were intended by the donor. These candles must therefore by kept for the use of the Altar; but the material for the cushion may be got; and I shall pay for it out of Church funds.

Always sincerely,
P.A. Sheehan, P.P.

281. FROM: DONERAILE, CO. CORK.

Text: MS PA DON I/196; a card, no date.

Dear M. Ita,
I shall say Mass @ 8.15 tomorrow morning.
Of course I shall be happy to have Emily here tonight.

Always sincerely,
P.A. Sheehan

282. FROM: DONERAILE, CO. CORK.

Text: MS PA DON I/197; a card, no date.

Dear M. Ita,

Perhaps you could gently hint to Fr McWilliams that I have not been able to offer him the usual compliment of a dinner, as I do not wish to put additional pressure on Anne, who is already fatigued enough from visitors, door-callers, etc.; I am sure he is much happier with yourselves; but I should not like that he should think us indifferent.

P.A. Sheehan

[283]. FROM DONERAILE, 13 OCTOBER 1913

Text: MS, University College Cork, Papers of Mrs William O'Brien, UCC/WOB/PP/AS/45(A), on mourning paper

My dear Mrs O'Brien,

I cannot express to you my feelings of appreciation on reading your beautiful article on my dear brother.

It was so true, so touching, so sympathetic, coming straight from the heart of one who loved him. William's leading article also was a heartfelt tribute to the affection that existed always between them – never clouded for a moment during all these years – an affection rooted as he said in their boyhood days and blossoming to the last.

I can truly say that the like affection binds me, intensified, if possible, since I came to know you and appreciate all your kindness and goodness of heart.

Believe me,
My dear Mrs O'Brien,
Ever gratefully and affectionately,
Yours,
D.B. Sheehan

[284]. FROM: DONERAILE, 14 OCTOBER 1913

Text: MS, University College Cork, Papers of Mrs William O'Brien, UCC/WOB/PP/AS/41, on mourning paper.

My Dear William,

I have been looking for some book to send you to hold as belonging to your dear friend and read by him and I think you may like this book if you have not already read it. If you happen to have the book I can send you another, but I dare say you have read them all.

May I say how much I was touched by your article in Monday's *Free Press* in which you poured out the strength and riches of your affection for him.

Ever Yours affectionately,
D.B. Sheehan

[285]. FROM: SEAFIELD, QUEENSTOWN, 11 NOVEMBER 1913

Text: MS, University College Cork, Papers of Mrs William O'Brien, UCC/WOB/PP/AS/49, on mourning paper.

My dear William,

If you have any way of influencing the Mallow Committee re the memorial to the Canon, I would be so thankful if you could do something to stop the touting and writing for subscriptions which is going on. I tried to stop the whole thing in Doneraile as he would not wish it, and they would not listen to me. I am putting up a Memorial Cross on his grave, and I hoped, when I failed to stop the Memorial, that it would be only some small thing in the Church to his memory, a tablet on the wall or something useful in the Church.

I cannot say how humiliating to me and his memory, is this canvassing for money, for erecting some stone or mortar memorial. He would feel this bitterly, as you know, and I have to bear it now, and hear comments on the way in which pressure is being put on outsiders to subscribe to the Doneraile or Mallow project.

As an old friend, I would ask you to try to stop this miserable business and you could get Fr Madden to help in doing so.

I think those who are pushing these rival projects show poor respect for his memory whereas a small and simple voluntary tribute from those who knew him and loved him would be pleasing to all, especially if it took the form of a charity – a gift to the poor and the stricken. This alone would be his wish and surely they should not forget it, if it is not possible to stop the whole thing altogether. I know you will feel with me in this view, and therefore I ask your assistance.

Very sincerely yours,
D.S. Sheehan

Letters to which dates cannot be assigned

286. FROM: MALLOW, 28 APRIL.

Text: MS PA DON I/89

My dear Columba,

This week we are winding up our stations; but quite probably next week I shall put myself right with you all by running over to Doneraile. I must not specify any day however, lest I should fail; and lose my good character of being immoveable as granite when I make a promise.

All well here,

Yours always,
P.A. Sheehan

Nota Bene !!
Keep that story of the cocks to yourself. It is only intended for private circulation and it is wonderful how these ridiculous things come back and cause trouble. I hope Reverend Mother is really well after Lent.

287. FROM: MALLOW, 8 SEPTEMBER.

Text: MS PA DON I/92

My dear Sr Columba,

It strikes me as barely possible that you or some of the sisters may have heard of a quiet, experienced person who would undertake the duties of housekeeper here. If so, let me know. About 12 months ago Fr Madden was kind enough to recommend some suitable person from Doneraile parish; but I was unable to take her into my service. Perhaps some such person would be still available.

I would have gone over before this, if only to see your two devoted sisters from Dakota; but Fr Barry is away on holidays. The young postulant who went from our orphanage here will prove very useful and zealous.

Frank doing well; but thinks of leaving Surgères for Nantes for Faithful Companions. I assume she has written you on the subject.

In great haste and with fond remembrance to Reverend Mother and Community

Yours always,
P.A. Sheehan

288. FROM: MALLOW, 10 SEPTEMBER.

Text: MS PA DON I/93

My dear Columba,

I am afraid I cannot go to Doneraile tomorrow but probably I shall run over on Wednesday.

With regard to the young girl you speak of, her want of training would be a great drawback, in as much as I am quite unable, even if my tastes ran in that direction, to train such people myself. My present servant would suit me very well; but on the rare occasion when I ask a few priests to dine, she is perfectly helpless, having had no experience, I fear such would be the case with the young girl you speak of. In fact, I find that she would have no chance of learning anything here unless she came previously trained. A servant who has been *in some good house* would suit me best.

I am in no hurry; as I have not yet given notice to my servant. But I have suffered so much from domestics, as to make me wish that someone would establish an order of lay-brothers for domestic service; or that it might become fashionable to import a few Chinese.

Yours always,
P.A. Sheehan, C.C.

289. FROM: MALLOW, 13 NOVEMBER.

Text: MS PA DON I/94 a card.

My dear Columba,

The heliotrope was a mild and not unpleasant surprise. I shall never complain of a little task, even in metaphor, and you know it is a consolation to us poor mortals, who have similar weaknesses, to find a little pardonable weakness amongst the Celestials.

I would not like to promise to accept your invitation for Monday. I have large amounts of contracts and engagements on hands; and am not sure of a day. But I shall make it a duty to see you soon.

We have just closed our examinations. They were very successful; and even I who am a most querulous and exacting individual, felt quite softened by the great success of my poor little girls. I think May got 1[st.] for everything.

We are opening our Young Men's Society hall tomorrow evening. I hope it will be a success. You have not said a word about Frank lately; and lately she has been very much in my thoughts.

Keep well! And help us in any way you can.

Yours always,
P.A.S.

290. FROM: MALLOW, 20 NOVEMBER.

Text: MS PA DON I/95

My dear Columba,

I am sorry I cannot go over tomorrow. I am on sick duty: and my confreres will be both away. I wish you all a pleasant feast and happy returns. I am glad to say that Sister Ita's father is now on a fair way to recovery.

Don't be distressed because that poem was such a conundrum to you. It was so to many learned theologians and other august people. I thought I saw some meaning in it; and some poor people whom Fr Russell calls my *Sister Poets* thought it very fine. But we, poets, living up in cloudland have a language of our own and we must not be supposed to come down to small intelligences that grope their ways in the valleys. This will give you food for meditation 'till I see you again.

You heard of our concert: it was wonderful. I was never so proud of Mallow. Everything went so smoothly and the audience, comprised of all classes, was so orderly and respectable. I don't think any town in the South could produce such an entertainment. The only time in my memory that approaches, and perhaps surpasses it, is that wonderful grouping of little girls in Doneraile a couple of years ago.

The memory of that makes me jealous. It was the most artistic thing I have seen in Ireland. I wish I could produce such a tableau here.

All well here. May has developed a slight cold; and everyone else is suffering from influenza. I hope you'll have a happy feast; and that the clergy will be there in great numbers.

Best wishes to Reverend Mother,
P.A. Sheehan, C.C.

291. FROM: MALLOW, 24 DECEMBER.

Text: MS PA DON I/90.

My dear Columba,

I had made a granite, cast-iron resolution that I would not send a single Christmas card this year. But the evil things have come falling like snow-flakes upon me and I must get rid of them somehow or other. So I have picked out the prettiest and 'tis yours. I wish there were an Act of Parliament against them.

I hope you are not tired after your three hours effort the day of distribution. It was a wonderful tour-de-force.

I had a happy little letter from France. Our friend there is doing well.

Best wishes for the happy season to Reverend Mother and all friends.

Yours Always,
P.A. Sheehan

Don't be scandalized at this worldly notepaper. I must get rid of that too.

292. FROM: MALLOW, TUESDAY.

Text: MS PA DON I/97; a fragment.

My dear Columba,

A line from the midst of dust and chaos to say I got your invitation to Monday's ceremony the Friday after: and that I shall run over soon to see you and have a long talk over everything.

Could you get me a servant. I want one who would be strong and quick above all [Letter has been cut at this point]

293. FROM: NO ADDRESS

Text: PAHRC/HJHP/SL/4, Manuscript Copy[332]

Dear Mr Lysaght,

I hold you now in fee – your morning with all its dreams and despondencies and lyric tenderness, your noon with all its beautiful retrospects and hopes.

Now, let us have your evening thoughts "or the teacups" and the fire – a grand psalm of Christian hope and optimism. You can do it.

Yours etc.
P.A. Sheehan

332 A note precedes the transcription: "Acknowledging receipt of some other of his works he says".

Biographical Notes

Ashlin, Fr Stephen Coppinger (1836–1918), parish priest of Doneraile (1881–1895), brother of the architect George Coppinger Ashlin (1837–1921), and nephew of Bishop William Coppinger (1791–1831) of Cloyne and Ross. Fr Ashlin was administrator of the parish of Queenstown (Cobh) 1876–1881 and acted as an intermediary between the bishop of Cloyne and his brother during the building of Queenstown Cathedral. In 1881 he was appointed to Doneraile where he carried out substantial alterations to the interior of the parish church to plans drawn by his brother. He retired in 1895 and eventually moved to Twyford Abbey, London, where he died.

Atkins, Dr T. Gelston (1855–1924). Son of the architect William Atkins, Gelston Atkins studied medicine at the Queen's College, Cork, and qualified in surgery and midwifery. He was consulting surgeon to the Cork Maternity Hospital and surgeon to the South Charitable Infirmary, Cork City. He published extensively on midwifery, malignant diseases and gangrenous appendicitis. He was also a member of the Gynaecological Section of the Royal Society of Medicine. Dr Atkins was a member of the Fountainville, Firville, Mallow, Co. Cork branch of the Atkins family.

Baron Russell of Killowen, see Charles Arthur Russell.

Baroness Castletown of Upper Ossory (from 22 January 1883), see Lady Castletown of Upper Ossory.

Barry, Dr William (1849–1930). Born London, of Irish parents, educated at Oscott Jesuit School and at the Gregorian University, Rome, he entered priesthood in 1873; Rector of St Peter's, Leamington; Professor of Theology at Oscott 1877–1880; appointed to Dorchester in 1888. As 'Canon Barry' he wrote articles for the *Dublin Review* and the *Contemporary*. His work on the medieval papacy was censured by his Catholic superiors. His novels include *The New Antigone* (1887), a pro-Catholic novel of ideas in the form of a witty attack on free love and free-thinking, socialism and the New Woman, was reprinted three times in the year and ran to seven editions by 1906; *The Two Standards* (1898), more overtly Catholic, with an artist hero based on Wagner, satirising high finance; *Arden Massiter* (1900), its hero a young English socialist involved in Italian revolutionary politics; *The Wizard's Knot* (1900), is dedicated to Douglas Hyde and Standish H. O'Grady and finds humour in the Celtic revival; *The Place of Dreams* (1893) contains ghost-stories. He also published *The Papal Monarchy* (1902); *Newman* (1903); *Renan* (1905); *The Traditions of Scripture* (1906); *Roma Sacra* (1937); *The Triumph of Life* (1928).

Beecher, Patrick (1870–1940), ordained for Waterford and Lismore in 1896, taught in the United States and in Canada before being appointed Professor of Sacred Eloquence and Pastoral Theology at Maynooth in 1904. He published *The Holy Shroud: a reply to the Rev. Herbert Thomas, SJ* in 1928; and translated F.X. Shouppe, SJ, *The Pulpit Orator* (1914).

Belloc, Joseph Hilaire Pierre René (1870–1953) was an Anglo-French writer and historian who became a naturalised British subject in 1902. He was one of the most prolific writers in England during the early twentieth century. He was known as a writer, orator, poet, satirist, man of letters, and political activist. He is most notable for his Catholic faith, which had a strong impact on most of his works, and his writing collaboration with G.K. Chesterton. He was President of the Oxford Union and later MP for Salford from 1906 to 1910. He was a noted disputant, with a number of long-running feuds, but also widely regarded as a humane and sympathetic man.

Berry, Fr John founder of the homes for Catholic boys in Liverpool.

Birrell, Augustine (1850–1933). Politician, barrister, academic and author, he was Chief Secretary for Ireland (1907–1916) and mainly responsible for the passage of the Irish Universities Bill (1908), which established the National University of Ireland, and about which he consulted with Lord Castletown.

de la Bouillerie, Msgr. Alexandre-François-Marie Roullet (1810–1882), Bishop of Carcassonne, and subsequently Archbishop of Perga and Coadjutor of Cardinal Ferdinand François Auguste Donnet, Archbishop of Bordeaux. Eldest son of the Angevin Count de la Bouillerie, *trésorier* of Napoleon, Louis XVIII and Charles X, peer of France and Minister of State, he was born in Paris; studied for the priesthood in Rome where he was ordained in 1841 and said his first Mass in the Cappella Borghese of Santa Maria Maggiore. On his return to Paris, he taught at the seminary in Saint-Nicolas du Chardonnet before being appointed Vicar General and Archdeacon of Ste. Genviève. He was an ardent promotor of eucharistic devotion, introducing the *Quarant'Ore* to Paris as well as perpetual adoration. He was consecrated bishop of Carcassonne in 1851; transferred to Bordeaux as Coadjutor in 1872. He was a member of *L'Académie des Jeux floraux* of Toulouse, one of Europe's oldest literary academies. He died in Bordeaux in 1882. Among his writings are: *Méditations sur l'eucharistie,* Brussels 1851; *Hours before the altar: or Meditations on the Holy Eucharist*, New York, 1856; *Petits poèmes de Mgr de La Bouillerie*, Bar-le-Duc, Typographie des Célestins, 1875.

Brady, Bishop John (1840–1910), was born at Kilnaleck, Co. Cavan, educated at All Hallows College, Dublin, and ordained for the archdiocese of Boston in 1864. He was appointed titular bishop of Alabanda and auxiliary to the archbishop of Boston in 1891. He died in Boston on 6 January 1910.

Browne, Robert (1844–1935), was born at Charleville, Co. Cork, ordained for the diocese of Cloyne in 1869, dean of Maynooth 1875, Vice president 1883,

President of Maynooth 1885, and Bishop of Cloyne 1894. He completed the building of the College Chapel at Maynooth and of St Colman's Cathedral, at Cobh (Queenstown).

Browne, Wilfrid, OMI, (died 1917) was a native of the diocese of Beverley and died at Colwyn Bay.

Bruneau, Dr Joseph Marie Alexandre, SS (1866–1933). A Sulpician priest, born at Saint-Galmier, France, 18 April 1866. He studied at the seminaries of Saint-Jodard, Alix, Lyons, and Issy, and at the *Institut Catholique de Paris* with Alfred Loisy. He was ordained on 15 June 1889. His first assignment was to teach in the seminary of Autun. In 1894, he was sent to the United States, to teach Scripture and Dogma at St Mary's Seminary, Baltimore. In 1896 he was appointed superior of philosophy at St Joseph's Seminary, Dunwoodie, New York. From 1906–1909 he was superior of philosophy at St John's seminary, Brighton. In 1909, he returned to Baltimore where he remained until 1933. He was the author of numerous works on Scripture and the priesthood. He translated Sheehan's novels into French – dedicating the French translation of *My New Curate* to Yves le Querdec, *non de plume* of George Pierre Fonsegrive-Lespinasse, editor of the modernist leaning *La Quinzaine*. He died at Evian-les-Bains in the Haute-Savoie 26 August 1933. He was an early supporter of the historico-critical approach to biblical research and, along with George Tyrell and Walter McDonald, contributed to *The New York Review* which began publication in June 1905 at Dunwoodie but ceased in June 1908 in wake of the publication by Pope Pius X of *Pascendi Dominici gregis*. In the aftermath of the affair, several of the staff in Dunwoodie were transferred to parochial appointments. Bruneau had dissociated himself from the group of Sulpicians in Dunwoodie who refused to obey the orders of their Superior General and resigned from the order. During this controversy, he was transferred to Boston and eventually back to Baltimore. Fr Heuser, the editor of the *American Ecclesiastical Review* and general censor for all Catholic publications in the United States during the initial phase of the modernist crisis, continued to publish articles by Bruneau in the *Review*. Among his published works are: *The Harmony of the Gospels* (1898); *The Infancy of Christ* (with A. Durand 1910); *Our Priestly Life* (1928).

Castletown of Upper Ossory, Lady (1853–1927). The Hon. Ursula Emily Clare St Leger, only surviving child of Hayes, 4th Viscount Doneraile (1818–1887), who died of rabies contracted from a pet fox, and Mary Anne Grace Louisa Lenox-Conyngham. She married Lord Castletown of Upper Ossory in 1874. She died at Doneraile Court on 11 March 1927. Through her marriage to Lord Castletown of Upper Ossory, the management of the Doneraile estate passed into the hands of her husband. That administration proved catastrophic for the Doneraile estate. In a letter to Justice Oliver Wendell Holmes (25 March 1911), Canon Sheehan reported: "The Castletown affair was very tragic ... [Lord Castletown] sold out all the purchased estate; and had speculated wildly (so it was said) in foreign investments, which proved useless".

Castletown of Upper Ossory, Lord, Bernard Edward Barnaby FitzPatrick (1848–1937), 2nd Baron Castletown of Upper Ossory of Granston Manor in Queen's County, Co. Laois. After Eton, he graduated in law and modern history at Brasenose College, Oxford. He spoke German, French and Irish. During the Paris Commune, he served in the Red Cross ambulance corps. In 1871, he received a commission in the army and served in Egypt (1881–1882) and in South Africa during the first Boer war. Succeeding his father in the House of Lords in 1883, he pursued a moderate nationalist line which saw him supporting Home Rule, the Wyndham land act and Lord Dunraven's *Irish Reform Association*. In addition to several offices, he was Chancellor of the Royal University of Ireland (1906–1910) and supported Birrell's University Bill, the framework for which he was instrumental in developing. Lord Castletown had a passionate interest in Celtic heritage and, in 1898, was among the founders of the Celtic Association, an organisation concerned with the preservation of the languages, literature, music, dress and customs of the Celtic peoples and gave considerable assistance to Douglas Hyde in the foundation of the Gaelic League. Lord Castletown published a considerable number of short stories, articles, and works on subjects including folklore, the Fitzpatrick family, and his travels abroad. His association with Doneraile began in 1874 when he married the Hon. Ursula Clare Emily St Leger, only child of the 4th Viscount Doneraile. In 1907 he assumed the administration of Lord Doneraile's estates. An autobiography *"Ego": Random records of sport, service, and travel in many lands* was published in London in 1923, followed by *Here and there about the world* in 1932.

Coleman, Fr Ambrose OP, (1858–1942). Born at York, he studied initially at York and at Dundalk. He joined the Dominicans in 1874 and studied philosophy and theology at Tallaght, Co. Dublin and in Rome. Returning to Ireland, he was assigned to various houses of the Dominican Order including Cork, Dublin, Newbridge and Galway. Although he wrote on a wide variety of subjects, his speciality was history. He edited Stuart's *History of Armagh* and updated O'Heyne's *Irish Dominicans*. In 1897, along with Fr Glendon, he founded the *Irish Rosary*. He was a member of the Royal Irish Academy. He died at Tallaght.

Conway, Catherine (Katherine) Eleanor (1874–1926), journalist and poet. Born of Irish parents in Rochester, New York, she was educated in Rochester and Buffalo. After working as an editor and journalist in New York, she joined the Boston *Pilot* 1883. In 1904 she became the paper's first female editor. In 1908 she became editor of *The Republic*. Many of her poems, which she began to write in 1880s, concern religious themes. She was regular contributor to the *Irish Monthly* and a correspondent with Fr Matthew Russell, SJ.

Crawford, Francis Marion (1854–1909). The son of an American sculptor, he was born in Italy and educated at the universities of Cambridge, Heidelberg and Rome. Having tried to make a professional career as a baritone singer, he turned to writing. His first novel *Mr Isaac* (1882), set in colonial India, was an immediate success. In 1885, he settled in Sorrento from where he published a long series of novels and historical studies, among them *Marzio's Crucifix*, *Saracinesca* (1887), *Sant'Illario* (1889), *Greifenstein* (1889) and *Don Orsino* (1892). He died at the Villa Crawford in Sant'Agnello di Sorrento in 1909.

Cremen, Dr Patrick John (born 1844). Of Sydney Place, Cork City, he was a member of the Queen's University of Ireland and of the Royal College of Surgeons, Chief Medical Officer of the Cork Union Hospital and physician of the North Infirmary in Cork City.

Dallow, Canon Wilfred (died 1917). He was educated at Ushaw College, Durham, and matriculated at London University. He was appointed to St Werburg's, Chester (1882–1883), Seacomb (1883–1885), and parish priest of St Joseph's, Moreton, and Chaplain to Upton Hall, Birkinhead in 1885. He was elected a member of the Royal Society of Antiquaries of Ireland in 1889.

Dennehy, Henry Edward (died 1902). Parish priest of Kanturk, Co. Cork (1874–1902) and author of the historical novel *Alethea: The Parting of the Ways*, published under the pen name of Cyril by Burns and Oates in 1896. He published a further novel in 1901: *A Flower of Asia: An Indian Story*, Burns and Oates, London.

De Vere, Aubrey Thomas (1814–1902). Born at Curraghchase, Co. Limerick, he was the third son of Sir Aubrey de Vere de Vere and nephew of Lord Monteagle, Chancellor of the Irish Exchequer. In 1832, he entered Trinity College, Dublin, and graduated in 1837. From 1837–1846 he travelled in England where he came into contact with John Henry Newman. He set out for Rome 1851 in the company of Henry Edward Manning. He was received into the Catholic Church at Avignon on 15 November 1851. Newman appointed him professor of Political and Social Science at the Catholic University in Dublin. He eventually withdrew to Curraghchase where he died in 1902. Among his poetic works are: *The Sisters* (1861); *The Infant Bridal* (1864); *Irish Odes* (1869); *Legends of St Patrick* (1872); *Legends of the Saxon Saints* (1879); and *St Peter's Chains* (1888).

Egan, Maurice Francis (1852–1924). American ambassador extraordinary and minister plenipotentiary to the Kingdom of Denmark (1907–1917), he was the son of an Irish emigrant from Co. Tipperary, and a graduate of Georgetown University. His father encouraged him to pursue a career in law but he chose journalism and literature. He was professor of English at Notre Dame (1888–1896) and at the Catholic University of America (1896–1907). During the presidency of Theodore Roosevelt, he acted as an unofficial contact between the government and the American hierarchy. Roosevelt appointed him Ambassador to Denmark in 1907. A noted Catholic writer, he published several works including *Lectures on English literature,* New York 1889, *Glories of the Catholic church in art, architecture and history,* Chicago 1895, *Selections from the prose and poetry of John Henry Newman*, Boston 1907, (together with Justin McCarthy, Lady Gregory, Charles Walsh and Douglas Hyde) *Irish Literature,* Philadelphia 1904, *Ten years Near the German Frontier,* New York 1918, *Recollections of a Happy Life*, New York 1924.

Faber, Fr Frederick William (1814–1863), born at Calverley, Yorkshire, he was educated at Harrow and at Balliol College, Oxford, where he became a follower of John Henry Newman. In 1843 he was appointed rector of Elton in Huntingdonshire but resigned in 1845 and followed Newman into the Catholic Church. He founded the Wilfridians, a religious community which eventually merged with Newman's Oratory at Birmingham. Faber founded the London Oratory, initially at King William Street, and subsequently at Brompton. He was a prolific hymn writer, his most famous being *Faith of Our Fathers*, and encouraged the practice of congregational hymn singing among Catholics.

Finlay, Fr Thomas, SJ, (1848–1940), taught at the Catholic University, Dublin, member of the Senate of the National University of Ireland, trustee of the National Library of Ireland, and a commissioner for intermediate education. A prolific writer, he founded the *New Ireland Review* (1894–1911), subsequently (from 1912) *Studies.*

FitzPatrick, Bernard Edward Barnaby see Castletown of Upper Ossory.

Franzelin, Johann Baptist (1816–1886). Born in Aldein in the Südtirol, he was educated initially by the Franciscans at Bozen and subsequently by the Jesuits. He entered the Society of Jesus at Graz in 1834. He studied at Tarnapol, Lemberg and at the Collegium Romanum. He was ordained in 1849 at Le Puy in France where he taught oriental languages before being transferred to the Collegium Romanum as assistant professor of dogmatic theology and lecturer in oriental languages 1850–1857. He was a consultor for the preparation for the First Vatican Council and played a significant role in drafting the conciliar decrees. He was created Cardinal in 1876. Of his works, the most notable is: *De Divina Traditione et Scriptura* (Rome, 1870) which was considered a classic work. Others works include *De SS. Eucharistiæ Sacramento et Sacrificio* (1868);

De Sacramentis in Genere (1868); *De Deo Trino* (1869); *De Deo Uno* (1870); *De Verbo Incarnato* (1870); and *De Ecclesia Christi.*

Galbally, Edward J, (1872–1943), was born in Carslile and educated at St Cuthbert's, Newcastle and at Ushaw College, Durham. He emigrated to the United States in 1895 where he became associated with Fr Herman Joseph Heuser in the running of the *American Ecclesiastical Review*, becoming chairman of its publication committee and eventually its managing editor. In 1929 he received a doctorate in letters from St Joseph's University. He was a member and manager of the American Catholic Historical Society. In 1933, through the Dolphin Press, for which he had responsibility, he published *Herman Joseph Heuser DD; founder of the Ecclesiastical Review*. He was also responsible for the editing and publication of Fr Heuser's biography of Canon Sheehan and brought the proofs to Doneraile where they were corrected by Mother Ita.

Gibbons, Cardinal James (1834–1921), Bishop of Richmond and subsequently Archbishop of Baltimore.

Grove White, Colonel James, (1852–1938) of Kilbyrne, Doneraile and Kyrenia, Cyprus. Born aboard HMS Vulcan, then anchored in Melbourne harbour, he joined the British army and received a commission into the 51st regiment and the Middlesex Regiment. He saw action in the Zulu wars and in the Boer wars. In retirement, he devoted himself to antiquarian and historical research and was a regular contributor to the *Journal of the Cork Historical and Archaeological Society*. His *Historical and Topographical Notes, Etc. on Buttevant: Castletownroche, Doneraile, Mallow, and Places in Their Vicinity* (1905–1913) is a primary source for the history of North Cork.

Hawker, Robert Stephen (1803–1875). Son of a medical doctor, he was born in Plymouth; educated by his grand-father, a Calvinist minister, and at Cheltenham Grammar School, he went up to Pembroke College, Oxford, in 1822. Married Charlotte Eliza I'Ans in 1823; took his BA in 1828 and MA in 1836. He was ordained a deacon in 1829 and priest in 1831 by the Bishop of Bath and Wells. He was appointed to Morwenstow in 1835. Mrs. Hawker, who was a good German scholar and had translated Schiller and Goethe, died in 1863. Hawker married secondly Pauline Kuczynski in 1864 and by her had three daughters: Morwenna Pauline (1865), Rosalind (1867) and Juliot (1869). His declining health obliged him to move to Plymouth. On 14th August 1875 he was received into the Catholic Church. He died the following day and was buried in Plymouth. Among his publications are: *Tendrils* (published under the name of Ruben), London 1821; *Pompeii*, Oxford 1827; *Records of the Western Shore*, Oxford 1832; *Poems,* Stratton 1836;

Ecclesia: A Volume of Poems, London 1846; *The Poetical Works of Robert Stephen Hawker*, London 1879.

Henry, H.T. professor of music at St Charles Seminary, Overbrook, Philadelphia. He published several volumes of poetry and hymns with the *Dolphin Press.* He was a long time contributor to the *American Ecclesiastical Review.*

Heine, Christian Johann Heinrich (1797–1856), born in Düsseldorf to a Jewish family and initially destined for commerce, was educated at Bonn and Göttingen, where he studied law. He began writing poetry before 1820 and published his volume, *Gedichte*, in 1822. His 1824 visit to Luneburg, Cuxhaven, Heligoland, Hamburg, and the Harz eventually resulted in the satirical *Die Harzreise* (1826–1831) which attracted lasting attention. In 1827, he published his most important work, *Buch de Lieder*, a collection of poems of dreams and romantic melancholy. Heine moved to Paris in 1834 and earned a living as a journalist and correspondent for the *Allgemeine Zeitung* mainly on political and social questions as well as on the history of literature. On completion of the doctorate at Göttingen in 1825, he was baptized and in 1841 married Eugénie Mathilde Mirat.

Heuser, Herman Joseph (1851–1933), was a prominent Catholic intellectual and prolific writer who influenced scholarly and clerical life in the United States and abroad through his publications, including the journal the *American Ecclesiastical Review* (1889–1975), which he edited for many years. Born on 23 October 1851 in Potsdam, Germany, Fr Heuser was the first child of Herman Joseph and Julia Neese Heuser, and had a sister two years his junior, Julia. Heuser attended secondary schools in Berlin and Breslau focusing on religious education. He also took classes in science, language, art and music. His family emigrated to the United States in 1867 leaving him behind to continue his studies in Breslau. He emigrated to the United States at the age of seventeen and in 1868 he began to attend a diocesan preparatory seminary in Glen Riddle, PA, where he served as a 'seminarian professor', leading instruction in Latin, French and Gregorian chant. In 1871 he began teaching at St Charles Borromeo Seminary at its new campus in Overbrook, PA. Following his ordination on 2 February 1876, he was appointed seminary professor at Overbrook and taught there for over fifty years. Heuser also served as an adviser to the Pontifical Commission on Anglican Orders in 1896. In 1905 Heuser received a Doctor of Divinity, *honoris causa* from Pope Pius X. In 1907, during the Modernist controversy, Heuser was appointed by the Apostolic Delegate as general censor for all Catholic publications in the United States. Along with editing the *American Ecclesiastical Review*, Heuser also organized and directed the Dolphin Press of Philadelphia, which printed many ecclesiastical works. From 1900 to 1908 he published *The Dolphin*, a general Catholic literary magazine that began as a book supplement to the

American Ecclesiastical Review. His biography of Canon Sheehan of Doneraile was published by Longmans of London and New York in 1917.

Hinkson, Henry Albert (1865–1919) barrister and novelist, husband of Katerine Tynan.

Hodkinson, James and Company. Ecclesiastical painters and decorators, the Company was founded in 1852 by James Hodkinson (1826–1916) who trained under A.W.N. Pugin. James Hodkinson was born in Manchester and went into business, decorating Cathedrals and Churches throughout England, Scotland and Ireland. In 1862, seeing a business opportunity, James Hodkinson moved permanently to Ireland, settling in Cork and subsequently at Henry Street, in Limerick in 1876. James Hodkinson was succeeded by his sons Louis, Harry and Alfred in 1916, and eventually by Louis's sons Aubrey and Malcolm in 1955; and finally in 2004 by Aubrey's son Randel Hodkinson. James Hodkinson and Company decorated the Chapel and the Mortuary Chapel at Doneraile Convent in the 1880s. The Company painted the Convent Chapel in 1919 and again in 1960.

Hogan, Dr John (1858–1918), born at Coolragh, Co. Clare, studied at St Sulpice, Paris, and at Freiburg-im-Breisgau. He was ordained for the diocese of Killaloe in 1882, appointed professor of Modern Languages at Maynooth in 1886, editor of the *Irish Ecclesiastical Record* in 1892, Vice President of Maynooth in 1910 and President in 1912. He died in 1918. Among his publications are *The Life and Works of Dante Alighieri*, London 1899; *Irish Catholics and Trinity College*, Dublin 1907; *Maynooth College and the Laity*, Dublin 1910. In 1902, he published a critique of *Luke Delmege* in the *Irish Ecclesiastical Record.*

Hogan, Fr John Baptist, (the Abbé Hogan) (1829–1901). Born Ennis, Co. Clare, he was reared in France by his uncle who was priest of the diocese of Périgueux. Educated at the seminaries of Bordeaux, he transferred to the seminary of Saint Sulpice in Paris in 1849. He joined the Sulpicians and was ordained in 1852. He was professor at Saint Sulpice 1852–1883; first president of the newly founded Theological Seminary in Boston 1884–1889; president of the graduate Theological Seminary of the Catholic University of America at Washington 1889–1894; and president of St John's Seminary, Brighton, Massachusetts 1894–1901. He received Dr James Field Spalding into the Catholic Church at Washington on 15 January 1892. He published *Clerical Studies*, in the *American Ecclesiastical Review* 1891–95.

Holmes, Oliver Wendell, Jr (1841–1935), an American jurist and Associate Justice of the Supreme Court of the United States (1902–1932). He was noted for his long service, his concise and pithy opinions and his deference to the decisions of elected legislatures. He is one of the most widely cited United States Supreme Court justices in history and is one of the most influential American common law judges through his judicial restraint philosophy. Holmes retired from the Court at the age of 90. He also served as an Associate Justice and as Chief Justice on the Massachusetts Supreme Judicial Court, and was Weld Professor of Law at the Harvard Law School, of which he was an alumnus. His correspondence with Canon Sheehan was published in 1974.

Horgan, John Joseph (1881–1967) born in Cork, educated by the Jesuits at Clongowes Wood, he qualified as a solicitor in 1902. His uncle had been a curate in Mallow and had had the young Sheehan in his choir. He was actively involved in nationalist politics, served as chairman of the Cork Opera House and on the board of the Cork Harbour Commission. Among his published works are: *Great Catholic Laymen,* Dublin 1905; *Home Rule, a Critical Consideration* (1911); *The Complete Grammar of Anarchy,* Dublin 1918; *From Parnell to Pearse: Some Recollections and Reflections*; Dublin 1948.

Hudson, Fr Daniel Elred (1849–1934). Born near Boston, he entered the Congregation of the Holy Cross at Notre Dame in 1871 and was ordained in 1875. After ordination, he was appointed editor of *Ave Maria,* a weekly magazine, and remined as editor until 1929. His correspondence includes letters from Fr Herman Heuser, Fr Matthew Russell, SJ, Maurice Francis Egan, as well as from Canon Sheehan of Doneraile.

Huysmans, Charles-Marie-Georges (1848–1907), French novelist who published under the name of Joris-Karl Huysmans. Born in Paris to a Dutch father and French mother, his father died when he was eight years old. For more than thirty years he worked in the French interior ministry. In 1874, he published *Le drageoir aux épices,* a collection of poems influenced by Charles Baudelaire. His early novels, *Marthe, Histoire d'une fille* (1876), *Les Sœurs Vatard* (1879), *Sac au dos* (1880), *En ménage* (1881) and *À vau-l'eau* (1882), concieved within a circle which included Guy de Maupassant, Léon Hennique, Henry Céard, all reflect the influence of Zola's naturalism. His succeeding novel, *À rebours* (1884) amounted to an experiment in decadent literature which Zola disowned. From decadence, Huysmans moved towards the symbolism of Stéphane Mallarmé and to Catholic writers such as Jules Barbey d'Aurevilly, Villiers de L'Isle Adam and Léon Bloy. *En rade* and *Là-Bas* appeared in 1887 and in 1891, the former, an exercise in brutal realism, the latter expressing a thinly disguised autobiographical and pessimistic disgust of the modern world and an attempt to find an alternative in the middle ages which led him to historical and contemporary satanism. In 1895, Huysmans converted to the Catholic Church and describes that long and painful process in his novel *En route* (1895). *La cathédrale* (1898) is a study in symbolism in the context of the cathedral of Chartres and was followed by several papers on the majesty and beauty of Christian art and architecture. *L'oblat* (1903) is an account of his attempts to live the monastic life. Huysmans' conversion is to be seen in the context of a spate of similar conversions among French writers which included Paul Bourget, Charles Péguy, Ferdinand Brunetière, Paul Claudel, Léon Bloy, François Mauriac and Jacques Maritain. As one of the principal exponents of the *renouveau catholique,* he died in Paris on 12 May 1907.

Keller, Canon Daniel (1839–1922). Born at Iniscarra, Co. Cork and educated at the Vincentian Shcools in Cork, at Maynooth and Paris where he was ordained in 1862. He was apointed curate of Killeagh, Professor at St Colman's College, Fermoy and curate in Queenstown from where he was appointed parish priest of Youghal in 1885. He succeeded as dean of the Cathedral Chapter in 1899. He had been incarcerated for his activities during the agrarian troubles surrounding the Plan of Campaign (1886–1891). He had been proposed by the parish priests of Cloyne as one of the candidates for the provision of the see of Cloyne in 1894. He was friendly with Sheehan and invited him to spend the second half of his period of convalescence at St Mary's Presbytery, Youghal, in 1889.

Kelly, Fr Charles, DD, parish priest of Towanda, PA (1876–1899), in the diocese of Scranton.

Laffan, Josephine May see May Sheehan.

Lady Gilbert, see Rosa Mulholland.

Lord Chief Justice, see Charles Arthur Russell.

Lord Killowen, see Charles Arthur Russell.

Lowell, James Russell (1819–1891). American poet, politician, and diplomat, he was born at Cambridge, Massachusetts, and graduated with a law degree from Harvard Law School. He was appointed professor of languages at Harvard in 1854. He campaigned against slavery. In 1857 he became editor of *The Atlantic Monthly*. In 1877, he was appointed ambassador to the Court of Spain and remained there until 1880 when he was appointed American ambassador to the Court of St James's. He returned to the United States in 1885. His published poetical works include: *Year's Life* (1841); *Miscellaneous Poems* (1843); *The Biglow Papers* (1848); *A Fable for Critics* (1848); *Poems* (1848); *The Vision of Sir Launfal* (1848); *Under the Willows* (1869); *The Cathedral* (1870); and *Heartsease and Rue* (1888).

Lysaght, Sidney Royse (1856–1941). A poet, novelist and landowner in the parish of Doneraile with substantial interests in the iron and steel industry in England and Australia, he married Kathrine Clarke of Waddington, Lines, in 1886. Their son, Edward Edgeworth MacLysaght (born 1887), was a Member of Irish Free State Senate, genealogist and Chief Herald of Ireland. Among his poems are: *A Modern Ideal* (1886); *Horizons and Landmarks* (1899); *Poems of the Unknown Way* (1901). His novels include: *The Marplot* (1893); *Her Majesty's Rebels* (1907); *My Tower in Desmond* (1925); and *The Immortal Jew* (1931).

Malebranche, Nicholas (1638–1715). French Oratorian and rationalist philosopher. In his works, he sought to synthesize the thought of St Augustine and Descartes, in order to demonstrate the active role of God in every aspect of the world. Malebranche is best known for his doctrines of Vision in God and Occasionalism. Known by many as "The Occasional Philosopher," a term coined by David Hume.

Mannix, Daniel (1864–1963). Born Charleville, Co. Cork, ordained for the diocese of Cloyne 1890; Professor of Philosophy and Theology at Maynooth 1891–1894; vice president and President of Maynooth 1903. Named titular Bishop Pharsalia and Coadjutor of the Archbishop of Melbourne on 1 July 1912, he was consecrated on 5 October 1912 and succeeded to the archdíocese in 1917.

Mauri, Prof. Angelo (1873–1936). Born in 1873, he pursued a brilliant academic career which saw him obtain the doctorate in Law at the University of Genoa, as well as doctorates in literature and philosophy at the University at Milan and a doctorate in economics at Freiburg. He practised as a lawyer but was drawn to journalism, working briefly at *Il Corriere della Domenica* and *La Rassegna Sociale* before assuming a position at *L'Osservatore Cattolico* in Milan. He moved to Turin at the request of Cardinal Richlmey as editor of his newspaper, *Il Momento*. Through his involvement with the *Congresso Nazionale Cattolico*, he was increasingly drawn into the Catholic political sphere of Giuseppe Toniolo and Padre Antonio Gemelli. Through concerted activity, the government of the city of Milan was taken from the liberals and anti-clericals. His involvement in politics evolved onto national level through his work with the *Partito Popolare* for which he was elected a deputy to the Italian Parliament and was nominated minister for agriculture in the short lived government dismissed in 1924. With the rise of Mussolini to power, he retired to private life having adopted a clearly anti-fascist position. For a time, he taught economics at the Catholic University of Milan. Mauri recognised the importance of Canon Sheehan's writings for his Catholic movement and undertook their translation and serialization in *L'Osservatore Cattolico*. He died in 1936. His publications include: *Il salario libero e la concorrenza servile in Atene* (1895); *I cittadini lavoratori dell'Attica nei secoli V e VI a.C.* (1895); *L'Hofrecht in Italia* (1895); *L'abate Naudet* (1896); *La crisi rurale in Italia* (1897); *Le finanze di Milano nel Medioevo* (1898); *Idee municipaliste* (1899); *Un programma sociale* (1908); *Per i paria della proprietà* (1918); *La guerra del petrolio* (1923); *I nuovi sviluppi dell'economia agraria* (1927); *La dottrina economica di Pietro Verri*, (1929).

McCarthy, John (1815–1893), born at Fermoy, Co. Cork, educated at Maynooth, ordained 1842, was curate and parish priest of Mallow for 35 years, appointed Bishop of Cloyne 1874, he died in 1893. He became legal guardian of the Sheehan children following the death of their mother in 1864.

Meynell, Wilfrid (1852–1948), newspaper publisher and editor sometimes writing under the pseudonym John Oldcastle. Born in 1852 to Quaker parents, he converted to Catholicism in 1870. He was introduced to publication by the Catholic-convert Fr William Lockhart, who was his model for professional Catholic journalism and Christian charity. Meynell married writer and poet Alice C. Thompson in1877. They had seven children. He became editor of the *Weekly Register* and founded the magazine *Merry England* in 1883. Meynell wrote several books and supported the work of literary figures, including the poet Francis Thompson whom he rescued from dissipation.

Miller, Joaquin Miller (1837–1913) *nom de plume* of the American poet Cincinnatus Heine Miller, the "Poet of the Sierras", also known as the "Byron of the Rockies". Born in Indiana, he began publishing in 1868 with a volume entitled *Specimens*. While in London in 1871, he attracted considerable notice in literary circles and published *Songs of the Sierras* which was favourably received by figures such as Dante Gabriele Rossetti. He eventually settled in California from where he published a long series of poetical works which included *The Danites of the Sierras* (1910).

Morton, Edmond, educated in Paris, was ordained for the diocese of Cloyne and served as a curate with Patrick Augustine Sheehan in Mallow. Fr Morton was appointed parish priest of Ballyhea in 1902 and died on 2 December 1931.

Mother Alphonsus (1852–1938). Ellen O'Keeffe, born 1852 to Daniel and Mary O'Keeffe of Glountane, Co. Cork; entered St Joseph's Presentation Convent, Doneraile, 1874; received into the community 1875; made final profession 1877; died 1938. She was Superioress of the convent for three terms: 1900–1906; 1912–1918; 1924–1930.

Mother Austin (1835–1909). Born Margaret Anne Carroll to William and Margaret Carroll of Clonmel, Co. Tipperary, she entered the Sisters of Mercy at St Marie of the Isles, Cork City, in 1853 and made religious profession under the name of Sister Teresa Austin in 1856, and left as a missionary for Providence, Rhode Island. Between 1857–1859 she was assigned to the communities in Hartford, Rochester, Buffalo and Manchester. At the request of her religious superiors, she began to collect material to compile a biography of Mother Catherine McCauley, foundress of the Sisters of Mercy, which was published in St Louis in 1866. She was part of the founding group of nuns in Omaha, Nebraska, and subsequently of the group of nuns who founded the institute in new Orleans in 1869, where she was superior and mistress of novices from 1869–1891. She initiated numerous projects among the white and black populations of Mississippi, Florida, and Alabama, and Belize in Central America. She wrote numerous books, articles and other publications and translated many of the French spiritual classics into English to support the work of her community. She also published *Leaves of the Annals of the Sisters* *of Mercy* in 1881, 1883, and 1889. In 1891, she left the motherhouse in New Orleans to found the Mercy Order in Alabama at Selema, but transferred the motherhouse to Mobile in 1895. She was a close friend of Mother Baptist in San Francisco. She died on 29 November 1909.

Mother Baptist (1829–1898). Born Katherine Russell, third child of Arthur and Margaret Russell of Newry, Co. Down, she entered the Sisters of Mercy in 1848 at Kinsale, Co. Cork on the advice of her uncle, Charles Russell, President of Maynooth. Professed in 1851, she was chosen to lead a group of sisters to found a convent in San Francisco. She embarked from Dublin in August 1854, and sailed to Nicuragua from Liverpool. Having crossed the isthmus of Nicuragua, she embarked on the steam ship *Cortes* for San Francisco, where she landed on 8 December 1854. Very quickly she established a convent and founded St Mary's Hospital in 1857 as well as schools, orphanages, and homes for destitute women. From San Francisco, the community spread to Sacramento and elsewhere in California. She was a sister of Fr Matthew Russell, SJ, editor of the *Irish Monthly*, and of Lord Killowen, Lord Chief Justice of England 1894–1900.

Mother Berchmans of Jesus (1850–1898). Ellen Fitzpatrick born 1850 to Denis Fitzpatrick and Mary Slattery of Effin, Co. Limerick; entered St Joseph's Presentation Convent, Doneraile, 1869; made final profession 1870; died 1898. She was Superioress 1894–1897.

Mother Bridget (1851–1915). Kate Kearney, born 1851 to Edmond Kearney and Ellen O'Gorman of Effin, Co. Limerick; entered St Joseph's Presentation Convent, Doneraile, 1875; received into the community 1876; made final profession 1878; died 1915. She was Superioress from 1897–1900.

Mother Catherine (d. 1912). Elizabeth Cheevers of New Ross, Co. Wexford, entered the Convent of Mercy, Mallow, Co. Cork in 1864. She had spent most of her early life in Illinois, U.S.A.. Professed in 1866, she was superioress of the founding community in Kanturk, Co. Cork, in 1868. There she began primary and secondary schools and undertook the provision of nursing care in the local poor house. She was recalled to Mallow as superioress in 1890. Here she expanded the convent primary and secondary schools using the proceeds of a family legacy which came to her from the United States. She died in 1912.

Mother Francis (d. 1933). Mary O'Connell of Knocknanuss, Ballyclough, Co. Cork, was the eldest of five O'Connell sisters to enter the Convent of Mercy at Mallow, Co. Cork. She entered in 1859 and was professed in 1861. She was among the founding group of the Convent of Mercy at Kanturk, Co. Cork. She eventually returned to Mallow, where she died in 1933.

Mother Ita Ignatius (1867–1950). Presentation Convent, Doneraile, she was born Hannah O'Connell on 22 March 1867 to John O'Connell and Johanna McAuliffe of Knockane, Ballyclough, Co. Cork. She entered religious life on

8 December 1888 and made final profession on 9 January 1891. A cousin of Canon Sheehan, she acted as his confidential advisor and parochial secretary for many years, examining and proof reading his manuscripts, as well as offering critical comment on them. She commissioned Fr Herman Heuser, to write Sheehan's biography and supplied him with the Canon's papers for that purpose as well as material collected from his circle of friends and correspondents. In order to ensure early publication of the book, she came to an arrangement with the chief military censor to have packets containing the material for the biography expedited directly from his office in London to the United States. Mother Ita served as Superioress of the convent for three terms: 1906–1912; 1918–1924; 1930–1936. She died on 10 December 1950.

Mulholland, Rosa (1841–1921). Irish novelist, poetess and playwright. Born in Belfast, she originally wished to become a painter but, with encouragement from Charles Dickens, she persevered with writing. Following the publication of her poem *Irene* in the *Cornhill* magazine with illustration by Sir John Millais, her first novel, *Dunmara*, was published in 1864 under the pen name of Ruth Murray. In 1891, she married John Thomas Gilbert, librarian of the Royal Irish Academy, who was knighted in 1897 in recognition of his services to archaeology and history. Subsequently, she lived at Villa Nova, Blackrock, Co. Dublin. In addition to more than thirty novels and children's stories, Lady Gilbert also published (1905) a biography of her husband. Her literary circle included Katherine Tynan, Sarah Atkinson, Charlotte O'Connor Eccles, John Shaw, editor of the *Evening Mail* and George Atkinson, proprietor of the *Freeman's Journal*. Her sister, Ellen, married Charles Arthur Russell, Baron Killowen, a nephew of Dr Russell, President of Maynooth College, and brother of Fr Matthew Russell, SJ, editor of the *Irish Monthly*.

Murphy, Katharine Mary (1840–1885). Born in Ballyhooly, Co. Cork, she contributed poetry and prose compositions to the *The Nation*, *The Boston Pilot*, *Sharp's London Magazine*, and *Punch*, under pseudonyms including "Brigid", "Bessie" and "Elizabeth Townbridge". She succeeded to her father's coal business on Pope's Quay in Cork. She was related to the fiction writer and journalist Denis Holland (c.1826-1872) and to the eminent London physician Sir Richard Quain of Carrigoon, Mallow, Co. Cork. Her sister died in infancy, her brother became a distinguished medical doctor in Australia. She died on 10 April 1885 at the North Infirmary in Cork and was buried at Ballyhooly. Among her best works are: *Condemned to Death, Just for My Mother* and *How Tom Dillon Became a Zouave*. Cf. *Our Poets, no. XIV, Katharine Murphy, "Brigid"*, in *Irish Monthly*, vol. 13, n. 146 (August 1885), pp. 433-440; Richard Nagle, *The Popular Poets of Ireland*, Boston 1887, pp. 607-630; and also Letter no. 2, p. 35.

O'Brien, Fr John (1838–1917). Born at Garrenjames, Imogeela, Co. Cork, he emigrated to the United States with his parents in 1850 and went to work on a vegetable farm run by his uncle, William Foley. His interest in the priesthood was aroused in 1856 by the Reverend Maurice Power, parish priest of Killeagh, who was collecting funds for the building of Killeagh church and stayed with the O'Brien family. He studied at St Charles Academy and at St Joseph's Seminary, Troy, New York, and was ordained in 1868. Following ordination, he was appointed Charlestown, Mass., as a curate and in 1871 to Concorde, Mass, as parish priest. He was transferred to East Cambridge in 1873 and remained there until his death in 1917. In 1888 he founded the *Sacred Heart Review* as a local publication but it quickly developed into a national publication and was formally incorporated in 1894 with Fr John Colbert as executive editor. The motto of the Review was*: A Catholic Newspaper in a parish in perpetual mission* while the sub-title read: *To select well among old things is almost equal to inventing them.* The *Review* contained sections dealing with local, national and international news, and had a nation-wide subscriber base. It was important for its reporting of the Catholic Church in general and the Church in New England in particular; its pieces that explicate and defend Catholicism; and its advertisements. A complete series of the *Review*, running to 60 volumes, is conserved in the library of Boston College.

O'Brien, Mrs William, see Sophie Raffalovich.

O'Brien, William, MP, (1852–1928), son of a solicitor's clerk, was born at Mallow, Co. Cork. He was educated in Mallow and at Fermoy before commencing law studies at the Queen's College in Cork. He began a career as a journalist with the *Cork Daily Herald* and eventually moved to the *Freeman's Journal.* In 1881, he became editor of the *United Irishman,* an organ of the Irish National Land League. Increasing involvement with the land agitation of the 1880s, he developed and implemented the no-rent campaign. In 1883, he was elected MP for Mallow, beginning a political career which would see him representing a number of Irish constituencies until 1918. In 1890, he published a novel *When We Were Boys.* He married Sophie Raffalovich the same year. Her considerable fortune and moral support ensured that O'Brien continued his political and journalistic career with independence. In the Parnell crisis, he favoured neither side in the split in the Irish Parliamentary Party. In 1898, he established the *United Irish League* dedicated to agrarian reform and Home Rule. In 1909, he founded the All-for-Ireland League, a movement which was politically conciliatory and which attempted to win over unionists to the Home Rule cause. In 1910, he founded the *Cork Free Press* which acted as an organ for the new political movement. He stood aside at the 1918 election thereby making his seat available to Sinn Féin. Among his publications are: *Christmas on the Galtees*, Dublin, 1878; *Irish Ideas,* London, 1893; *A Queen of Men, Grace*

O'Malley, London,1898; *Recollections*, New York, 1905; *An Olive Branch in Ireland,* London, 1910; *The Downfall of Parliamentarianism*, Dublin/London, 1918; *Evening Memories being a Continuation of Recollections,* Dublin, 1920; *The Responsibility for Partition,* Dublin/London, 1921; *The Irish Revolution and how it came about,* London, 1923; *Edmund Burke as an Irishman,* Dublin, 1924.

O'Connell, Hannah see Mother Ita Ignatius.

Phelan, Fr Michael (1858 –1934), born Johnstown, Co. Kilkenny, he was educated at Carlow College and ordained for the the diocese of Golbourne in Australia in 1880. He joined the Jesuits in 1893. His younger brother was Bishop of Sale in Victoria.

Porter, George, SJ, (1825–1890), Archbishop of Bombay.

Plunkett, Sir Horace (1854–1932) was a pioneer of the agricultural co-operative movement and opened Ireland's first cooperative at Doneraile.

Raffalovich, Sophie (1860–1960), daughter of the Russian Jewish banker Herman Raffalovich and his wife Marie, was born in Odessa and reared in Paris. Her elder brother, Arthur Germanovich Raffalovich, was the London financial agent for the Imperial Russian Government and a noted economist, while her younger brother was Marc-André Raffalovich, the French poet and patron of the arts. In June 1890, she married William O'Brien and, with her wealth, financed his political and journalistic career. She converted to Catholicism prior to her marriage and in her writings promoted themes current among writers associated with the *renouveau catholique*. She frequently published in the *Irish Monthly,* and the *Catholic Bulletin*. Books published by her include *Under Croagh Patrick*, London 1904; *Silhouettes Irlandaises: au pied de Croagh Patrick,* Paris, Guillaumin 1904; *Rosette a tale of Paris & Dublin*, London 1907; *Unseen friends,* London/New York 1912; *In Mallow*, New York, 1920; *Around Broom Lane*, London 1931; *My Irish friends*, Dublin/London 1937. Following her husband's death, she returned to France where she escaped deportation during the Nazi occupation. She died at Eplessin, near Amiens, in 1960.

Reade, Charles (1814–1884), son a country squire from Ipsden in Oxfordshire, he was a fellow of Magdalen College, Oxford, barrister, novelist and dramatist, best known for his novels *The Cloister and the Hearth* (1861) and *Hard Cash* (1863). He was regarded as Dicken's natural successor and enjoyed much popularity during his lifetime. His novels were imbued with a scientifically researched and minute realism, the details of which often overpower his narrative.

Ruskin, John (1819–1900). Only son of wine merchant who had made a considerable fortune, he became the first Slade Professor of art at Oxford. He travelled widely in Britain, France and Northern Italy and devoted much time to writing, drawing and painting. He documented medieval architecture before its destruction through neglect, restoration, industrialization and revolution. His first book, *Modern Painters* (1866) was a defence of Turner. He published his *Stones of Venice* (1851–1853). From the 1850s, under the influence of Carlyle, his attention turned to social and political matters. Initially, Ruskin support the naturalist school of painting but subsequently supported the Pre-Raphaelite movement which he regarded as capable of promoting a complete reform of art and society. Ruskin came to believe that the objective of art was to communicate truth and the moral outlook of the artist. From 1878, Ruskin suffered intermittent bouts of mental instability. He died in London.

Roz, Firmin (1866–1957). Born at Limoges, he was a teacher, essayist, critic and historian. He wrote extensively on the United States and on English literature, including *Le roman anglais contemporain* (Paris, Hachette, 1912) as well as publishing a series of articles on Ireland in *La Revue politique et littéraire* for 1904 having been a guest of Lord Castletown at Doneraile Court in 1903. He was elected to the *Académie des sciences morales et politiques* in 1936. He died in Paris in 1957.

Russell, Charles Arthur (1832–1900), born at Newry, Co. Down, educated St Malachy's College, Belfast and at Castleknock College, Dublin, he qualified as a solicitor in 1854. Called to the English Bar in 1859, he took silk in 1872. He was widely regarded as the foremost advocate of his generation. He was MP for Dundalk 1880–1885 and for Hackney South 1885–1894. Appointed attorney general in 1886, he was named Lord of Appeal in Ordinary in 1894 and raised to the peerage taking the title of Baron Russell of Killowen, in the County of Down. In the same year he was appointed Lord Chief Justice of England, the first Catholic to attain that office since the reformation. In 1858, he married Ellen Mulholland, sister of the writer Rosa Mulholland. Three of his sisters were nuns and his brother, Matthew, became a Jesuit and, subsequently, editor of the *Irish Monthly*. He was a nephew of Dr Charles William Russell, President of Maynooth 1857–1880. His account of a trip to the United States was published as *Diary of a Visit to the United States of American in the Year 1883*, New York 1910. He also wrote *New Views On Ireland. or, Irish Land: Grievances: Remedies*, London 1880; *Arbitration: Its Origin, History, and Prospects: Address to the Saratoga Congress*, 1896.

Russell, Matthew, SJ (1834–1912). Born in Newry, Co. Down, he was educated by the Vincentians at Castleknock and at Maynooth. In 1857, he entered the Jesuits and was ordained in 1864. In 1873, he founded *The Irish Monthly* which was initially to have been a devotional magazine but quickly developed into a literary publication. He remained editor of the magazine until his death. Among contributors to the magazine were Denis Florence MacCarthy, Lady Fullerton, Charles Gavan Duffy, Stephen Brown, Dora Sigerson, Rev. T.A.

Finlay, Rose Kavanagh, John O'Leary and his sister Ellen, W.B. Yeats, George Sigerson, Mary Fagan, Frances Wynne, Oscar Wilde, M.E. Francis, Katherine Tynan, and Hilaire Belloc. He published: *Erin – Verses Irish and Catholic* (1889); *Vespers and Compline: A Soggarth's Sacred Verses* (1900); and *The Life of Mother Mary Baptist Russell. Sister of Mercy* (1901); *At Home Near The Altar* (1911). He was also a regular contributor to *Ave Maria* magazine published by Fr Daniel Hudson of Notre Dame, South Bend, Indiana.

Russell, Katherine (1829–1898), see Mother Baptist.

Ryan, Margaret Mary, published poems in the *Irish Monthly* from 1874 to at least 1900. She lived at 4 St Joseph's Place, Kilkenny. A letter from her is mentioned in the calendar of Canon Sheehan's manuscripts published in *Journal of the Mallow Field Club,* no 20 [2002], p. 74. In her reply of 4 March 1904, Miss Ryan strongly encourages Canon Sheehan to commence writing his *Life of Christ* which he intended as a response to Ernest Renan's *Vie de Jésus* (1863).

Sheedy, Morgan Madden (1853–1939), following matriculation, he was admitted to the first philosophy class at Maynooth on 27 September 1871 as a student for the diocese of Cloyne. In 1876, he went to the United States where he settled in Pittsburg. He was ordained on 23 September 1876 by Bishop John Tuigg, following which he was appointed professor at St Michael's seminary in Pittsburg. From 1881 he held a number of pastoral appointments before his nomination to Altoona in 1894, where he served for 45 years. He published frequently in the *American Ecclesiastical Review.* Following Canon Sheehan's death he collected funds in the United States on behalf of the Mallow monument committee. Father Sheedy was also the first rector of the Cathedral, when the Diocese of Altoona was established in 1901. He is buried in the courtyard between the Rectory and the Cathedral. He died 25 October 1939.

Sheehan, Bernard Augustine (b. 1902). Canon Sheehan's nephew, born in Dublin in January 1902. He was known as Jeff.

Sheehan, Denis Bernard (b. 1854). Canon Sheehan's younger brother was born in 1854. He entered the Irish Civil Service and became an auditor of the Board of Local Government in 1895 and was assigned to various postings throughout Ireland including Monaghan, Dublin, Clonmel, and Queenstown. He was executor of Canon Sheehan's will in which capacity he had the disposal of his papers, many of which he passed to the Presentation Convent Doneraile.

Sheehan, Eva. Canon Sheehan's niece, born in March 1911.

Sheehan, Hannah see Sr Columba.

Sheehan, May (b. 1876). Josephine Mary Laffan of Cloverhill, Pallas Green, Co. Limerick, was born in 1876. She married Denis Bernard Sheehan at Cloverfied in March 1901.

Sigerson, Dora (1866–1918), daughter of the Dublin surgeon and author George Sigerson and of the writer Hester Varian, began publishing poetry in 1893. She quickly became a notable figure in the Irish Literary Revival counting Alice Furlong, Rose Kavanagh, and Katherine Tynan in her circle of literary friends. In 1895, she married the English journalist and critic Clement Shorter. Among her publications are: *Verses*, London 1893; *The Fairy Changeling and other poems*, London 1898; *Ballads and Poems*, London 1899; *The Country House Party*, London 1905; *The Story and Ballad of Black Roderick*, London 1906;*The Troubadour and Other Poems*, London 1910; *The Sad Years*, London 1918; *Sixteen Dead Men and Other Poems of Easter Week*, Dublin 1919; *The Legend of Glandalough and Other Ballads*, Dublin/London 1921; *Love of Ireland: Ballads and Poems*, Dublin/London 1921; *The Tricolour: Poems of the Irish Revolution*, Dublin 1922; *The Sparks they Flew Upward*, London n.d.; *The Woman who Went to Hell*; London n.d..

Smith, William (1808–1872) philosopher, poet, and writer, educated at Radley school and Glasgow University. His poems *Guidone* and *Solitude* were published together in 1836. In 1839 he published his *Discourse on Ethics of the School of Paley*. In the same year he began his connection with *Blackwood's Magazine* which continued to nearly the end of his life. His novel, *Ernesto*, a story connected with the conspiracy of Fiesco, appeared in 1835. In 1851 he received an offer from Professor Wilson to supply temporarily his place as professor of moral philosophy at Edinburgh, but he was diffident, and had begun to write *Thorndale*, and the tempting offer was declined. *Thorndale, or the Conflict of Opinions*, was published in 1857, and, notwithstanding its length, speedily gained acceptance. *Gravenhurst, or Thoughts on Good and Evil*, was published in the same year. It confirmed and extended the reputation acquired by *Thorndale*. His health began to decline in 1869, and he died at Brighton on 28 March 1872.

Spalding, Dr James Field (1839–1921). Born at Enfield, Hartford, Connecticut, to Asa Leffingwell Spalding and Mary Reynolds Dixon, he was educated at Williston Seminary, and entered Williams College, as Freshman, in 1857. During 1863–64 he was Tutor in Greek at the College, 1863–1864; and from 1865 to 1870 Associate Master of Round Hill School in Northampton. In 1869 he entered the ministry of the Episcopal Church and became rector of St John's, Northampton. In 1870, he was appointed rector of St John's, Ithaca, New York; in 1872, of Holy Trinity, Portland, Conn.; and in 1879 he was appointed Vicar of Christ Church, Cambridge, Massachusetts. He married Anne Harper in 1864 and had three sons: Martha Raymond (1865), Henry Dixon (1869), and Philip Leffingwell (1871). In November 1891 he preached a sermon at Christ Church in which he announced his resignation and his decision to seek admission to the Catholic Church which took place at Washington on 15 January 1892. By April of the same year, reports circulated in the newspapers that he had reverted to episcopalianism. He subsequently